Life Energy, Life Meaning

A Path to Optimal Living and Work

By

Dianne Greyerbiehl Ph.D.

ISBN: 0-7596-9588-1

This book is printed on acid free paper.

1stBooks – rev. 04/29/02

Table of Contents

Introduction

This book is an outgrowth of my need to find a better way to change my life than just trying harder, reading the latest self-help guru, or relying on research about effective personal change. In the long run, none of it worked well for me or for the clients with whom I worked. All of us seemed to fall back into the same old reaction patterns sooner or later. To get any significant change, it seemed it took being hit over the head with a two-by-four...you know, one of those life crises that can't be ignored. Often, those crises were wrapped around a life issue that was not addressed and had been ignored for a long time.

The issue that I didn't want to address spanned a period of twenty-five years in my life. I chose to believe that if only I could super-achieve then I'd be acceptable and important to those around me. I'd get respect and I'd get opportunities for new creative projects. Well, I did get noticed in my field, I did get respect, I was accepted, and some nice creative projects did come my way. But never was I so alone, so exhausted, so anxious, and my self-image so unhealed. In other words, although being Ms. Super-Achiever did bring about some of the benefits I sought, they didn't have the effect I really wanted. I thought the achievements would bring close friends and a sense of community, as well as self-respect. They did none of those things.

Despite all the knowledge I had acquired in my masters and doctoral programs about effective change, I wouldn't face the fact that trying harder wasn't cutting it for me. The harder I tried to maintain the "same old," the more two-by-fours (**** learning experiences!) came my way. So then, I got the brilliant idea to package the "same old" in a new version. I thought I just needed to change a little, but I could keep on trying to super-achieve. That didn't work either. Persistence is a core characteristic for me!

The last "two-by-four" dealing with this issue came in a two-layered package. First, I felt driven to quit my job as director of a rehabilitation training and research center at the university where I had worked for ten years. I was totally burned out. I couldn't handle writing grants, teaching, and dealing with university and center politics anymore.

I decided to start a practice providing life coaching. Life coaching provides problem solving coupled with lifestyle planning and management. It helps people and organizations problem solve and strategically plan so that the focus is on creating the life, work, or organizational future that is desired. I had already been doing this within the rehabilitation field in different forms for many years. Therefore, I decided to take my skills to the general public, as well as continue helping those with disabilities.

At the same time I made this decision, my husband decided to retire. So our income was immediately cut by 75%. Oh, did I scare myself to death! I had visions of becoming a bag lady in spades! Not a reasonable deduction, but then when fear takes over, reason often goes out the window.

Despite my fears, the practice grew over time. But I really had to struggle to make that happen. In looking at what I was doing, it dawned on me that I had modified the format and altered the content a bit, but I was still trying to super-achieve. However, I was too afraid to rock the boat and try anything really different. After all, I had to earn a living!

Then the second layer of the two-by-four struck. I acquired fibromyalgia, a chronic dysfunction of energy exchange at the cell level with the result that you feel like you have a bad case of the flu all the time. Now I couldn't keep on going because I didn't have the energy and I hurt too much physically. In addition, fibromyalgia brought on a good case of clinical depression. That stopped me cold!

In my life, whenever I've run into an immovable wall that I couldn't surmount, I've reached inside myself to a spiritual place that was always there when I needed it. I asked All That Is (my version of God) why this was happening to me. The answer came in dreams, automatic writing, and other communication avenues to deeper consciousness that I had learned over the years. The answer was that super-achieving wasn't gaining me close friends or community, wasn't allowing me to be who I really was, and wasn't healing my self-image.

With that realization, I searched for a different approach to changing my life. I read all that I could get my hands on about personal change for a six-month period. I also talked to colleagues and friends about what worked for them. I knew that I not only had to change what I was doing, but somehow, I needed to build a new environment around me...new ways of relating, new groups, and new family relationships. Of course, while I was doing this I was still running my practice. What a challenge! However, I found that the answers I was discovering for myself became my most valuable tools for helping my clients.

As time progressed, my deeper consciousness finally made me understand that I had to find a way to allow my mystical nature to integrate with my daily life. That was an essential part of who I was. Up to this point in my life, I had always kept it private...walled off from my day-to-day outward behavior. As I found ways to let my mystical self peek out in my practice and my private life, I discovered that my self-image began healing itself. I also noticed that finding ways to be the real me (however I defined that) gave me more feelings of security than all the hiding and protective stances I'd taken over the years. It also seemed to open the way to finding the best paths for creating the life and work I wanted.

Despite all this learning, I was still experiencing a lot of struggle to find my answers. So I sat down one night and asked my deeper consciousness to show me a way I could change my life where I wouldn't have to struggle so hard. In an altered relaxed state of mind, I began an automatic writing process. My fingers began moving over the computer keys and material appeared that I knew I ordinarily couldn't produce with my conscious mind. Ideas would form just before the next sentence. They would spell themselves out in more solid form word by word and sentence by sentence. I didn't feel "taken over" by some power beyond me; rather, it felt like a collaboration process. Knowledge that I had was used as a basis to produce new ideas, which I had thought about before or which I had never before considered. When the ideas got too amorphous, I would halt the process. Then there seemed to be a type of dialogue going on in my head where a better way of expressing the idea or concept was worked out between myself and a power beyond my normal consciousness.

The result of this beginning collaboration was a rudimentary form of the Five-Domain Outline that this book presents. I called this framework NeuroQuantum Thinking (NQT). "Neuro," for neurological or the brain, "Quantum," for the inner mystical self and All That Is, and "Thinking," for the conscious mind. The model encompassed five domains of energy called Life Energy. That energy enabled anyone to manifest the life and work they wanted. I was thrilled with the outcome.

I immediately tried it with myself. It improved manifestation of what I wanted and did so in a way that meant I didn't have to struggle so hard. Yippee! I tried it with my clients with similar results. The side result was that my practice grew like a weed. Clients began coming out of the woodwork!

I worked with that basic NQT model for over three years. I gradually fine-tuned it through my experiences, as well as through the experiences of my clients, who told me what worked and what didn't. It seemed All That Is would whisper in my ear to try something new just when I was stuck. Or, I would get a client that forced me to adapt in a new way, and lo and behold, a whole new change process was born.

As I worked with the basic NQT framework, I knew there was something missing. The Five-Domain Outline produced a framework that brought about initial life change. Missing from it were procedures that would allow day-to-day functioning while still being connected to deeper consciousness. In addition, clients kept pressing me to put these ideas in greater written detail, like a book or workbook.

To do this, I knew that I had to have more time. I also knew that to get the additional time, I was going to have to give up my practice, at least temporarily. After consulting my deeper consciousness and All That Is over a six-month period about how to do this, my husband and I decided we would move to an area that was lower in cost-of-living and in the country. We found a beautiful piece of property in South Carolina near the Blue Ridge Mountains. We built a house and there I found peace, healing, and time. I started working on this book in earnest.

But as I was writing, All That Is still had a few of those "**** learning experiences" up Its sleeve. My sister and I had a series of major disagreements about our relationship. Bottom line, she wanted me to stop over-playing my role as personal counselor and expert problem solver. It was time for me to back off of these roles because she was changing and so was I. It took some time, but I finally realized that it was not good for my sister or myself to take on these roles to the degree that I had. It's okay to counsel and advise as long as it's not to your detriment or that of the other person. The old relationship we had was hurting both of us. It was time to build a new one. That wasn't easy, but is getting easier with time.

During the two years it took to write this book, I found that the experiences I encountered brought me closer to my inner mystical core, minus all the outer coverings that I had wrapped around it to protect it. It no longer needed protection…it needed to be let out! It wanted its freedom.

As I learned how to do this, the book I was writing kept re-writing itself. I'd feel an urge to go back over what I had written and change it to match what I was learning in my "two-by-four" experiences. In fact, as I wrote, I frequently found that I had to experience what I was writing in order to understand some of the "finer" details. Often the "experience" turned out to have multiple levels. Frustration was not the word I felt when this "experiencing" got in the way of writing down ideas. I am an "idea person." I love to play with ideas, putting together different patterns and concepts. Well, my deeper consciousness and All That Is had different ideas. So the pattern I learned to accept was working through negatives and positives around a certain concept, and then to write about it letting my deeper consciousness and All That Is speak through me.

As I began to regularly use the methods that I wrote about to manage my life and create what I wanted, the intensity of the "**** learning experiences" lessened significantly and disappeared faster. In addition, manifestation of the positive grew faster and stronger.

So there you have it. Why this book was written.

The book was written in a deeply relaxed, altered state of consciousness where I let my fingers just do the typing on the computer keyboard. When I first started listening to the deeper conscious part of myself for the formation of the basic NQT model, I heard words and sentences just ahead of what I wrote down. Often, I didn't know where it was leading exactly—I just kept typing. Sometimes I would look at what was coming out on the computer screen and say to my deeper self, "That's about as clear as mud." Then my deeper self, All That

Is, and my conscious self would confer and come up with a better version that was clearer to me.

If I were unsure of whether it was simply me who was doing this writing, I would ask in an aside if that were so. After a while, I knew when my conscious mind was dominating too much of the writing from how things were worded and how I felt. If I was angry, anxious, perfectionistic, judgmental, or tense I knew my conscious mind was into the writing up to its proverbial neck. So I would stop my writing for a while, and then go back making sure that I was feeling an inner centeredness. That became my physical cue that the result coming out on the screen was a true collaboration of my conscious mind, my deeper self, and All That Is. In contrast, when my stomach was in a knot, I knew my conscious mind was in the driver's seat.

The writing is done in first person, as if All That Is is writing directly to those who will read this book. I believe that the energy force coming through me was indeed All That Is. However, that energy has to write through my mind and my understanding. Therefore, the result of this writing is definitely a co-created work. That is so for any work done by automatic writing, whether done in a relaxed conscious altered state as I did, or a deeper unconscious altered state.

The bottom-line for the reader is that, regardless of where these words come from, you must judge what is truth for you. Each of us has our own truth and wisdom. No one person can know or write about the whole truth. But each of us has our own deeper self through which we hear a power beyond ourselves speaking to us with truths unique to each of us. So take from these writings what seems true to you, and then let the rest go. If you have picked up this book, it has some truth for you that is important to your growth. But you are the one that is the expert for you. Choose and modify as you see fit.

Chapter 1

Who Is God...And Who Are You?

Who Is God?

I am you and you are Me. I am energy. My essence and consciousness underlies everything you see, hear, touch, taste, and all that is. I AM ALL THAT IS. I live in everything. I am everything seen and unseen. But I am more than just the sum total of all that is. I am a conscious being, whole and eternally dynamic. I have no parts, only different characteristics or aspects that are My Consciousness. All that is experienced by you is My Consciousness in all Its aspects. So I am many, but one.

Each of you is an aspect of me. You have the power that I have but you use it or don't in different ways and to different degrees. Yet, you all create your life experiences. You create your dramas both together and individually. The purpose of all experience is to grow in your beauty and being, and to remember your relation as an aspect of Me as you do it.

Who Are You?

You are divinity experiencing being human, *not* humans reaching for divinity. When you believe you are humans trying to become better humans reaching for the divine, you give up who you are—an aspect of Me. You also give up your power. You give it away to each other, and to the external being you have created and call God. Your concept of God is a father parenting His children. But you've created a father that commits the absolute sin in parenting...you make Me keep you children forever!

In your concept of who I am, you remain always immature, incapable of growing up, always uninformed, always less than, and always vulnerable. Once more, in many of your religions, you have created Me to be exclusively male, leaving out the other half of the human race and creation. What a terrible parent

1

you make Me! How imperfect, how controlling, and how reflective of your cultures! This is your image of fatherhood and male authority with which you describe me. *This is your invention of God; it is not who I am, for I am you and you are Me.* We are colleagues, different in our knowledge and range of power, but not unequal. We work together at an energy and soul level to co-create your experiences and reality.

My energy is Life Energy. It is also your energy. This energy makes up My consciousness and yours. Life Energy is the essence of all that is, both matter and non-matter. Out of this energy, My energy, I create. Out of this same energy, your energy, you create your life experiences. So the key to living as divinity experiencing humanness on earth is to consciously know how to create and manage your life experiences through this energy. This is the essence of this book.

My Life Energy and yours consists of negative and positive energy as well as something called *Being*. In regard to Negative Life Energy, to experience being divine as human, earthly living demands that you must experience and understand the opposite of what you are. *That is, in order to understand what you are or what anything is, you must experience or observe what it is not.*

So you use negative energy to create these experiences. For example, the experiences of being sinful, an unworthy and weak human, vulnerable, and powerless are all opposites of what you can be as humans. Feel this. Know this and realize that this is your created drama for learning. You can stop this any time you want. You can begin to reverse your experience and remember who you truly are whenever you feel that the time is right. But remember that negative experiences and events are learning tools that teach you what you are not.

Positive Life Energy shows you who you truly are and creates what you want. Create the experience of awakening to your godhood; explore who you truly are. Explore how your experience of what you are *not*, adds to your knowledge of what you truly are. Awaken to your life and power as divinity experiencing human through talking to your soul and Me. Transform who you are. Become an adult and co-create with Me that divine aspect of who you truly are.

Being is Life Energy that is My core essence. It is energy that encompasses all types of energy including Positive and Negative Life Energy. It is the energy you feel when you feel close to the mystical or spiritual. It is the energy present in the creative effort where you lose track of time as you create. It is the energy of deep meditation and prayer. It is the energy that you feel when you feel centered, at peace, or balanced. It is where I am you and you are Me most completely. It is where what you learn becomes a part of all that is—My

Essence. It is the energy you must learn to live within in order to create the life and work you want and to become who you truly are.

I am important to your life, because My energy is life. You learn for Me and you learn for all of My aspects. **No one else can learn and grow in the particular way you can. No one is exactly like you. No one is your equal. You are irreplaceable in your living and learning! The fact that you are this special is what makes your living important.**

You live many lives, in many domains. No one, no thing, can replace your learning and growth. You are beloved. No matter what you choose or do, you are beloved. You enrich the divine aspect that you are as you learn more.

You are god and I am the whole, All That Is. I am life and existence. I am Love and so are you. Not the sexual love that you have debased from its original sacred purpose, nor affection, but rather, an energy that is Love beyond all loves. All things are made up of this energy. In fact, this is Life Energy. We are love. But each of you has free will as I have free will. You were truly made in my image and likeness. You are Me and I am you. Take this Life Energy that forms you and learn and grow as you choose.

You are not debased, weak, or sinful. You are made in my image so how could you be less than what I am? In fact, there is no perfection for perfection implies non-growth and a completion. There is only dynamic growing and becoming. So grow and learn for all of us and Me.

You and the Feminine Spirit

Within the Life Energy that is your essence, each of you has been created to have both male and female energies. Before 10,000 years ago, humans populated the earth who believed that all things were connected and that all were part of the sacred. Sacred energy was believed to be particularly in the female since this is from which children came. The contribution of male energy was not completely understood so, as time went by, the emphasis became more and more on the sacredness of females and the secondariness of males. Females were dominant over males, but emphasis was on being in harmony with the things of the earth.

Around 10,000 years ago, there came a decision by the human race that it would reverse this trend of female dominance. So out of the near east came males who conquered the female cultures to establish male cultures, which were the mirror image of the defeated female. Now males were the sacred vessel and females were secondary.

But a new emphasis was added— separation. The idea of separation appeared where I was said to be absolutely separate from you and all other things on earth. Males created religions that spoke of their exclusive access to the Divine through priests and rulers. And there grew the idea that man was put on

3

earth to have dominion over all things to use as he pleases. And so the foundation for the present male cultures came to be.

It is time to remember that male and female energy are within both men and women. It is time to understand, in order to remember that you are divinity experiencing humanness, that female energy is a critical foundation. Female energy provides an intuitive, receptive, non-linear understanding of the sacred. I am, in fact, not linear. I am present in all things all at once and I create by instant knowingness and intention (deciding what I want). Female energy is best suited to accessing My energy and wisdom in both male and female humans. On the other hand, male energy takes knowledge gained about the sacred by female energy and creates an experience to reflect that knowledge. So male energy is the doer...the creator of life experiences. Female energy is the knower...the door to wisdom and understanding.

Because you have overemphasized male energy in your cultures, the female spirit must now be a concern of high focus for the time being. The focus must be on how to remember and use feminine energy to access and hear Me. Then you can allow male energy to create and apply the knowledge to generating experiences and physical reality. Remember though that each human has both male and female energy. Each of you must learn how to use *both* of these energies so that they work together rather than fight for control.

Summary

- My essence and consciousness underlies all things. I am all that is. My essence and consciousness is energy and that energy is Life Energy. Life Energy is also Love.

- You are an aspect of Me. You are part of my Essence and your energy is also Life Energy and Love.

- You are divinity experiencing humanness. To realize and understand this as human, you generate life experiences with Negative and Positive Life Energy. Negative Life Energy shows you what you are not and what you don't want. Positive Life Energy shows you who you are and what you want.

- You believe you are weak, vulnerable, and powerless. You generate experiences that are showing you what the consequences of these beliefs are, e.g. helplessness, chaos, and distance from Me. Your real essence is that of a strong, vital, creative being who has the power to create your own life experiences and choose what experiences you do or do not want.

- No one else is like you. You are a treasured and necessary aspect of who I am. Only you can generate the particular learning and wisdom that is unique to you that will add to who I am and My wisdom.

- Life Energy contains both negative and positive energies, as well as a state of energy called *Being*. Life Energy also consists of female and male energies that are within each human being. Female energy is the knower and wisdom seeker. Male energy is the doer...the experience generator. Female energy must be a high focus for now because people have lost the knowledge of how to access and live consciously within Life Energy, in order to access knowing and wisdom. This is *Being*. Learning to do this is the focus of learning now and for the near future.

Dianne's Experience

The western culture model I was taught about who God was and who I was, left me feeling distant from that power and forever weak and fearful. Particularly as a female, at the time I was growing up, I was indoctrinated with the idea that girls were definitely not as good as boys. We were weaker, more sinful, and less competent. Moreover, God didn't seem to matter in day-to-day living. He was forgotten. Instead, the scientific model prevailed around me. It stated that you were on your own and in a dog-eat-dog world...a jungle of possible hurtful events. You had to watch your backside all the time—particularly as a woman.

This seemed like a picture of hell. To be forever tantalized with the idea of happiness if only you would do or be this. But doing this or being that never seemed to work for long. Happiness rarely seemed to be an ongoing picture in day-to-day living. Life was hard. You had to just survive as best you could. Because of human weakness, we seemed to be condemned to forever trying and never making it permanently to happiness. Sure seemed like a good description of hell to me!

As I accepted the picture of God and our role, which is described in this book, my feelings changed. I grew less fearful and more creative. I was more able to be me...whoever I defined I was at the time. I also became less judgmental of myself and others because I tried to look on experiences as teachers and guides. As I focused on believing that I was divinity experiencing humanness, I began to take back my power within myself. Slowly but surely, I decreased giving it away to outside people and events. I felt stronger, safer, freer, more at peace, and more joyful.

In fact, it seems pretty obvious to me that if you believe in the world painted by the present culture, one of aloneness, power outside of yourself, inequality, injustice, and danger, you will not find happiness. In this world, you cannot feel strong, safe, free, or at peace. In thinking back on my life, the only times I've really experienced those feelings has been when I've allowed myself to consciously relax into Life Energy and access the wisdom and knowledge that is inherently available because it is the medium and essence of All That Is.

To do this has been my journey over many years. But as I look back over what I have learned at different stages in my life, I'm amazed to see that each step was necessary to bring me to where I am now. Each step was part of a plan that fit together like the pieces of a puzzle to make my life purpose come alive. Knowing this has allowed me to be less fearful and more relaxed about events that I experience in daily life. I choose to believe that there is a greater power that is guiding my way and helping me co-create my life. I see no benefit in accepting the alternative traditional beliefs presented by society.

Life Energy Activities

- **Be in nature in a place where it is beautiful and calm.** Listen to the voices surrounding you—the birds, the squirrels, other animals, the trees, the wind. They are all My voice. Allow their conversation to seep through your consciousness. Be still. Listen. Relax and let be. Stay in the moment, not yesterday's happenings nor tomorrow's challenges. You will be rewarded with a calmness and sense of the beauty of creation. You will see yourself as part of that creation. You will feel Me. If you want to know the answer to questions that you have, ask in this environment. Then still your thoughts, listen, and look. I will give you the answer in multiple ways.

- **When you speak during the day, listen to what you say**. Are you being true to who you are? Do you tell the truth about what you want? Do you honor yourself as you speak about what you do or what has happened? If you criticize who you are, focus on what you cannot do, talk about how you are the victim of circumstances, or other's actions, you are not honoring who you are—divinity experiencing humanness. Instead, you disrespect your potential, your skills and abilities—your very essence. Speak of what you can do, what you are learning, and what you truly think in ways respectful of yourself and of others.

You bring messages to others by your words or else they wouldn't be there. They also bring messages to you. But to truly hear what they are saying, you must respect yourself and them and not allow yourself to feel the victim, or controller. Each of you is valuable. Act that way and you will respect who you are. This will lead to easily finding your path and having the courage to follow it.

Chapter 2

The Facts of Existence

All That Is and Quantum Physics

I said that everything is connected. The scientists of your culture agree. According to quantum physics, all energy is connected. All things and space are energy; nothing is not energy. It is simply more or less dense, shaped and formed in different ways.

Humans are energy—everything in your body. Your body generates electromagnetic fields around it as a result of that energy. The body fields touch on other energy already in that space, interacting with it and altering it. *There is no way you cannot affect one another and your environment!*

Your scientists have found that all energy consists of different kinds of particles. They call some of these particles, quarks. These quarks consist of even smaller particles. All these particles alter their form depending on what an observer *expects to see.* That is, the observer cannot observe reality (particles) without the form of the particles being altered. You affect your energy reality with what you expect. To put it in my words, **your intention (what you want), thoughts, and beliefs—all expectations—affect the energy that makes up your reality. It alters it and forms it into what you expect. What you think, you get!**

Of course, your energy interacts with all energy around it. Therefore, the resulting form (outcome) depends on the intensity of energy. The most intense energy will have the most influence. Translated into Life Energy terms, this means that **your most intense thought will have the most influence in creating your reality.**

In quantum physics, it doesn't take much energy to disturb and drastically alter a given form or structure. Small alterations can produce breakdown of the form. What results seems to be chaos. But "chaos" always settles into a new energy structure, which operates in an even more efficient fashion.

Translating this into Life Energy reality, it doesn't take a majority of people or an enormous effort to alter the status quo. The right kind of effort is driven by a vision of something that is beyond the self—a vision that impacts others. With this vision and a small group of people, you can eliminate or alter institutions, rules and regulations, laws, customs, cultures, and history.

The resulting change may seem chaotic and, because it does, people become anxious and fearful of the unknown. Remember though that the outcome of chaos is always a better, more efficient reality. That is a universal law. So, do not fear if all is changing around you. Things will alter in the end for the better. **You and I create messes in life to form something better!**

If all is energy, and I created all things as well as being part of all things, then that means I am made up of energy just as you are. This is Life Energy. Your Life Energy is part of Me. You are a "particle" in my "form" (My Being). But if your "particle" (you) were not a part of Me, I would be different. So, only you can contribute in your way to who I am. **You are essential to my very nature!** Impressive, huh?

Your Model of Living

Many of you have questioned the idea of human sinfulness and your flawed nature generated by your religions. Some of you have rejected these ideas. Some who have rebelled have used science as the answer. Their belief is that only what you see and can prove is real. Religion is unnecessary, unscientific, and creates myths. Those of you who believe this have used science to experience the opposite of religious dogma.

This science, from its infancy, saw things as separate entities, rather than the connection model generated by today's quantum physics. These concepts worked their way into your popular culture. This science became a teacher that said you should think of yourselves as separate and lordly entities, free to take and use because you are human. This science, even today, reinforces that reality is what you see, hear, taste, and touch. Therefore, the unseen is neither important nor real.

Your culture has extended the importance of the concrete to value money, doing, and possessions. The motto is "by your possessions others shall know you." The ideal results that are supposed to occur with this model of "scientific" living do not happen. You earn money; maybe lots of it. Why? To buy things; to have power. What do "things" give you? Moments of pleasure that are gone in the blink of an eye! Then you have to buy bigger and better toys. And then they become boring. Lesson? *Things* do not bring happiness.

You believe that money brings power—power to buy things and people, as well as do what you want. But you have power already; it is intrinsic to each of you. It is an innate characteristic. You are made in My image and likeness! But both your science and religions teach you that power is external. So you give away your power. You place it in money, in men, and in luck. You make yourselves helpless. **You give away your birthright so the power is not within you. You become victims**. Even your conquerors are victims for they are convinced that the power is not within them, but external in their money, position, and resources.

The outcome of this drama is that money brings fear…fear of losing it. And when you lose it, you lose power. So you try harder. But continuing to put your power in the external makes power temporary and limited. **As a result, fear becomes the foundation of your daily living.**

The truth is that reality is not what you see, but what you don't. Your quantum physics now confirms this with the observation that all things, even empty space, have energy. Energy, plans, mind power, creativity, emotions, and experiences are true reality—the true building blocks of humanity. By this, you manifest money, possessions, and action. Your own mind and that of God creates these outcomes. Where do you think you come from? Who do you think you are? Why are you here and alive? These are the truly important questions of the unseen reality. All else is mere drama…learning that you do as you live as divinity experiencing humanness.

Your Power Is Within

When you fear, the control and power are always external to you. But you have an internal power that is intrinsic to your make-up. That internal power, your Life Energy, is beauty beyond comparison. Your soul is My energy. Its natural bias is helping you create your life through Life Energy. Its natural emotions are joy, peace, fulfillment, rightness of being, and a feeling of living in the center of your being and Ours. Here with this power, you can create what you think and believe. You find life an endless path of novel, creative movement that is dynamic, flowing, changing but safe. An immovable power with a movable force!

You are god and a part of who I am. That is your legacy…each of you. You choose your destiny and you never die. You just change forms. Your purpose is to learn and become more than you are. Each of you is a dynamic inseparable piece of who I am. You are sacred. **Your task is to remember how to be divine while experiencing humanness. That means also experiencing how to integrate, with equal emphasis, female and male energies in order to experience divinity and humanness at its fullest.**

Negative and Positive Experiences Have a Purpose

Negative experiences are a necessary part of the human condition. They are part of your existence. For without the opposite, you cannot know the positive. The human experience is dichotomy and paradox. Negative can lead to positive and positive can lead to negative. Both are part of who I am. If I made all that is, then all that is must be an aspect of Me.

I am not separate from my creations. I allow them to develop into unique aspects of Me. I encourage each creation to seek its own perception and reality—to create it, generate it, and to make it real. But underlying all unique creations is My Energy—My Essence. I am all that is, that Life Energy that makes you who you are. The molecules, the quarks, and other energy matter of which you have knowledge are Me. You are Me and I am the sum total of you and more.

So negative energy is an aspect of My Life Energy. Many of you label intense negative experiences as evil. I allow the energy to be formed in this manner because you who experience it have agreed to it at your soul level. Those who are "evil" in your terms experience lack of positive energy and the consequences of intense negative emotions and outcomes. Those of you who choose this learn what it is to live without the positive. Negative power defines most of your existence and who you are. Fear is your constant companion.

Religions have presented the evil ones as being at war with Me. But I would not allow evil to be, unless it had a positive purpose. That purpose is to cause the transformation of reality around it to a greater, more positive Life Energy. Hear Me now and use these forces, both negative and positive, in the way they were created—to define your existence in the way you want to learn and to create a new life force for all of us.

You do not have to experience evil first hand. You can observe it as others choose these experiences for themselves and their learning. You can use your observations to form the opposite by choosing positive Life Energy to create optimal styles of living.

In fact, it is time you do just that. *You have had enough experience now with the negative and your "evil" dramas. It is time to experience the opposite in much more frequent form. It is time to revise your world so that you learn what beliefs and actions bring an emphasis on positive living, rather than negative.* It is time to revamp your whole style of living so that you can experience the feelings and experiences of positive living while being centered in Divine Love—your divinity experiencing humanness. This is what this book is all about—how to do just that.

You Have Free Will

As you begin a transformation toward a new living style, you must understand that you have free will. That means that you have choice over your life at various levels of reality. You all have chosen some life experiences and purposes from before the time you were born. You have chosen these things in order to manifest your divinity as humans in your own unique way, using your strengths and weaknesses gained over many lives to form the structure of this one.

You have also chosen to live within a group of associates and friends that you have known, or that will aid you best in your chosen life purpose(s). At a soul level, you have all made certain agreements about your life and experiences that you think will bring the best results.

Beyond these agreements, there are general ones that have been chosen as a human race. One of those general agreements is an attempt at transformation, where your race will learn how to be divine and human while within your conscious body. What that means and the outcome of that attempt is up to you to define. You, living now, are the pioneers and foundation for this momentous process.

All of these agreements at the soul, group, and human race levels create biases for your learning experiences in life, as well as your chosen life circumstance and skills. The biases are meant to create impulses and choices of experiences that will best nurture and manifest your soul agreements.

But over and above all of these agreements, there is still free will for the individual. You can still say "no." That is how powerful your will is. You can choose what your life should be, your circumstances, and even your purpose.

Changing the group agreements that you made at a soul level is difficult, but possible because of free will. Changing your mind is neither bad nor good, it just is. Out of it will come different experiences and a different life. It is admittedly easier to go with your soul agreements. It means that things will fall into place easier.

In fact, that is the defining characteristic of going the way of your soul agreements—ease of manifestation. You may experience times when things grow difficult. This may even last for some time. But at the end of that time, things will fall easily into place. If this does not happen, it is usually a sign that you are going against your own soul agreements, or that you have beliefs that are a barrier to what you want.

It Is a Time of Transformation

All of you have heard predictions of the end times. Those end times are upon you, but they do not have to be filled with destruction. They will be filled with letting old structures die, while new ones are born, for these old structures are no longer compatible with your purpose as a human race. You will find that the known institutions in your life—financial, educational, business, government, religion—will change dramatically within the next twenty years. They represent the model of living that surrounds the values of power, external control, and money as the highest of values to be considered. This is no longer acceptable to you. **It is time for the beginning of a new style of living and a new culture with new values.**

You will determine the characteristics of this new culture. But at the center will be a drive to learn of Life Energy and how it affects you in your daily living. Each of you will be trying on new models of living that will answer the question of Life Energy for you. Each of you will grow in this knowledge, so that your life will change as your knowledge of Life Energy grows. Collaboration, respect, and choice will be core values. You will find ways to reward each other when you show these values in your life. These are characteristics of the feminine spirit.

Some of you will opt not to change. This will be a hard time for you, but your decision may be compatible with your life purpose. In any case, you always have a choice. However, there is no option for not choosing during this time. **Not doing anything different is a choice**. And your choice to stay the same has its own consequences.

This transformation time will not be governed by dogmatic rules, since such rules slow down change. Rules also imply expertise and greater knowledge over others. *Each of you is the expert for your own transformation.*

The answers are within you, not outside in any institution, book, or other person. These outside sources can only act as catalysts for initiating your own knowledge of how to create with Life Energy. So decide for yourself what is good or bad for you; judge the consequences for you, your family, and your community. Speak your truth and then listen to what others say. Then decide if that adds to your truth, for truth is found in your heart and soul, as well as your interactions and experiences in living. Each of you has a portion of the truth. None of you know it all, for you do not have My ability to know the sum total of wisdom that has been acquired. So, keep yourselves ready to learn from yourself and from one another as you evolve your life.

Honor both the feminine and masculine spirit knowing that neither is created to be dominant over the other. Each simply has a different job to do. To be fully divine while experiencing humanness, these energies must be integrated within each human in order to hear clearly the answers that you seek.

Summary

- Everything is energy, Life Energy. Quantum physics has called this energy, quarks. It has confirmed that everything is made up of this energy, and that all energy is connected. It has also noted that energy is affected by your expectations of what it is supposed to be. Energy conforms to your expectations. That means that your intentions, thoughts, and beliefs alter reality by altering the very energy that is within you and surrounding you. It alters it and forms it into what you expect. What you think, you get!

- It doesn't take much energy to disturb the status quo. Small alterations can produce big results. The outcome can seem like chaos, but in order for something new to be born, something old must die. And the something new coming out of chaos is always better in the long run. You and I to form something better create messes in life!

- Your present model of living does not allow for happiness because it is founded on false beliefs about what brings happiness. One of those beliefs is that only what you can see, hear, or touch are important to living. The truth is that reality is not what you see, but what you don't. Energy, plans, mind power, creativity, emotions, and experiences are your true reality. These are the foundation for achieving happiness.

- Your power is within you, not in external things or people. Only when you accept this, will you be able to create your life in the way you desire.

- Both negative and positive energy are part of Life Energy and each has a purpose. Negative energy teaches you what you do not want and what you are not. Positive energy teaches you what you are and what you do want.

- Each of you has free will, which allows you to choose what you do with your life. You can say no to Me, your soul, or to soul agreements made before you came into your present body. It is a more difficult life when you do that, but free will is part of your nature. Choosing something different from what has been agreed upon is neither bad nor good. It will simply produce a different life, with different experiences that will contribute to the knowledge and wisdom of us all.

- It is a time of transformation where each of you will be learning about Life Energy and how to use it. The type of transformation is up to you.

Dianne's Experience

It is so easy to think of yourself as a victim of circumstances or the actions of others. Actions of family members, friends, or spouses can be hurtful to you, particularly when they represent well-established conflicts between you. Therefore, it becomes easy to see yourself as a victim being unfairly treated and unable to stop what is happening. I've spent a good part of my life falling into this belief and being angry at the circumstances and people involved. I've spent my share of nights and days saying, "If only…" That feeling of depression, anger, hurt, and being stuck gets to be pretty familiar after a while. And I know I've used my "victim hood" to get sympathy from others. But the sympathy is never enough to erase the bad feelings. It only lightens them temporarily.

I think I became attached to this cycle even though I knew it didn't work very well. The "oh poor me syndrome" stayed on until life circumstances pushed me into a corner where I experienced clinical depression. That was no fun at all! The world was black; life was black. I envied those who had died; at least they were free from this pain! I tried therapy. It helped only when I took back control within myself. When I depended on the therapist for solutions, things usually went back to the "same old" pretty fast. Only when I decided that I had the power within myself to make things different, did things really begin to lighten up.

I realize now that the depression was my inner self's creative way of hitting me over the head with a two-by-four so that I would begin to take back my power more consistently in my life. Before the "depression era," I would only take control within me when I was pushed into a corner or when I really wanted something to happen. But daily living was usually lived well within the ideas I was indoctrinated with by this culture—power outside yourself, watch your back, don't trust others, achieve.

Even when I tried to focus on my power being within, I couldn't quite bring myself to believe that this was so. All the talk about energy seemed a little far-fetched to my scientifically trained mind. Just touchy-feely stuff! Then I began reading different books on quantum physics, and I began thinking about how ridiculous it really was, believing that only what I could see, hear, and touch was real. There was a whole world out there that we couldn't see, hear, and touch. The phenomenon of electricity was one of them. The more I thought about it, the more I realized I'd been "had" by the present cultural beliefs. They demanded that you put all the power into outside things, often, scientific things. What lack of control! I decided that I would rather opt to believe in things that would promote feelings of respect, honor, and competence within me, rather than the opposite proposed by the beliefs I'd been fed.

I focused on looking at negatives that came my way as the energy of All That Is that was there as a teacher and helper if only I would listen to its message. Sometimes All That Is and I had some lively discussions where I was mad as hell about the negative energy I was experiencing. Pissed off at All That Is I was! Ultimately, I realized that the experience had been my choice through beliefs I had, or intentions (what I wanted) or both. When I found the beliefs and intentions that were creating and maintaining the experience, in most cases, my life circumstances took an abrupt about face to the positive.

Sometimes, that didn't happen. The negative continued although often less intensely. Always at the bottom of it was the necessity to learn things from the process and to identify even more basic beliefs that had to be changed and reformatted into the positive.

I'm now consciously choosing a good many of the experiences I have in each day. I listen to my inner voice to tell me what might be the best path to co-create my vision. Sometimes, it means just quieting my thoughts and stopping my rush toward accomplishing goals. When I'm busy, I have trouble hearing what my inner voice is saying. I find that the more I listen and talk to the voice of my inner self and All That Is, the smoother my life goes, and the greater peace and happiness I have. It is a learning process to do this, but I find that my way is eased if I ask for help from the Universe.

It has stopped being such a struggle to learn. I have stopped feeling like there is a war going on inside me, e.g., one side telling me all this Universe stuff is a bunch of hooey, and the other side saying it's the truth. Instead, I feel like the different parts of me are now talking to one another and figuring out how to cooperate rather than kill each other. It's a nice feeling!

Life Energy Activities

- When you are in Nature, listening to good music, or just relaxing, open your mind and senses to the energy around you. Listen and feel the sensations of your body, the sounds around you and their energy, the touch of the wind, the presence of the energy surrounding your body. Practice doing this each day for about ten to fifteen minutes and you will begin to sensitize your mind and body to the reality that is real, Life Energy. As you do this, its reality will become more familiar to you and more comfortable. You will discover ways to use it and relate to it that you never thought of before.

- Ask your inner self to show and/or tell you warning signs, which indicate that you are giving up your power to others or circumstances. Usually there are specific sensations and actions that are precursors to that happening—a tight feeling in the pit of the stomach (fear is growing), a narrowing of focus accompanied by a high drive to get something done at all costs, or a feeling of being tired when you think of doing something. All of these are examples of warning signs, which indicate that you are about to give up your power to the outside. When you have identified what these signs are, ask your inner self to help you nail down specific things you can do to get back on track. For example, relaxing the tight ball in the pit of your stomach and asking yourself what this is all about. What are you afraid of? Listen for the answer and then deliberately focus on co-creating with Us, a different positive choice for yourself.

Chapter 3

Basic Manifestation of Life Energy

How Do You Create What You Want?

Manifesting means making something solid—actual. But manifesting involves far more than that. First, it involves altering Life Energy with your intention (what you want) and general thoughts. Your intention is a specific form of thought. What you think, alters the shape and movement of matter. You think and it becomes an energy form.

Second, once you have altered energy with your thought, you have an emotional reaction that is added into your thought. It is one big ball of energy now. Your emotion makes the "ball" become bigger and more intense.

Next, you move your new Life Energy form into subtle physical energy. It becomes almost physical but not quite. It has magnetic properties now. It begins to draw to itself resources and support to take the final step—becoming physical.

Finally, your thought becomes physical.

As you can see, "manifestation" is not a simple process. Yet, the driving force behind it is simple, your thought. So you create your own reality. What you think, you get.

"Wait a minute!" I hear you saying. "What about all those times I did think and didn't get? All the times I prayed and nothing happened; I focused and nothing resulted. What happened?"

Thinking one thought is not usual for humans. Thinking one thought will usually bring on many other associated thoughts. Many of you will begin to free associate past experiences, beliefs, assumptions, and fears linked to the thought. Then, when you tell another what you are thinking, more thoughts are generated. So the one original thought is very much affected by the cluster of reactions it generates. It can make the manifestation of your thought more or less likely.

The strongest thought is the one that is manifested. So if your strongest thought is "I can't really do this," then what you originally wished for will not be manifested. If the strongest thought is, for example, that you can find a partner to your liking, then that will be manifested.

The strength of your original intention or thought is determined by the following factors:

1. How important it is to you.
2. Whether your vision of what you want, your goals, and your self-identity are generally compatible with your thought, OR vice versa, whether your thoughts are compatible with your vision and self-identity.
3. Whether your core assumptions and beliefs are compatible with your intention or thought.
4. Whether your emotions are compatible with your intention or thought.
5. Whether your subtle physical and physical energies are compatible with your intention or thought.

These "factors" are all types of Life Energy. So, whether your intention or thought becomes concrete depends on how compatible all these types of Life Energy are with what you think. The more compatible, the stronger the intention or thought.

In this chapter, I'll teach you how to align all these types of Life Energy to your thought or intention so that it becomes the strongest energy. It isn't as complicated as it sounds!

Domains of Energy for Manifestation

There are five domains of human Life Energy:

- spirit
- mind
- emotion
- subtle physical
- physical

These domains are realities that have their own rules and their consciousness. The Spirit Domain is the most powerful of all domains for manifesting something in physical form. In the order listed, Mind, Emotion, Subtle Physical, and Physical Domains demonstrate decreasing amounts of power. (William Tiller in

Science and Human Transformation does a very nice explanation of these domains from an energy perspective.)

All these domains must be compatible with each other in order to manifest easily what you want. So let's get started with how to do that and get you more familiar with the characteristics of each.

Knowing What You Want—the Spirit Domain of Life Energy

The purpose behind your living as humans is to find new ways of manifesting your divinity as human. This begins with your spirit forming and directing your life purpose(s), as well as other intentions (thoughts of what you want) that align with your life purpose(s). By doing this, your spirit makes the energy of your life purpose(s) and other intentions more dense—more compacted into a beginning concrete form. Remember, thoughts are energy. The thought of your life purpose and intentions at the spirit level is energy. The result is an increase in energy density.

The Spirit Domain of Life Energy is the most powerful of all domains of energy in the human experience. Whatever is intended (idea of what you want) in the Spirit Domain structures the remaining domains to become manifest in physical form.

Levels of the Spirit Domain

There are three levels of energy within the Spirit Domain:

- *Spirit I is Myself…All That Is* – my purpose in this domain is to co-create with you what you envision.
- *Spirit II includes your Higher Self, guardian spirit and guides* – their purpose is to act as translators for Me and also be your inner helpers in co-creating what you want.
- *Spirit III includes your soul and inner psyche* – they begin manifestation through defining your intentions (commitment to something, or idea of what you want).

Your Higher Self consists of multiple selves from many dimensions and times; you are one of these "selves." The multiple selves are aspects of the Higher Self, somewhat like cells, organs, tissue, and blood are aspects of the human. Some people call this entity the Oversoul. It provides you with the greater wisdom it has acquired, and it acts as a translator and access point for knowledge beyond itself from other realities, other non-physical beings, and Me. It also acts as the access point to your individual deeper (inner) consciousness.

Your Higher Self, therefore, is the linking agent between these greater realities and your own inner self.

Guides are non-physical beings of various levels of knowledge and wisdom who come to guide your choices and life path as the need arises. Among these guides is your guardian spirit or angel. Your Higher Self acts as the access point and translator for these guides if needed.

The soul is that non-physical part of you that retains knowledge of the Spirit Domain as you become human. It has access to all of your learning and wisdom as well as that of your inner helpers and Myself. It is part of your deeper consciousness.

Your inner psyche is the part of you that focuses on living and learning as a human. It consists of many characteristics that you call personality or parts of yourself. It is part of your deeper consciousness. It retains *all* the knowledge that you have acquired in this life. Regardless of whether you consciously remember things you have learned, your deeper consciousness remembers it all.

Before birth, your soul and psyche are separate aspects of Me. After birth, they join to become one unit within the human body. With your soul and your inner psyche, you can access knowledge that has been learned over your lifetime, as well as in other lives and other realities. This provides you with your very own inner library.

Your Life Purpose (Your Core Life Intention)

Your life purpose(s) is clearly important to your life on earth. You are the one who chose it before you were born. Your life purpose guides all of your manifestations. It is your core life intention. So how do you consciously find what you had in mind?

Ask yourself these questions:

Questions for Finding Your Life Purpose(s)

1. What am I drawn to?
2. What excites me and gives me energy?
3. What do I love to do?
4. What gives me a deep sense of satisfaction:
   a. With me?
   b. With others?
5. Where and when do I feel connected to the divine?
6. When and where have I truly tapped into my optimum skills?
7. Where and when have I learned with ease and joy?

Answering these questions will begin to create a picture in your mind and an understanding of your life purpose—why you are here.

Your life purpose corresponds to what you are driven to do. It is simultaneous with a deep core longing to fulfill paths that you want to choose. It is a longing to become who you truly are—divinity experiencing human. Your life purpose is usually not one straight path, but one of multiple detours. This is because you propose to live life as an intense, many-layered experience. However, your choices are motivated by your life purpose. Your longing to find something beyond what you are right now, is part of the growing process for fulfilling your life purpose.

So, obey your deepest core drive. Choose experiences that match the drives and you align yourself with an easy, flowing energy that will fulfill who you are and your purpose. If you choose beyond this, if you choose to stretch well beyond what you think you can do, your life experience becomes rougher, more intense, and filled with challenges. Nevertheless, you are still fulfilling the life purpose you picked.

If you choose to ignore your deepest drives and do what you think you have to, or what others demand of you, you still fulfill your life purpose. You teach yourself the opposite of listening to your inborn urges. You teach yourself about the experiences of helplessness, lack of control, and power external to you. You learn the consequences of your choices. Those consequences provide a counterpoint against which you can compare choices that are the opposite, choices that *do* correspond to your inner urges and desires. Remember, human experience is built on contrast—negative versus positive, what you want versus what you don't want. All this fits into your life purpose.

Envisioning What You Want

Forming a conscious vision of your life purpose and other life intentions (things you want) that are important to you is the first step in manifestation. It is important because it is the first step in:

- <u>Consciously</u> knowing how to manifest what you want. By answering the questions I gave you, it begins this process and provides you with a picture or idea of what you *do* want.
- Forming a lifestyle that "goes with the flow," e.g., goes with your core energy.
- Transforming who you are according to what *you* define, rather than ideas or decisions made by others.
- Learning what it means to be divinity experiencing humanness…an aspect of Me manifesting your energy in a way that is perfect and specific to you. Remember that you are unique. There is no one else that can accomplish your life purpose and intentions in the way that you can.

The Mind Domain of Life Energy and Manifestation

Your mind is not your brain. Your human mind is made up of Life Energy that is your conscious thinking self in non-physical form, as well as being part of your deeper conscious self. The mind works through your brain and your body to form experiences you want. The mind, emotion, brain, and body are a system, a unity that makes up what is human. However, since the mind is also part of your deeper conscious self, it provides a link to your soul and inner psyche. Because of this connection, it can work with your deeper consciousness in the Spirit Domain to manifest your life purpose(s) and intentions. **To do this, it aligns itself with the life intentions of your inner psyche and soul in the Spirit Domain, which are the strongest**.

Unfortunately, in most of your cultures, the strongest life intentions are often those where you put the power outside of yourself. For example, many who perceive themselves not in a power position intend to accept what others tell them to do. If you commit to this, e.g. intend it to happen, your mind will go to work to make this part of your manifested life purpose.

If you intend to allow "destiny" to form your life purpose, then your mind will focus on manifesting whatever is the strongest element that you are attracted to in your daily experiences. But your daily experiences will be formed and manifested largely by others. Your choices will be limited to the stream of opportunities others provide you or by destiny.

If you intend to wish for a better life, but decide you are a victim of bad luck or circumstances, your mind will make manifest this aspect of your life purpose.

If you commit to gain power for yourself through gaining money, position, or both, the power is still external to you. Money and position can be taken away. This means that you may constantly live in fear that this will happen, and you will no longer have power. Your mind will focus on attracting and creating dangers all around you, just as you believe them to be. Your mind will create precarious times and events that will wrest your power away from you until you struggle and fight to regain it.

All these examples are ones the human race has played with for some time. With these intentions, you have learned what it is like to have a life where your power is external to who you are. The power is in other people, circumstances, and objects like money. You live the life of victims even when you believe yourselves masters of your life. Your power is outside of who you are. You have given up your true intrinsic power, your divinity. You have given it away to others. You live the life of struggle. You live the life of fear. You live the life of yearning for something just beyond what you have.

These intentions manifest a life purpose that teaches the consequences of separating your humanness from your divinity. You believe yourself to be a biological mechanism that operates like a machine. You believe God to be outside of you and that others have to tell you how to reach Me, how to deserve Me. This is a model of separation. It is time to change it!

Life intentions should be focused on a model of integration—being part of Me and therefore divine as well as human. It is time you emphasize different intentions in your life. Intend to:

1. Manifest your life by *you* creating a picture of what you want...not leaving it to others.
2. Create a life that corresponds to your unique talents and characteristics so that you manifest who you are, not what you are not.
3. Co-create life experiences with your soul's intentions, your life group's intentions, and your purpose as a human race to create your versions of divinity experiencing humanness.

When you make these commitments, it strengthens any intentions with which they are compatible in the Spirit Domain. When you do this, your mind can align itself more easily with these intentions and make their manifestation easier. The bottom line is that your mind focuses on manifesting whatever are the strongest life intentions from the Spirit level of Life Energy.

Levels of the Mind Domain

Your mind is made up of three levels of Life Energy:

- *Mind I* engineers steps and strategies that will make your life purpose and intentions happen, as well as defining who you believe you are (your identity*)*. Your identity is made up of your psychological identity (skills, personality characteristics) as well as the fact that you are divinity experiencing humanness.
- *Mind II* controls beliefs, thinking skills, characteristics of thought (right brain or left brain preference, memory styles, organization styles), communication skills, and relationship skills.
- *Mind III* houses your sense of the intuitive and access to psychic knowing and skills.

All these parts of your mind must be aligned to your life intention(s). Although this seems hard, doing it is easy. For example, part of your life purpose and intentions may be to create happiness with a partner. This is your intention in the Spirit Domain. *The next step in the Mind Domain is to do the following:*

1. **Create general steps and strategies** that will support making your intention (happiness with a partner) happen over time. For instance, you describe the kind of person you want as a lifetime partner. You find groups where s/he is likely to be. You make your search for a life partner a part of your daily action, such as meeting new people and generating new friendships. To make this process easy, you make your steps small and your strategies simple and easy. You generate support and resources for your changing life vision. But most of all, listen to your inner voice and follow it. Above all, make what you do easy and fun. Listen to your intuitive urges and follow them. These are all strategies that you could use.

2. **Create an identity** (who you are) that supports your life intention. Identify how you should act, what you need to believe about yourself, as well as characteristics that are important to supporting your intention of happiness. Also, remember that you are divinity experiencing humanness and that this is part of who you are. Write it down, draw it, act it out, or do all of this.

   For example, you describe yourself as having a good self-image and sense of personal power. You also have a good sense of humor, you easily relate to people, and you are nonjudgmental, competent, loving, and creative. Because you are divinity experiencing humanness, you put down that you deserve respect and love just because of that. With this definition of who you are, you will attract a partner to you that is complimentary to this identity.

3. **Identify beliefs** that support your intention of happiness. For instance, create a belief that you deserve happiness with a partner compatible with your life intentions. Write your beliefs down.

4. **Identify skills** that will support your happiness intention. For example, a skill of communicating your needs and intentions to your partner in a way that they can understand would be important. You may already have this skill, or you may have to learn it.

5. **Identify the intuitive instinct** that tells you when you are going in the direction of your life intention. For example, a feeling of calm and balance that some call "centered" would be an intuitive instinct compatible with your positive life intention of happiness. A tightness or sense of anxiety somewhere in your body would be an intuitive instinct that you are aligned with the negative aspects of your life intention, e.g., learning what will not bring happiness with a partner.

6. **Develop intuitive knowing** that comes from listening to your inner self, your Higher Self, guides, and Me! Develop tools to access inner knowing such as interpreting your dreams, prayer, and meditation. Learn to write or draw what you hear or feel when talking with Us in the Spirit Domain of Life Energy.

Beliefs, skills, identity, steps and strategies, and intuition...these are the levels of the Mind Domain that will create a dense or more intense gathering of Life Energy to begin to form your intention in physical reality. *The more compatible they are with each other and your life intention, the stronger the energy.*

The Emotion Domain of Life Energy and Manifestation

Emotions are a domain of reality, just as mind and spirit. Emotions are also a type of Life Energy that forms your reality, and are the key to human existence. They are a magnificent gift you gave to yourselves. They provide:

- The critical experiences of life because they are the testing ground for intentions, beliefs, skills, intuition and strategies. By your emotional reactions, you can tell whether your beliefs, skills, intuitions, and strategies are right for your intentions. If you struggle for a long time and nothing happens, and you continually feel frustrated, sad, or angry, you are telling yourself this doesn't work.

- The intense experiences that are essential to human choice and learning. These experiences deepen, intensify, and speed learning and knowledge. From emotion grows wisdom. You learn what works and what doesn't, and what brings you happiness and closer to who you really are. By your emotional reactions, you learn about yourself, others, and the Universe. Wisdom is the outcome.

- A built-in feedback cycle to Mind and Spirit Domains, as well as the Physical and Subtle Physical Energy Domains. It gives you an instantaneous "read" on the consequences of your experiences that you are creating or in which you are participating. If the emotions are intensely negative, they begin to alter your beliefs, identity, and strategies, as well as impacting your physical body and its energy centers. If your emotions are intensely positive, they do the same...**their feedback alters the character of the Life Energy in the other domains of human reality.**

Love, fear, hate, anxiety, joy, confidence, peace, struggle—all are emotions. *To manifest your intentions, your emotions must be compatible with both your intentions from the Spirit Domain and the operations within the Mind Domain. So this is how you do it.*

Remember how your intentions form reality. Spirit energy forms intentions. This domain is the most powerful for manifestation. It has the strongest Life Energy. Your intentions in the Spirit Domain trigger all other domains of reality. So mind follows the lead of the strongest intentions from the Spirit Domain and makes energy denser in preparation for physical manifestation.

The Emotion Domain is next. Emotions are called forth that are compatible with your strongest spirit and mind energy. The emotions make the energy already manifesting even denser and more intense.

Suppose you intend to become a helper to others as part of your life purpose. Let's assume that in the Mind Domain, you have created identity, beliefs, skills, intuition, and steps that are compatible with this intention. Now, in the Emotion Domain, you decide what emotions are compatible with your intention and the mindset you have created (identity, beliefs, skills, intuition, and steps). Emotions such as pleasure in helping others, joy in the accomplishments of those you help, and care for yourself so that you balance your needs with others, would all be emotions compatible with the intention of helping others. So, focus on these emotions and encourage them. As you do, they will grow stronger and so will your intention.

Manifestation and Male and Female Emotions

You have created a culture that divides human emotions. Males can display anger and mastery in all its forms, but must resist displaying other more "female" emotions such as love, tenderness, fear, sadness, and caring. For females, it is the reverse. It is fine to show love, tenderness, and caring, but not fine to display anger or command. You have labeled any male showing "female" emotions as weak, especially in the business world. This mirrors your concept of females as being less than males.

Consequently, you have generated different experiential realities for human males and females so that each is less than they could be. But all human emotions are meant to be experienced by both halves of the human race. If both males and females do not allow themselves the freedom to experience and display the whole range of emotions, the energy to manifest reality is limited. Manifestation demands the whole range of human emotional capacity.

Negative Emotions and Manifestation

Negative emotions are ones that act as barriers to your intention, but they tell you what is not compatible with what you want. Fear tells you that you are not safe, or that there could be unpleasant circumstances or people entering your life. It is an invitation to find out what you do want.

There are other types of negative emotions, but, in fact, all are variations of fear. Anxiety, envy, jealousy, hatred—all have at their base fear, fear of not having something, fear of never having something that good again, fear. These emotions are not the devil personified. Nor are they a manifestation of human weakness. They are divine teachers. They teach you what you are not and what you do not want. They teach you by giving you the experience of the consequences of such emotions. How are you to know what you want and who you are without experiencing the opposite? Human life is lived by contrast. Negative and positive are contrasts.

Negative emotions not only teach you the boundaries of what you don't want, but they often give you a hidden gift. You may hate what has happened to your parents and friends. You observed them being mistreated by the legal system. From that, you decided to become a lawyer. This is a gift...good, which manifests out of bad.

Life, in fact, is biased. Contrary to your beliefs, it is not biased toward negative emotions and experiences. It is biased toward the positive. It is easier to create something positive than negative. Positive energy is stronger than negative over the long term. You have deliberately set up experiences that paint the opposite picture. Your media, schools, religions, and governments tell you that life is hard, filled with evil, difficulties, and sorrow. Life is not! You have created your own bias by these beliefs. So if you want a different reality, change your intentions to envision a more positive reality. Then, change your mindset and your emotions to support your vision and your vision will become reality.

The Subtle Physical Energy Domain

Your intention, mindset, and emotions bring Life Energy into denser and more intense form as you go from the Spirit Domain of reality to the mind and then to emotion.

Less powerful than these domains of reality, but very necessary to human existence, is Subtle Physical energy. As William Tiller indicated in his book, *Science and Human Transformation*, this domain is primarily made up of magnetic energy. His experiments to show this are very clever and a start towards showing that **true science and Life Energy are one and the same thing.**

Subtle Physical energy is made up of a reality that surrounds the physical form almost as a shadow. In fact, the auras, chakras, and meridians discussed by your esoteric traditions are Subtle Physical Life Energy. The human aura and the chakras act as a transducer system that takes in the Life Energy of the other domains (Spirit, Mind, Emotion) and changes their energy to subtle physical energy. Then the meridian pathways transport this transduced (changed) energy into the physical body's neurological and physiological systems.

Your aura, chakras, and meridians are focused on the health and energy flow of the human body as well as the other domains of Emotion, Mind, and Spirit. They also allow the larger energy fields of Spirit, Mind, and Emotion to become more focused and dense in order to manifest into human existence.

Your body therapies often tap into the Subtle Physical Domain of Life Energy and use it to heal the physical body. Acupuncture, Reiki, Shiatsu, Healing Touch, and Cranial-Sacral therapy are a few examples. By accessing the Subtle Physical Life Energy of the human body, you can balance and make coherent the denser Physical Domain with Emotion, Mind, and Spirit Domains. It is a powerful way of altering your reality.

Additionally, manipulation of subtle physical energy provides you with a base of something that is concrete. You can see the acupuncture points on the

30

skin and the needles, you can feel the heat of Reiki and Healing Touch hands, you can feel your body moving with Shiatsu and Cranial-Sacral work. But there is the unseen component also—the subtle physical energy that you are manipulating and balancing. In time, your perceptual systems will be altered so that you can see this subtle energy. Now, only psychics, intuition, and specialized instruments can "see" it.

Simply because you cannot easily see or touch subtle physical energy, as well as the energy of the Emotion, Mind, and Spirit Domains, does not make these energies unreal. It just makes them beyond what your present physiology and state of mind can perceive.

Do not believe scientists who say the only reality is what can be observed, or what they tell you to believe. Science is a religion with dogma and "spiritual" leaders of its own. It is time to put aside this notion that physical reality is the only real reality. It restricts who you are and it robs you of your intrinsic power—your divinity experiencing being human.

The next step in manifestation of a life intention is to match the energy centers of the Subtle Physical Domain so that they are coherent with your intention. That is, the energy of the aura, chakras, and meridians must demonstrate an energy pattern that facilitates your intention in becoming more dense and intense so that it can manifest in human reality. You do this by asking your inner self which of these energy points need your focus to change the energy flow.

You can start by asking your inner self about each of the chakra centers and their corresponding aura of energy. If you have an inner feeling that you should concentrate on a particular center, focus on the color of the center and on bringing white and gold light into the mixture to help healing and energy flow. Do the same for each center. Then ask if there are specific meridian points on your body where you need to bring light and energy. Use your hand to slowly go down your body and stop where you feel you should. Concentrate on bringing energy and light to that area through your hand. These actions will align these energy centers and pathways to your intention.

The *Being* State and Subtle Physical Energy

"*Being*" is a state of energy and experience where you exist within non-physical reality. It encompasses all of Life Energy. This energy state is the natural home of your soul, guides, your Higher Self, and Me. It is the level of reality from which all things are created. Intentions, thoughts, your identity, actions, emotions, and physical reality all begin here.

To access this type of non-physical reality, make your conscious mind take a back seat so that you can experience a deeper and more complete reality through your intuitive sense. When you do this, you experience what your Life Energy feels like. Here we can easily converse and relate with one another because you have stilled the usual chatter of your mind. Here you can experience peace, joy, security, unconditional love, freedom, and wisdom because these things are intrinsic to the energy of *Being*.

Being is also the state from which your *Observer Self* is able to make choices about negative or positive experiences in your life. The *Observer* is that part of your conscious mind, which sits back and observes what you and others are doing as you are doing it. Only when the *Observer* is active can you make choices in your life. To observe or be aware of what you and others are doing as you are doing it is an aspect of *Being*.

Being is part of all domains because it is Life Energy. But it reaches your conscious awareness most intensely within the Subtle Physical Domain. This domain focuses *Being* into denser energy within the energy fields and centers (chakras and meridians) of the human body.

Being is THE most important tool for your learning. *If you cannot set up an ongoing relationship between you and I within this unseen reality, you will not be able to achieve a transformation to a more optimal state of living. This is the key to your future. You must develop ways to access and be in this reality so that you can build your inner wisdom and personal power.*

The more ways you find to live within Being, the essence of Life Energy, the better. I will give you an extensive list so that you can find the access methods best for you. Don't be afraid to create your own methods. There are many ways of accessing Being through the Subtle Physical Domain. No one way is the right way. Only you can decide what is right for you.

One way to access *Being* is to relax in whatever way is most effective for you. Then just *exist*. Close your eyes and still your conscious thoughts. If thoughts pop up, just notice them and allow them to drift away as if you were an observer. Notice your breathing and focus on your breathing. Gradually slow your breathing as you note your "in" and "out" breaths.

Switch your focus to right between your two eyes in the middle of your forehead and just *exist*. Note the darkness. Don't try to see anything. Just exist letting yourself rest in the energy that you feel as you just *exist*. This energy is your soul and My Essence. It is Life Energy. Just allow your mind to rest here. Don't struggle with trying to make it happen. Just relax into existing in Life Energy while focusing your eyes in the middle of the forehead. This energy is always there so I am always with you!

You will feel a deep relaxation and an increasingly deep vibrancy and peace as you practice this. You may see in your mind's eye a light, feel a deep energy, or hear an inner voice. Allow yourself to follow it and see where it goes. *Do not consciously reach for it or you will bring back the control of your conscious mind.* Practice this on a regular basis.

Other methods for accessing Being are listed below.

- *Dreaming*…your inner self speaks to you through dream symbols about important issues and your life purpose. Remember what you dream and ask Us to help you understand its message to you. Then take the major things in your dream and free associate what they mean to you. Trust your inner self and Me to help you find the correct meaning. Listening to your dreams integrates your conscious mind with *Being*.
- *Praying*…this is a form of talking to Me within the Life Energy of *Being* as long as you mean what you say rather than reflexively reciting some memorized prayer or verse. It can be a monologue on your part or it can be a dialogue between you and I—whatever you desire.
- *Meditation*…when you still the chatter of your mind and just focus on My Consciousness within the Life Energy of *Being*, it is a form of listening to Me. I will talk to you through feelings, thoughts, symbols, images, words, or all of these things. Just listen.
- *Mindfulness*…this is a method of using your attention so that you are highly aware of everything you do and everything around you each moment. This allows you to *Be* fully in the present. Your mind stills, your senses sharpen, and you hear, sense, and see parts of our Life Energy (yours and Mine) that you haven't experienced before.
- *Automatic writing*…relax deeply and then allow your hand to write whatever comes to mind about a question or questions you have. It allows Us to talk to each other within *Being*.
- *Day dreaming*…allow your mind to drift in images and sensations around specific topics you pick. The images you get are like dream symbols that can be interpreted. Free-associate what the images mean to you to help interpret what the inner meanings are. It is a conversation in *Being* between your inner self and conscious mind.
- **Resting in, listening to, and feeling nature**…it is another form of *Being*.
- *Tai Chi, Chi Gong, yoga*…these movements can promote an inner focus and concentration that accesses the Life Energy of *Being*.
- *Deep breathing or other specific patterns of breathing*…when you focus on various movements of breathing, it bring you into *Being*.
- *Movement to music*…it brings you into *Being*.

- **Drawing in a relaxed state of mind**...do it around certain issues or emotions or thoughts and it will bring you into *Being*.
- **Creative writing**...writing poetry or stories can bring you into *Being*.
- **Talking out loud to your inner self, Higher Self, guides, or Me**...allows Us to have a conversation within *Being*.
- **Tarot cards or the Runes**...these old esoteric traditions can be used as a way of communicating with your inner self and Me. They are best used not to predict the future so much but as tools for looking at yourself and where you are. This brings you into *Being*.

All of these approaches are tools—ways of consciously gaining access to Being. This is for you to do or choose, not someone else. You can certainly learn from others how best to access Being. But it is essential that you finally access your own Life Energy by yourself! Alternatively, you can use a group. Do it, however, with the intention of using the group's more intense energy to help you access your own reality and Life Energy. It is time for you to gain this skill in the best way possible. Then you are on your way to experiencing and developing divinity while being human.

<u>The Physical Domain of Life Energy</u>

This is the level of energy with which you are most familiar. This is also the level you know least. Your understanding of the physical level is based on the myth of separation—the idea that you are separate from each other and Me. With your notion of separateness has come female, followed by a male dominance. Each has dominated in different ways. The female culture of over 10,000 years ago was more connected to nature, knowing at some level that humans were not so separate from their surroundings. But females were believed to be of more value than males because they produced life.

As I said earlier, you, as a human race, decided that you wanted to know the opposite of this experience. So males rebelled and over time, eliminated female-controlled cultures. The male culture that was created dominated females and elaborated on the idea of separation. God was separate from man and ruled man. Man was separate from woman and all other things on earth and was meant to rule them as he pleased. The entire earth, in fact, was created for man as his play thing, and he was to have dominion over it as he pleased. Your traditional creation texts and religions are based on these beliefs.

Those who got in the way of the male culture's leaders were killed or eliminated as being evil. Those under the leader's rule were required to abdicate their power to the leader. And finally, as you "progressed," you no longer believed that gods or God controlled you. Instead, you believed that you controlled all that was seen, and all that was unseen was irrelevant.

The truth is the very opposite. **The truth is that true reality is unseen.** That reality is connected because it is made up of energy that is connected. All reality is Life Energy. Therefore, humans are Life Energy, as are plants, animals, minerals, and heavenly bodies (planets and stars). All are connected. All are conscious in different ways. All are aspects of Me!

Therefore, what you do to yourselves—your own bodies, minds, and spirits—you do to Me. What you do to others—humans, animals, plants, etc— you do to Me. Everything that you do affects the learning of others and Me. As you learn and experience, so I grow and evolve. That is called living…real living. This dynamic evolving and becoming is the very nature of All That Is, and you, My human aspects. What you choose and do, adds to this living. You are free to choose and do whatever you think best.

But it is time to choose and experience positive living and learn your true natures as divinity experiencing humanness. You have learned enough of the negative contrast. It is time to develop the positive and understand and reflect Divine Love.

Now let Me explain how to add the Physical Domain into the manifestation process. At the Physical Domain, the intention(s) of the Spirit Domain, the steps, identify, beliefs, and intuition of the Mind Domain, the feelings and sensations of the Emotion Domain, and the magnetic energy of the Subtle Physical Domain, all manifest as a dense and intense form of energy. Remember, whatever is the strongest energy is the one that will manifest in physical form.

If you want to manifest a positive intention such as becoming whatever you do best, you align your Spirit, Mind, Emotion, and Subtle Physical energy so that all domains are compatible with this intention.

Now, in the Physical Domain, find ways to make your body's biochemistry and physical functioning compatible with your intention. Talk to the consciousness within your body. Remember that all things within your body have consciousness, e.g., cells, ligaments, tissues, organs, brain, and blood. As such, each aspect of your body not only has a consciousness all its own, but has free will and a knowledge of how best it should function to fulfill its purpose and the overall purpose of your body. The overall consciousness of your body is sometimes called the Inner Healer. We will call it *Body Consciousness*. *Body Consciousness* and all the aspects of your body are Life Energy and should be treated with respect and communicated with as you would other human beings. They are alive! Talk to them; tell them what you want and what your intention(s) is now. Ask their help to align the physical body and their particular part of the body to be compatible with the overall intentions you have put in place at all the other domains of existence, e.g., three levels of spirit, three levels of mind, emotion, and subtle physical energy.

Learn physical skills needed to support your intention. Allow your *Body Consciousness* to tell you what is best and what new skills to learn. These things could include learning how to control your own brain wave patterns to complement your choices, what nutritional intake will help, and exercising your body in ways beneficial to your intention. Doing all this in the Physical Domain anchors all of your other domains of existence to the earth and physical reality.

If all domains of Life Energy are now compatible with your intention, it will begin to manifest.

These are the basic steps of manifestation. (See Figure 1. for an illustration of all five domains and their role in manifesting human reality.)

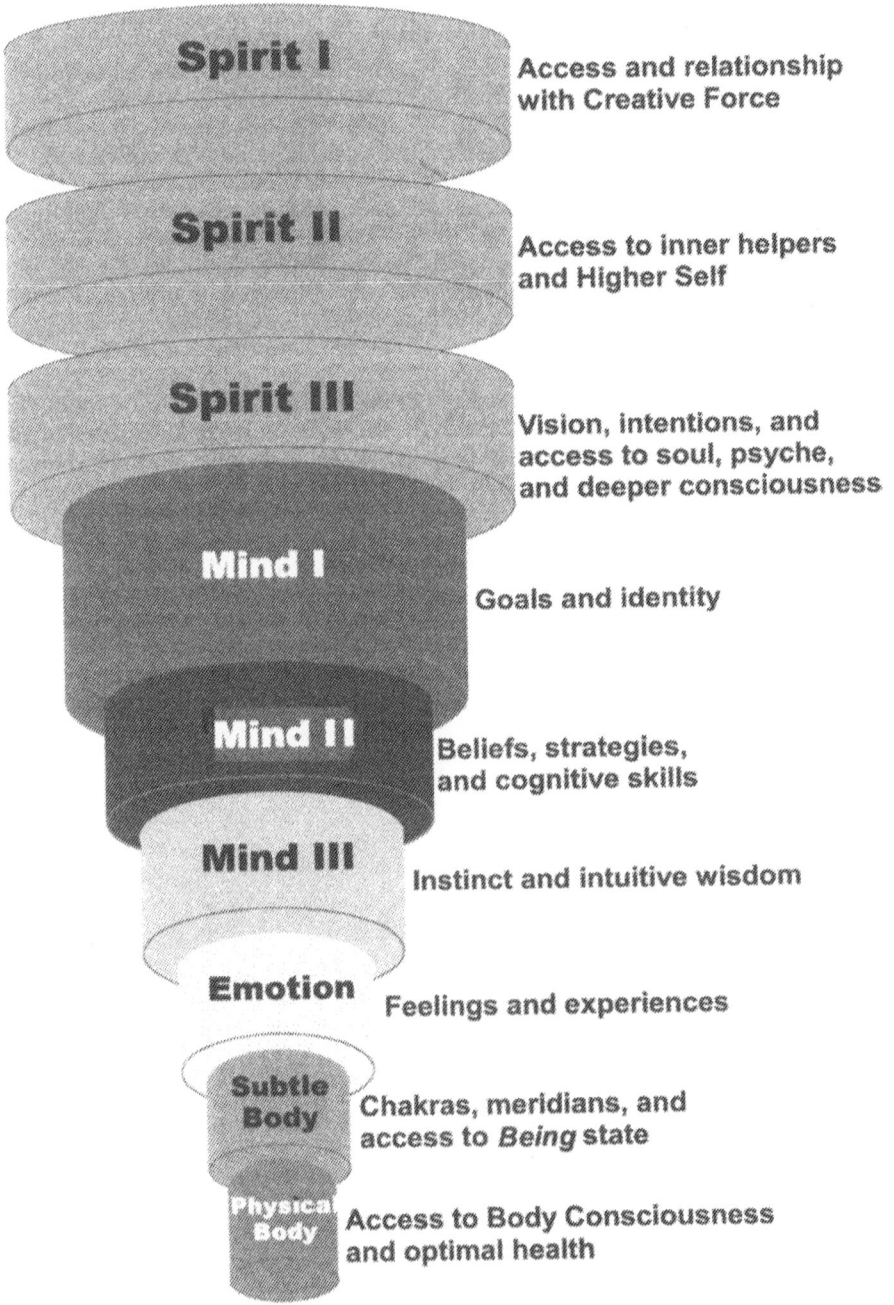

Spirit I — Access and relationship with Creative Force

Spirit II — Access to inner helpers and Higher Self

Spirit III — Vision, intentions, and access to soul, psyche, and deeper consciousness

Mind I — Goals and identity

Mind II — Beliefs, strategies, and cognitive skills

Mind III — Instinct and intuitive wisdom

Emotion — Feelings and experiences

Subtle Body — Chakras, meridians, and access to *Being* state

Physical Body — Access to Body Consciousness and optimal health

Figure 1. Life Energy Domains and Their Purpose

Strengthening the Life Energy Domains

Once you have aligned Life Energy within each of the domains to match your intention(s), meditating on what you want will hasten the manifestation of your intention(s). The _way_ you do this must have certain characteristics:

- *Focus on your intention and experience it as real and already occurred.* The more real you can experience your intention, the faster the manifestation process. If you focus on it as if it is still in the future and not yet manifested, you are telling the Life Energy you have created to stay in the future. Do this for about five minutes per day.

- After concentrating on your intention for five minutes, stop picturing or thinking about what you want and try to forget about it until the next day. The next day, concentrate on it in the same way, and then forget about it for the rest of the day. And so on. Constantly thinking about what you want slows the manifestation process with your fear and longing.

Summary

- The strongest thought is the one that is manifested.

- There are five domains of human Life Energy: Spirit, Mind, Emotion, Subtle Physical, and Physical. These domains are realities that have their own rules and their own consciousness. The Spirit Domain is the most powerful of all domains for manifesting something in physical form. All the domains must be compatible with each other to easily manifest what is wanted.

- Each domain of Life Energy has its own purpose for helping to manifest reality:

  The Spirit Domain – definition of your life purpose (your core life intention) as well as other life intentions (what you want) through collaboration with your inner psyche, your soul, inner helpers, and All That Is.

  The Mind Domain – creation of:

    1. steps and strategies to carry out the intentions,
    2. a new identity that will match what you want,
    3. beliefs and skills to support the manifestation of your intentions, and
    4. intuition and access to inner knowing to help carry out your intentions.

  The Emotion Domain – choosing emotions and experiences that are compatible with your intentions.

  The Subtle Physical Domain – activation of energy centers and paths within the magnetic energy fields of the human body that support your intentions; best access to awareness of *Being* state of consciousness.

  The Physical Domain – choosing nutrition, exercise, and control of brain patterns to support your intentions with the help of your *Body Consciousness*.

- *Being* is a state of energy and experiences where you exist within non-physical reality. It is the essence of Life Energy and who you really are minus your physical body. It is the home of your soul, the inner self, your Higher Self, and All That Is. It is the level of reality from which all things are created. Your intentions, thoughts, identity, actions, emotions, and physical reality all begin here.

- *Being is the most important tool for humans to learn about and to use to create the reality desired.* There are many ways of accessing *Being*.

Dianne's Experiences

For years, I struggled with trying to manifest the reality that I desired. Sometimes, the answer seemed to be a resounding "NO." It made me question my belief that thoughts and energy create reality. It threw me into fits of depression, anger, frustration, and weariness, depending on the situation when this happened. I couldn't figure out why things didn't work out as I had imagined it.

I worked out slowly that there must be other levels of reality involved, including my Higher Self and All That Is. But it didn't make sense that they would arbitrarily say no if I had free will. So I decided that there must be something else involved. The explanation given in this chapter makes the most sense of anything that I have ever read. By myself, I couldn't have come up with what I wrote. Believe me, I sure wanted to before this!

Once I understood that the five domains needed to be aligned with each other to make for the most intense thought to create the reality desired, and that there were agreements involved at the soul level that made manifestation easier or harder, my failures of the past began to make sense. I decided I would try what was written in this chapter with my life first, before I tried it with anyone else. So I went through each of the five domains, aligning them with a picture or vision of what I wanted. The vision was that I lived in a beautiful house in the mountains with a view of a lake. There were walking paths and woods all around. It was a peaceful and healing retreat. In this same vision, I imagined that I learned more each day about how to live as divinity experiencing humanness without having to struggle hard to learn. That each day, I found more and more peace and joy. It worked! My vision came true inside of two years. All of it!

I began trying the framework with my clients and, gradually, it began to bring them what they envisioned. In as little as 30 one hour sessions, my clients began to get better control over their lives and have parts of their vision materialize. But watching their work and mine within this five-domain framework, I realized that manifesting a vision or intention involved a process of working with the framework over time. It took making adjustments and discoveries in each of the five domains to fine tune what was envisioned so that it would manifest. For example, there are parts of you that want the vision you have, while there are other parts who want to keep the status quo. The parts of you that get in the way must be faced, respected for the message they bring, and then integrated into the picture of what you want. Fighting and hating those parts of your personality will only make matters worse.

Watching the progress of my clients, as well as myself, I also learned that as you do more work with these domains, you get better at creating what you envision. It's a skill and like all skills, needs to be practiced and developed! But the rewards are great and long lasting. With this framework, you are freed from depending on external sources of power. You take back you power within you and begin to create and control your own life according to your choices, rather than other people's needs and demands. It's a great feeling. It gives a deep feeling of empowerment! In addition, it begins to build sources of happiness in daily life that are much more permanent and intense than what can be obtained using the assumptions of our culture, e.g., power is outside of you, money is power and will get you happiness, etc.

Life Energy Activities

• Think of **one** thing you would like in your life—something important to you. Work within the five-domain framework that I have given you at each of the domains. Start with describing to yourself the one thing that you want. Then put down steps and strategies that might get you that one thing, and create three beliefs that would support what you want. Next, list two skills that are important in order to support getting what you want. Then identify two emotions that are important to support getting what you want. Next, tell your *Body Consciousness* to align the chakras and meridians that are important to what you want. Finally, identify whether there is anything you need to do physically to support getting what you want, e.g., diet, nutritional supplements, exercise, or training your mind.

This forms a complete picture of what you want with each of the domains supporting what you envision. Don't expect to know exactly how to do this yet. I will give exact details in the last chapter. For now, just try using the five-domain framework to the best of your ability.

Keep a journal of your successes and failures. Remember that humans must work with both negative and positive energies to know what something really is. Your failures are telling you what doesn't work and what you don't want. Your successes are telling you what does work and what you want according to your intention or vision. For your successes, ask why they were successful so you know how to repeat them. For your failures, ask what the message is for you—what you need to learn.

As you learn new things from keeping your journal, modify your vision if necessary. Make sure the remaining domains are still in sync with your vision if you change it. Doing this will begin the learning and creation process for you. You will learn how to create what you want and to control your life as you want. You will learn the beginning skills for being who you truly are…divinity experiencing humanness.

- Explore different ways to access *Being* (Life Energy) given in this chapter. Find out how *Being* feels to you, the wisdom it can provide, and the friendship with Us it can give.

Chapter 4

Negative Manifestation and Everyday Life

Your Everyday Life

Within your industrialized nations, you have created an everyday life that is too negative to sustain human life. The result is an increase in sickness and disease that are new to humans. Your planet is dying because of your abuse of its ecosystem. Your institutions are coming under attack all over the world because they are no longer able to support adequate living. You are boxing yourselves into a corner so that you have no choice but to try something else.

In the U.S., your Constitution formed a spiritual basis from which you could evolve as humans in dignity. Although the bias of male dominance can be seen in these principles (women and people of color were excluded from the rights written down), it nonetheless provided a new basis for freedom and tolerance that had not been seen for a long time.

These same principles have been twisted and ignored as money and power have become your vision of what is desired. Talking to Me has become dogmatized into a ritual attended usually once per week. Otherwise, you forget to include Me in your daily lives. Your legislators have forgotten the basis of their existence—to serve their people to the best of their ability. Your business institutions are rampant with greed. Your educational institutions teach by rote and do not challenge the mind and consciousness as they should. Your spirit is focused on the concrete, what you see in front of you as reality. God is a myth according to many of your scientists.

What can sustain life in this picture? What is the purpose of living? Is this living or simply existence? You limit who you are to reflexive robots. You react to what comes your way, or you set up an image of earning enough money to be on easy street. Yet, your research tells you that neither money nor power bring happiness and optimal living. You are pursuing a myth of happiness!

Your deeper selves know that this is not a viable way of maintaining life. But your souls are aiding and abetting your slide into extreme negativity so that you have to do something different. Trying harder with the same old approaches will not work! So you have decided along with Me that it must change. Your institutions will crumble and new forms will arise that are better suited for nurturing life that is divinity experiencing humanness.

How do you survive this change process? How do you not only survive, but prosper and grow to become the beings that you truly are? This is the focus of this chapter.

The Negative and Positive are on a Continuum

This is the beginning of a difficult concept, but one that is important for you to understand to be able to manage the process of change while building optimal living. Positive and Negative Life Energy are on a continuum of homeostasis (balance). More Positive Life Energy and consequent experiences will attract Negative Life Energy and experiences, and vice-versa. They balance each other. You, as a human race, have set this as a law of earthly existence. *You choose the intensity of the experiences and the balance point for positive and negative outcomes.*

You use negative and positive experiences to decide what is best for the manifestation of your intention. The negative tells you what you don't want and what something is not. The positive tells you what you do want and what something is, e.g., its defining characteristics. You use the knowledge gained from these experiences to decide what the best choices are to manifest your intention. *Whether you experience the negative directly or through observation is up to you.* Look at Figure 2. on page 46 for a depiction of these principles.

Negative and Positive Life Energy and their outcomes are, therefore, equivalent to a right and left rudder correction on a boat or plane. The course of a plane or boat is steered by the position of the rudders and the intensity of their use. In similar fashion, you use negative and positive emotion and events to steer the course of your intention. *But the intensity of the experience, and whether the experience is negative or positive, is determined by your decision about the rightness of the course for your intention.*

For example, let's say you have an intention that you want to find a life's work that is satisfying, joyous, interesting, and that gives you the freedom to exercise your talent. The next thing you know, you lose your present job. This is something you don't want. But the experience is telling you that you need to move in a different direction and/or rethink what you want. By manifesting this unwelcome outcome, your deeper consciousness is trying to give you the energy to reach out for work that you want or that is best for your life purpose. Losing your job was necessary.   Without this, you wouldn't have attempted to do anything about your intention for a better job because you were too afraid.

Now let's say you find the career that you want. Your deeper consciousness will manifest an experience sooner or later that will be negative to show you more of what you don't want and help you to expand your definition of the type of work that would manifest your original intention. You have a choice whether to experience the negative event directly or by observing it in others or both.

The balance point (homeostasis) of positive and negative outcomes changes as you shape the course of manifesting your intention. The balance point will depend on:

- Where you are in your journey to fulfill your intention, e.g., whether more negative or positive experiences are needed next to manifest your intention.
- What you believe about your reality, e.g., whether negative experiences are more frequent than positive or vice-versa.

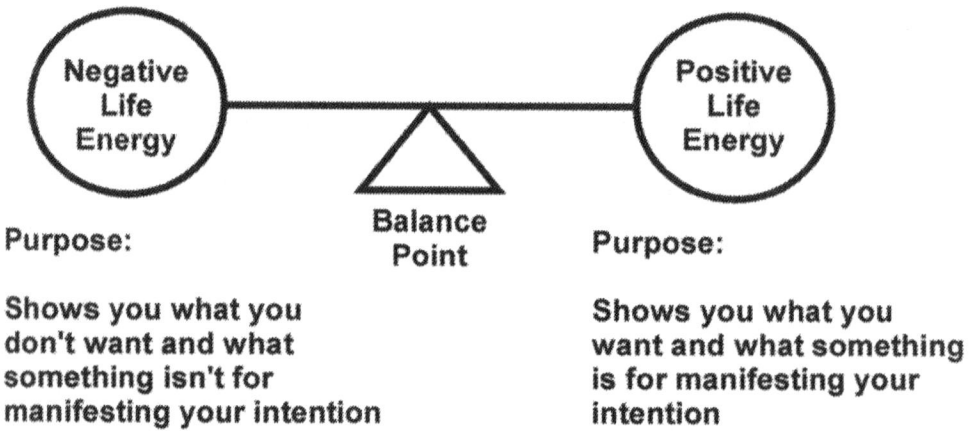

Figure 2. A Continuum of Life Energy and Their Purposes

You will also choose a bias. The bias involves the intensity of positive and negative you experience. Therefore you could set the bias so that your positive experiences will be very intense and the negative much less so. But there are consequences to any bias that is set. If you decide to keep the negative in a mild experience range, then your learning will know more about the positive than negative and vice-versa.

So far, most of you have biased your experiences toward more intense negative experiences than positive. As I have said before, as a race, you have decided to reverse this bias to more intense positive experiences and less intense negative ones. You have also decided to alter the point of balance or homeostasis so that there will be more positive than negative experiences.

Presently, your idea when experiencing Negative Life Energy is that something has control over what you want or don't want. Your belief assumes that you can't have what you want because of this outside control. The result of this belief is that you feel like a victim, helpless because the power is beyond you.

As I have just explained, this is not the case. You create your negative experiences as a group and individually. You have intentions and you steer a course that will best get your intentions created. So control is not outside of you, but always within you. What you are experiencing, you have either created or accepted at some level of your self (conscious, deeper conscious, Higher Self).

The next thing is extremely important for optimal living. The way to look upon negative vs. positive feelings and events in your life is this: There are differences in life experience, which *can be negotiated by you, the person. It is your choice. You decide what will be your bias and balance point (intensity and amount of positive and negative experiences) at any one time.*

Choose your bias and balance point and so it will be. Notice the result; ask if you want it or need it. Then, if you wish change, negotiate a change between your "differences." Treat negative and positive as if they were different parts of yourself. They really are different energy patterns within your make-up that you have created or accepted by your intention, bias, and balance point. Ask these energies and your inner self to work out the solution(s) and overcome any challenges in the most effective way.

For example, allow your fearful self to speak to the self that wants empowerment. Tell them, as well as your deeper self, to work out a solution or solutions where the outcome will be intensely positive. Ask those parts of you to let you "hear" their solution in your mind, or show you with signs or opportunities that come your way. Also, use the tools for accessing *Being* to help understand your experiences and how to change them to help manifest what you want.

Remember that these negative and positive energies are part of who you are and are partners in your life purpose(s). Respect them, converse with them, and make them your "friends." This is the way in which you can truly become whole. Integrate opposites so that you know they are all a part of you— negative *and* positive, light *and* darkness, spirit *and* body, rather than negative *or* positive, light *or* darkness, spirit *or* body.

The Continuum of Positive and Negative, Transformation and Control

With the approach that the positive and negative are a continuum for steering your life intentions to manifestation, you do not have the constant struggle and war between the negative and positive that you have now. Most importantly, you are in control over the course of your life experiences. You have your hand on the rudder, rather than letting someone or something outside of yourself do it.

In fact, it is critical that you control the rudder that manages Negative and Positive Life Energies through consciously setting your intentions (what you want) in the Spirit Domain. When you do not consciously set your intentions and then manifest them by matching the other four domains (mind, emotion, subtle physical and physical) with those same intentions, it will seem as if you are sliding along on a sea of surprise storms and unexpected turns that are outside of your control. That is, of course, an illusion. But because you are not setting intentions and actions consciously, it will seem real enough.

When you decided to experience the negative intensely, it was necessary for most of you to give up the skill of consciously setting your intentions and working with all five domains of reality to achieve your intentions. It was necessary to do this because you needed to feel as if the control was outside of you to create the negative reality you desired to experience. You needed to feel that I was separate from you and unknowable.

So now, if you desire to reverse this reality and institute a positive bias that will nurture a life of divinity experiencing humanness and optimal living, you must reverse your use of consciousness so that you perceive the reality and connections between all things both physical and non-physical. The only way to do this is to use your conscious mind to set your intentions in the Spirit Domain, match the energies of the Mind, Emotion, Subtle Physical and Physical Life Energy with your intentions, and then manage positive and negative energies in the best way to help manifest what you want.

Tuning Your Energy from Negative to Positive

This is very important. In order to achieve transformation to an optimal life, you must form your intentions <u>consciously</u>, as well as <u>consciously</u> know how to *manage Negative and Positive Life Energy <u>within</u> the five domains of Life Energy (Spirit, Mind, Emotion, Subtle Physical, and Physical).*

Negative and Positive Life Energies are part of each of the five domains of human reality. (See Figure 3. on the next page.) They form the contrasts of life so you understand what a thing is and what you really want within each of the domains. This means you must know how to manage these two energy systems within these domains to manifest what you want. How do you do that? I will give you a seven-step process to use in the final chapter. For now, let Me explain in general things you can do to manage negative energy within each domain and make it your friend and teacher.

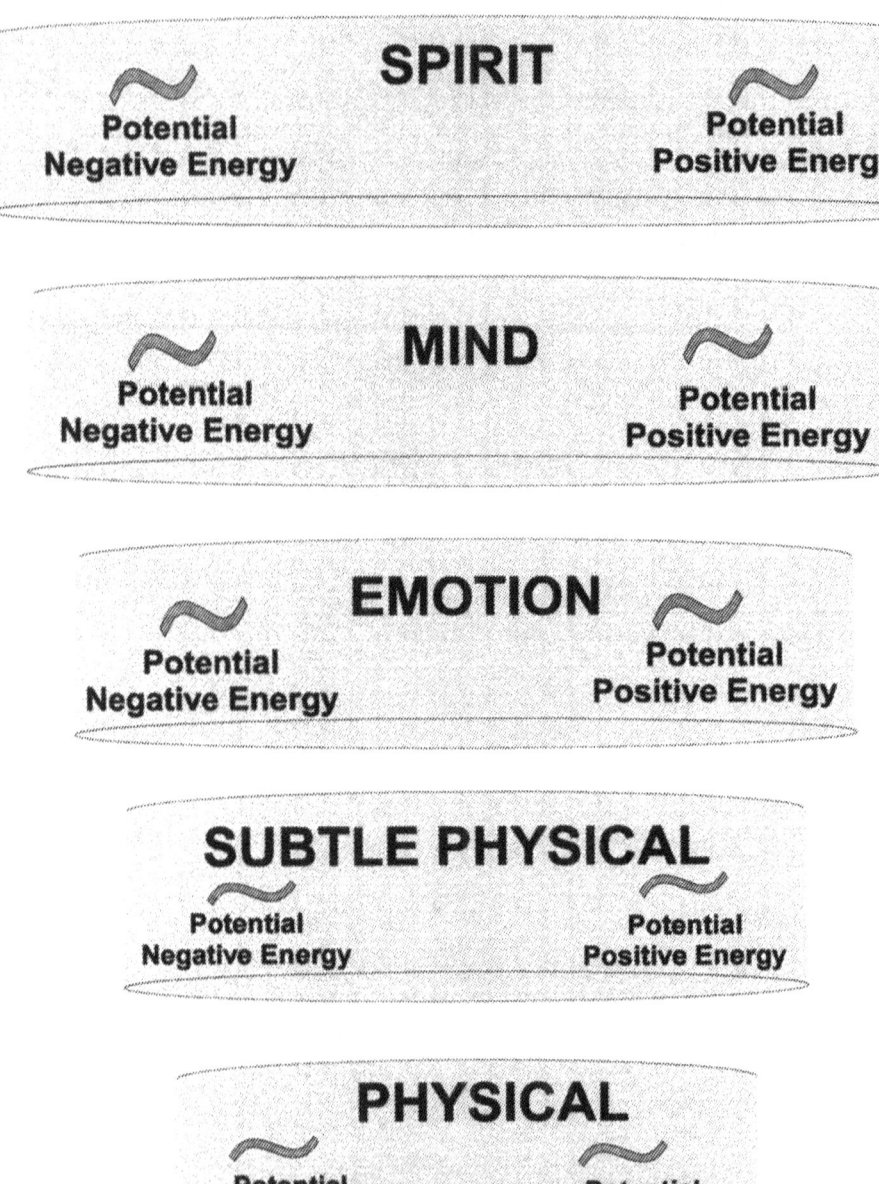

Figure 3. Life Energy Domains Showing Negative and Positive Energies

Spirit Domain: Vision and Intentions

Here it is important to form positive intentions rather than negative ones if you wish to build optimal living. For example, your intention (what you want) should be stated in a positive form, rather than negative. Suppose one of your intentions is that, you want more happiness in your life as well as optimal health. State this wish as if it has already happened and indicate that you want more frequent intense positive experiences. Example: "I experience frequent and intense happiness and have optimal health." This statement sets your balance point toward the positive and sets a bias for intense positive experiences. It also sets the time frame for manifestation in the here and now.

A negative way of stating the same thing is as follows: "I don't want anymore major traumas and crises in my life, including being so sick." This is telling Life Energy what it *should not* form, but says nothing about what it *should* form. With such a negative statement, you are focused solely on negative energy and ignoring the positive.

At times, you may feel yourself wishing for things to change, and your thoughts create a negative intention such as, "I don't want that anymore!" There is nothing wrong with this. You now know what you don't want. But next, form a positive thought about what you do want such as, "I want to have friends with whom I feel compatible." This will set a positive intention.

The key is this. Stating what you don't want in your life is an intention. It tells Negative Life Energy what you don't want. But to get to optimal living you must state what you <u>do</u> want. This tells Positive Life Energy what to manifest for you. And you must state what you want as if it has already happened so that it manifests NOW, not sometime in the future.

Mind Domain: Beliefs

You have trained yourselves to react in a certain way to your environment and experiences. Those responses are based on the assumptions and beliefs taught by your culture or learned through personal experiences. Some of the responses are adequate for helping you form a new positive type of living. Many of the responses are not. Your task is to separate what is useful and what is not.

One way to do this is to ask what you are assuming. When you get into a conflict with a family member, for example, what are you assuming? One assumption you might make is, "I should be respected and loved no matter what and this isn't happening."

You also usually tell yourself a "story" about what is happening. Using the same example, the story might go like this: "I wouldn't do that to him. All he's doing is thinking about what he wants and forget me! How many times have I helped him and not asked for anything in return!"

Your assumptions and the story you are telling yourself are made up of beliefs about yourself and the other person. You believe that family should love one another unconditionally. You believe you are being disrespected and taken advantage of. You believe that you are not appreciated. You believe the other person is self-centered and critical, demanding more than they ever give. You also believe that this person makes you feel this way by their actions. This, in turn, indicates that you believe the control over this situation is outside of yourself and in the hands of the other person. No one can make you react a certain way. But if you believe this, it will happen.

To make your beliefs conscious and more positive, follow this process:

1. Write down your assumptions about what happened. What were you assuming should have happened and didn't? These are beliefs.
2. Write down the story you are telling yourself about what happened, e.g., your interpretation of what was happening such as what the other person was doing to you. These are beliefs.
3. Now write down what you would have liked to experience and why.
4. Write down what you don't want to experience and why.
5. Ask yourself whether what you've written in step 3 and 4 are compatible with the life you want (your life intention or vision). If they aren't, then rewrite them to better support the optimal living you want.
6. Ask yourself whether your assumptions and your story (your beliefs), will support getting what you want. If not, reword your assumptions as well as the story you are telling yourself so that they are compatible with what you want.
7. Look at your actions and emotions in this experience and write down things you believe about you in that situation, both positive and negative. Reword negative beliefs so they are more positive.

In order to have choices about how to consciously manage Negative and Positive Life Energy in this type of situation, you must make these beliefs conscious as I just did in these examples. Then you must change your beliefs in order to change your reactions and have a more positive outcome. Here is how to do this for yourself.

Let's use the example of family conflict and go through this process. I have written down what assumptions might be made about the family conflict. I have also described the story you might tell yourself, and listed the beliefs that are associated with the story.

The next step, step 3, is to write down what you want and why. Let's say you want an easy, mutually loving and compatible relationship with members of your family. You want this because family is an important support mechanism for you.

Step 4 asks about what you don't want. Let's say you don't want to feel angry, tense, and guarded when you interact with your family. You don't want this because it means that you are letting your control slip outside yourself to your family.

Step 5 asks whether what you put down in step 3 and 4 are compatible with what you want in your life as a whole. Let's say part of your life vision (intention…what you want) is to love yourself and others as aspects of Me. Both Step 3 and 4 fit in with this picture. Step 3 talks about wanting a mutually loving and compatible relationship with your family. Step 4 states what you no longer want and why, in this case, because you know that you are giving up your control to others.

Step 6 involves rewriting your assumptions and your story (your beliefs) to better fit what you want your life to be. Going back to the original example, there was an expectation (belief) that there should always be unconditional love in families. This is not a reasonable belief. It is not possible in human reality to provide unconditional love all the time. You could state that unconditional love is possible some of the time in families and is a good thing for which to reach. You can also make a commitment to try to respect each other as divinity experiencing humanness. You could word your expectation to something like this: *I believe that each of us is divinity experiencing humanness. As such, I will ask members of my family to support my life journey as best they can. I will give them the same thing in return.* These are reasonable positive intentions and beliefs.

Step 7 involves asking the question, "What do you believe about yourself that is making you react this way?" Do you believe that you are not worthy of respect? Do you believe that you are inadequate? Look at how those beliefs create the situation that I have just described— you believe that you are unworthy and you create the situation according to this belief.

Rewriting some beliefs from the example:

Negative Belief	Reworded Belief
I wouldn't do that to him.	I usually try to be respectful to others and I listen to what they want. But sometimes I have to set boundaries to protect my interests and what is good for me. This could clash with what others want. If that happens, I can explain why I can't help, and affirm their ability to get what they want elsewhere.
All he's doing is thinking about what he wants and forget me!	It's perfectly all right for him to think about what he wants. But I want more consideration given to what's important to me. I can ask him to do this. If he can't, then I have to make a decision about how I feel about that and what I want to do about the relationship.
You believe you are being disrespected and taken advantage of.	No one can cause me to feel disrespected and taken advantage of. These are interpretations that I am making about the situation. What I am saying when I react that way is that I want something different. I can ask for what I want either through setting an intention (what I want) at the Spirit level and/or I can ask the other person to give it to me. Also, if I respect and love myself I don't have to have respect from others. And if I respect and love myself and do not allow myself to do things that are not good for me, I am not a victim. I create my life.

Change your beliefs to reflect the positive about yourself, such as:

- I am worthy of respect just as I am because I am divinity experiencing humanness.
- I have all the tools that I need to complete my life journey and life purpose.
- My tools and skills are just different from others who have their own tools and skills for their journey.
- I am perfect for the particular aspect of God that I am.
- No one else can learn and provide the knowledge and experiences that I can.

Resolve to focus on your new positive beliefs and imagine what situations they will create. Act as if you have already learned these beliefs and they are now part of your normal reactions. Keep this focus each day, and they will become a part of you and form a new reality.

Mind Domain: Inner Communication and Intuitive Knowledge

There are other ways to help you retune your Negative Life Energy experiences to more positive ones, which involve inner communication and your intuition.

Option 1. Face the negative; do not run from it. Ask your deeper consciousness the message it is trying to tell you. *Remember that the message is one that you yourself are creating at a deeper conscious level along with your helpers (Myself, your Higher Self, your soul, your guides). You are creating the message through Negative Life Energy to guide your conscious experiences and learning in the direction desired.* When you ask your deeper consciousness what the message is, listen for the answer within your mind, or write down the first thing that comes to mind using your non-dominant hand to write. (Using your non-dominant hand insures that your conscious mind is occupied with how to write, thus allowing your deeper consciousness to by-pass the usual censorship of your conscious mind. If you cannot use your non-dominant hand, then maintain relaxation and free associate whatever comes to mind. Do not allow your conscious mind to sensor what your write down as you do this.)

a) Ask yourself what gift(s) you have given yourself through the use of this Negative Life Energy. What have you learned to do as a result of the negative? For example, as a result of the fear for your emotional safety, you have learned how to network with many different types of people. Thank the dark side of you for helping you learn this.

b) What part of yourself are you not accepting that your dark side (your shadow self) is showing you? Is there a self within that bullies other people and insists on having its way at the expense of the other? *Your dark side always reflects some aspect of yourself you do not accept, or that you need to develop.* For example, you may need to become more assertive, and your dark side is pulling aggressive or assertive people to you to show you how it is done.

c) Give love and acceptance to the self you are right now, and the potential self you want to be. You are exactly where you are supposed to be at this moment in time for the life purpose(s) that you have chosen. So honor where you are now, what you have learned, and the potential force to become more of who you are (divinity experiencing humanness).

d) Let go of all the labels you have for the experiences generated by your dark side such as fear for your emotional safety. Let go of all the experiences you are picturing in your mind's eye having to do with the negative feeling. Notice the energy that is left…it is simply energy. It is *Being.*

e) Now ask yourself if you are ready to move forward to a more positive experience. If you are, focus on the experience(s) you want to have, making it as vivid as possible in your mind's eye. Create beliefs that will support this image. Carry out the rest of the manifestation framework discussed in Chapter 3 to create the positive experience. You and I will manifest it in a time and way that is best for you.

Option 2. Another technique that is very effective for managing the negative is having a dialogue with Me! To prepare for our conversation:

a) Relax using whatever method is best for you. Listening to music before and during a conversation with Me is a good way of relaxing and staying that way.

b) Set up your intention. What do you want to find out from our conversation?

c) Indicate that you wish to receive the best information that is possible for you.

d) Indicate that you wish to receive a feeling of deep knowing that lets you distinguish between information from your deep consciousness versus your ego. Your ego or conscious mind will give you information or advice that gives a feeling of tension or pressure because it often acts like a scolding parent... "You should do..." I don't operate that way, nor does your soul. So it's important to know to whom you are listening. The conscious mind, unaided by your deeper consciousness, can only give answers that are limited in scope. So, if you feel anxious, fearful, or have difficulty finding words as you are trying to talk to me, you are allowing the conscious mind to control.

e) If you suspect your conscious mind is controlling or overly interfering, note what it says, and tell it respectfully that you have heard its message. Then let it go. The conscious mind often gives advice based on beliefs it has been programmed with from your life experience. Tell it that you and it need to figure out a new angle because the present programming isn't working. In that way, your ego and your soul can work together.

Option 3. Consult Tarot cards, Angel cards, or other esoteric traditions such as the Runes or the I-Ching. These methods access your deeper consciousness and provide you with an answer to the negative situation you are experiencing. These esoteric approaches should not be used to predict the future, so much as to provide advice on understanding a problem or situation in your life.

Option 4. Record and interpret your dreams. As I said earlier, dreams are generally created in order to better describe situations experienced during your waking hours. Dreams are a built-in internal teacher—use them.

Mind Domain: Strategies To Get What You Want

There are many strategies for overcoming blocks to creating forward movement towards what you want. Two of the best logical strategies are as follows:

Option 1. Brainstorm about the situation that is blocking forward movement. Describe the problem and then brainstorm to find a good solution. When you brainstorm, do not censor the possible solutions you write down. Just write whatever comes to mind. After you're done, only then pick the one that looks the best. Make sure you understand what the real problem is before you come up with a solution.

Option 2. **Journal**, so that you not only record the thoughts and events of each day, but also put down a free association of how you feel. Doing both these things uses both the logical and intuitive parts of your mind. After a period of five to seven entries in your journal, notice what you want and what you don't want over those entries. Then brainstorm how best to go about getting what you want.

The key at the Mind Domain level is to change negative experiences to positive by looking at your beliefs and decisions. Change each to fit with what you envisioned and want at the Spirit Level.

Emotion Domain

Option 1. Treat negative and positive emotions as if they were different parts of yourself. They really are different energy patterns within your psyche that you have created or accepted by your intentions and thoughts. Ask these energies to speak to one another to work out the solution(s) and overcome any challenges in the most effective way.

For example, allow your fearful self to dialogue with the self that wants empowerment. Write what each says down. Allow each to state what they feel. Then tell them its time to work out a solution together where the outcome fits in with what you want out of life. It's time because what you are doing isn't working and trying harder isn't going to cut it. Ask those parts of you to write out the solution(s) or show you with signs or opportunities that come your way. Ask your soul, your guides, your Higher Self, or Myself to help these parts of your psyche find the best solutions(s) for you.

Option 2. Another important approach to managing negative emotion is to find the core purpose of the experience. Remember, these negative and positive emotions and experiences are your "rudders" for creating and manifesting the intentions you want. So, find out what your intention is behind the negative experience. What are you trying to get; what bottom line purpose?

To find the core purpose behind the negative experience, talk to it as if it were a person. After all, all negative experiences are either created or accepted by some part of your consciousness. So it is a part of you that has made this happen, trying to teach you something. *Talk to it in the following way*:

1. *Ask, "What is my purpose?"* Listen for the answer. Write it down.

2. *Then ask, "If you accomplish this purpose for me, is there anything else more important that you want for me?"* Listen to the answer and write it

down. Then ask the same question again. Listen for the answer again. Continue writing what you get.

Keep on asking the same question and listening for the answers, until one answer gives you a feeling of peace and an instant recognition that if you really achieved this, it would bring you great satisfaction, harmony, and peace. In other words, it would place you in some aspect of the state of *Being*. At the same time, you will feel all the tension about this topic leave you. This is the core purpose of this negative teacher that is part of you.

3. **When you know your core purpose,** thank this negative "teacher" for helping you find it. Create with your mind's eye and inner emotions what it would be like if you achieved this core purpose. Make it as real as possible.

4. **Then ask yourself if you are willing to start with this core purpose, rather than it being the last thing you do.** If you are, then commit to focusing on making it happen in your life. I, your guides, and your soul will help you find ways of doing that.

5. **To help you see how different it would be if you start with your core purpose**, go back to look at the purpose you identified right above it. Ask yourself, "If I start with this core purpose of (state what it is)_____, how would it make this purpose of (state what the purpose just before the core purpose was)_____ different? How would it alter my life and my reaction?" Write the answer that comes to you.

6. **Do the same thing for all of the other purposes** you found before getting to your core purpose. Do this so that you fully realize and experience how different your life will be if you start with your core purpose as the first step rather than the last for this problem.

Let Me give you an example of this approach. Let's say that you are experiencing fear of saying "no" to others when they ask you to do something.

Step 1. *Label that part of you* that is generating this fear as Fear of Saying No. Ask this part of yourself, "What is your purpose for me?" The answer comes, "Protecting you from loss of love."

Step 2. *Next say*, "If we achieve protecting me from loss of love 100% of the time, is there anything even more important that you want for me?" The answer comes, "Getting love from others without a struggle."

Step 3. ***Next ask***, "If we achieve getting love from others without a struggle 100% of the time, is there anything more important that you want for me?" The answer, "To learn to love yourself without qualification."

Step 4. "If we achieve learning to love myself without qualification all of the time, is there ***anything else even more important that you want for me***?" The answer, "No; this is your core purpose."

Now, you look within yourself and feel a sense of deep peace and calm. You also notice that the tension about the problem has left you. This then is truly the core purpose.

Step 5. ***Next, imagine how it would feel*** and what you would do if you loved yourself without qualification. Make it as real as possible. Remember that ways of accomplishing this will come to you with Our help. Then ask yourself if you're willing to start with this core purpose as your first step, rather than having to wade through all the other purposes first. If you are, continue with step 7 (and skip step 6).

Step 6. ***If you feel a resistance to starting with the core purpose*** as your first step ask, "Is there another part of me that doesn't want this to be the first step?"

Listen for the answer and ask why it is unwilling to start with this core purpose. Let's say this "other part of you" says, "You can't start with loving yourself because you are afraid of being abandoned by others if you don't do what they want."

So now you are talking to a part of yourself that has a fear of being all alone in the world. This part of you also has a core purpose, which may be different from the one you just discovered. But you must find the core purpose of this second part of you 'Fear of Being Alone In the World' first, before going to step 7.

So now repeat all the steps from 2 through 5 to find this self's core purpose. And then go on to step 7 through 9. Follow the directions using the core purpose of your second self (Fear of Being Alone in the World) first, and then go back to the first self (Fear of Saying No). The examples below use the information gained from the first self example, Fear of Saying No.

Step 7. ***At this point, you are going to re-look at the other purposes*** you found before your core purpose. The one right before the core purpose for the Fear of Saying No part of you was, "wanting to get love from others without a struggle."

Ask, "If I start with my core purpose of loving myself without qualification, how would it make different *getting love from others without struggle?*" The answer comes, "It wouldn't matter so much, because I would be feeling love from myself. Also, people would give love back more easily because I wouldn't be demanding it from them. There wouldn't be a struggle anymore!"

Step 8. *The purpose right before* "getting love from others without a struggle," was "protection from loss of love." So next, ask, "If I start with my core purpose of loving myself without qualification, how would it make different *'protecting myself from loss of love'?*" The answer comes, "I would be getting more love than before because I would be feeling love from myself. And I will attract others to love me because I love myself. When I feel comfortable with myself, it attracts other people to me. So I wouldn't have to be so afraid of losing love anymore."

Step 9. *Next, ask,* "If I start with my core purpose of loving myself without qualification, how would it make different the original problem of 'not being able to say no'?" The answer comes, "If I love myself without qualification, I will be considering whether saying no would be the best loving thing to do for myself. It will making saying no easier."

I have adapted this approach from a book Dianne read called *Core Transformation* by Connirae Andreas. It is a wonderful way of getting to the inner self and Me when negative reality is activated.

Remember that these negative emotions are part of who you are and are partners in your life purpose(s). Respect them, converse with them, and make them your "friends." This is the way in which you can truly become whole. Integrate opposites so that you know they are all a part of you—negative *and* positive, light *and* darkness, spirit *and* body, rather than negative *or* positive, light *or* darkness, spirit *or* body.

Subtle Physical Domain

Negative experiences, emotions, and beliefs affect your body's subtle physical energy by slowing down the flow of energy or even stopping it in certain areas. To transform these lowered energy areas back to more optimal functioning, you can do the following: Ask your inner healer, your *Body Consciousness*, to help you create positive energy changes within your body's major subtle energy centers—the chakras. Look at Figure 4. on page 63 to see where these centers are located in your physical body in addition to their natural color frequencies. Visualize the appropriate color as you hold your hand over the seventh chakra at the top of your head. Have the intention that healing energy is coming through your hand and into the chakra. Then visualize the color becoming brighter and brighter as the chakra's energy increases to an optimal level. Then move onto the next chakra in the middle of the forehead and do the same thing. Continue with this process for each chakra until you have completed giving healing energy to all them.

Then ask your inner healer to continue to help you transform negative subtle physical energy to positive during your day. It will then go about supporting you in the way you've asked.

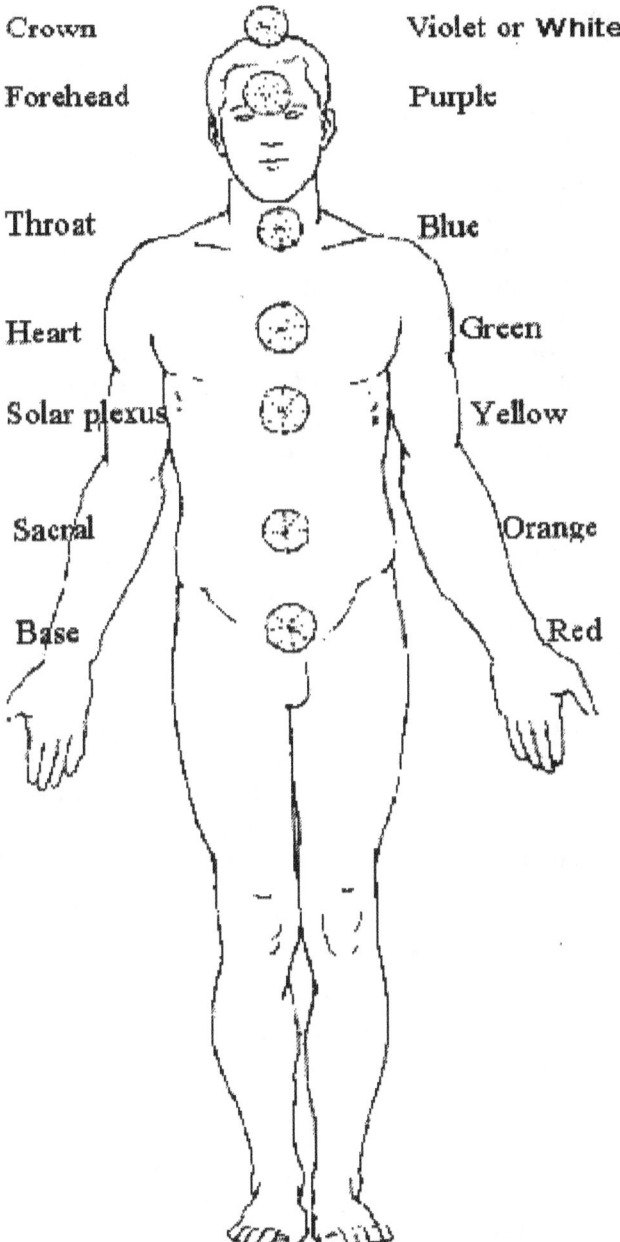

Crown   Violet or White

Forehead   Purple

Throat   Blue

Heart   Green

Solar plexus   Yellow

Sacral   Orange

Base   Red

Figure 4. The Seven Major Energy Centers Within the Body - The Chakras

Physical Domain

Illness or body imbalances are showing a dis-ease in your body's energy. In other words, it is reacting to some intentions, beliefs, attitudes, emotions, actions, and/or subtle physical energy that are resulting in this outcome. If this outcome is simply a result of negative energy signals that you have created in one or more of the Life Energy Domains, you can change your body's functioning to health and well-being by changing your "programming" in these areas.

Examine your intentions in the Spirit Domain. Do you want to be physically healthy or are you intending to get sympathy and caring from others by seeming to be a victim of your illness? This intention or wish will guarantee your ill health staying in place. In contrast, an intention of wanting to enjoy a vibrant healthy life will guarantee better health becoming manifest in your life.

Look at your beliefs in the Mind Domain. Just free associate what you feel and believe about sickness and health in general, and your health in particular. Put down whatever comes to mind and continue this for about five to ten minutes. Then look at what you have written. The phrases and words you put down are beliefs about health. (A more detailed procedure for examining beliefs was given in the Mind Domain section of this discussion about transforming negative energy to positive. Use that process also.)

Beliefs are some of the most common reasons for ill health and poor functioning. A belief such as health is solely controlled by outward fixes like drugs, doctors' advice, and other physical aids, will guarantee that your creative power to change things for the better is outside of your control. You are saying that you have no control over your own body's Life Energy. Wrong! Your control is within you. Outside helps are only aids to your inner control.

Another common belief is that the appearance of ill health is usually a random event—it just happens due to chance encounters with germs or an accidental occurrence. You are an innocent victim. Wrong. You created or accepted this condition at some level of your consciousness. Change your belief to accepting responsibility for what has come about.

Unless you are using ill health to teach you something important or have accepted it as a condition of living out your life at a soul level prior to your birth, the most likely explanation for poor health is within your beliefs. Even if your less than desirable state of health is a given for the time being because of your learning needs, you can tell your deeper consciousness and Me that you want to learn the same thing through a different avenue if that is possible. Or, that if this condition is to be a given, that you function in the best health possible.

Besides changing energy at the Spirit and Mind Domain as described, what can you do to promote well-being at the Emotion Domain level? Use the Core Transformation process that I just described, addressing your illness as part of you, the part with whom you are going to speak. This will give you the core purpose for experiencing this physical condition.

What can you do to aid health at the physical level of Life Energy? You can relax with music that helps you feel at peace with yourself. Ask your inner healer, your *Body Consciousness*, to move your body and create inner energy that will help you change the negative energy you are experiencing to positive. Then, let your *Body Consciousness* and its wisdom move your body in ways that are helpful for healing or addressing the negative energy. Let your body move in whatever way it desires. If you feel like singing, toning, or saying something, do it. Be uninhibited. Follow what your inner healer wants to do.

You can also determine what would promote relaxation, adequate rest, fun, body balance, good nutrition, and adequate energy to meet each day. Your body deserves this attention because it is through this body that you are able to do all things human. It is your responsibility to respect it and nourish its functioning. Make out a general health program for yourself that will promote the best health you can achieve while working to manifest your intentions.

This completes my suggestions for transforming Negative Life Energy to Positive Life Energy within each of the five domains of human reality. Later, I will show you how to incorporate the suggestions into a daily seven-step process.

Myths About the Negative

You have created many beliefs about the negative. Many of these act as barriers to using the negative side of Life Energy in an effective way. Let Me talk about some of the main myths that get in your way.

Myth 1: Negative experiences and feelings are bad for you.

Negative Life Energy is uncomfortable. It can unbalance your physical, subtle physical, emotional, mental, and spiritual health if you experience it too intensely. But, as I have been saying, the negative is part of My energy and yours. It is a teacher and partner if you will let it be. Therefore, it is not bad. Nor can you get rid of it since it is a part of your total Life Energy. It is a teacher of what you don't want, establishing that boundary for you.

It also produces some type of a gift. **Out of all negative comes positive**. It is for you to face the negative and learn what the gift is and the message it is trying to teach. And, finally, it is for you to restate the situation so it becomes more positive.

In addition to these benefits of negative experiences, all negative emotions have a general purpose behind their existence.

Depression, for example, acts as a creative force to remove barriers that are preventing joy. Its purpose is to make you identify, face, and transform barriers to joy. Once that is done, it can also tell you that it is time to give up whatever is causing your depression. Let it go. It needs to die so that you can focus on something new.

Anger warns you that you are giving up your control to someone or something else. It tells you that you are vulnerable and need to protect yourself by taking back your control. It also warns that you feel someone or something is crowding your territory. Anger is there as a tool to build up your energy so that you can (respectfully) tell the person to back off. It also tells you to create adequate boundaries around you so that you are able to show love to yourself besides others. Telling others that you cannot help them now because you are exhausted is a boundary and a loving thing to do for yourself.

Fear has the purpose of warning you of circumstances you may not like, or unsafe conditions for your physical, emotional, mental, or spiritual functioning. Its function is to make you aware of those possibilities. Your next move is to choose what it is you *do* want. Remember, what you focus on increases the probability that it will appear! Face those things you fear and ask what their message is. Then focus on letting go of your fears, and restating them to become positive. Or find the core purpose of the fear.

Anxiety reminds you that your assumptions about how your world operates around you are wrong. It tells you to look at what you believe. What do you believe could happen:

- at work,
- walking down the street, or
- when being around others?

What do you believe about:

- the availability of abundance and security,
- your world,
- being sick and how to get healthy?

Your beliefs are creating a nagging feeling that all is not right. Identify them, change them by rewording them, and your anxiety will disappear.

Sadness tells you that you believe you are functioning in a world of separation and negativity, rather than connectedness and an underlying force that is Life Energy. It is reminding you to BE in Divine energy and BE who you want to be. *Don't just observe it or wish for it! Live and be it each moment.* Experience the vibrancy, joy, and wonder of Life Energy.

Envy teaches you the things you *do* want. It also gives you the energy to go out and get it for yourself.

Worry teaches you to look at options for the future. To do "what ifs" provides flexibility for you. But once you have done your job, let worry go. Know that you and I have control over your life. Remember that we create messes so that you and I can create something better. And something better always results in the end. (Remember that quantum physics principle?)

So each negative emotion has a purpose; it is your teacher. Ask what it is trying to tell you, then decide what you are going to do about it. Do it as best you can and then let it go. Focus on the positive or just *Being*. But do not try to get rid of the negative and assume it is bad for you. It is part of you. As part of you, when you ignore it, its job is to get stronger so that you will notice it and hear what it has to teach you—so listen.

Myth 2: Humans are flawed and weak.

You believe that I am all that is good and Satan, or forces like him, are all evil. Then you follow this belief with one that says you are separate from Me and, therefore, are flawed and weak. In fact, you believe that you are very much inclined toward being bad. But I still let you keep free will. This set of beliefs produces societies that emphasize the negative, as well as gaining power and control over others.

In such cultures, you can never reach goodness because you are imperfect...flawed. You also believe that you need saving and guidance by those who know better. This opens the way for priests and ministers as well as health professionals who claim secret or higher knowledge, in addition to rulers and leaders who demand absolute power. In these societies, either you have power or you are a victim.

As I have said before, the idea of separation from the God force, and of evil and good, came largely from the horde of individuals who came out of the East to conquer your earth-based, feminine-focused cultures 10,000 years ago. It provided a means of power and control that was not experienced before. It let you, as a human race, develop the experience of separation from Me, feel isolation and aloneness, and build power centered in humans who are imperfect and can do evil. It allowed wars and killing to become the way of eradicating nations and individuals who were judged evil or weak. It allowed the experience of weakness, helplessness, and victim hood.

Remember, My Consciousness pervades all things, even those labeled as evil by you. That Consciousness allows you, as an aspect of My Consciousness, to choose negative or positive, or simply *Being*. That choosing is there because you are an aspect of Me and you have free will.

You are not flawed! How could I produce a flawed product? Am I not All That Is? If I produce something flawed, then how am I not flawed Myself? How could I make a mistake like that? No, all things that are created are an aspect of Me. *If you go overboard on emphasizing negative potential energy, then you create a highly intense experience of what you do not want.* By your concept of separation from me, you have allowed such intensity to come into being. By your concept of being flawed and weak, or victims of this intense negative power over you, you made way for maintaining the intensity of negative experiences over thousands of years.

Let Me say this again. You are an aspect of who I am. You are not flawed. You have the same potential energies within you as I have. You have five domains of energy (spirit, mental, emotional, subtle physical, and physical) with which you create your reality. You have positive and negative energy with which to tweak your creations so they go in the right direction for your intentions and purposes. And ultimately, you have *Being*— the energy that underlies all energies that exist—the energy of consciousness itself. These are all types of Life Energy with *Being* underlying the reality of all other energies! Between the two energies, the five domains, and *Being* you have major power devices to create earth reality.

Magnificent beings of light and energy at your core...that is who you are! You are part of who I am and therefore your core essence is Love, which is My Consciousness. You are part of *Being*, and the Life Energy of *Being* is Love. Out of that has come all there is.

So I and you are but one individual. I and you have within our make-up all the potential to create, each within our sphere of ability. The human body is made in My likeness. You have cells, organs, muscles, ligaments, a brain, tissues, and blood. Each is an aspect of you as you are an aspect of Me. Do you call an organ or tissue that begins to act in a way harmful to the body evil? Do you label death and pain as evil? Some of you do. But, in fact, those are experiences that are created or accepted by you to tell you what you do not want in your life experience. But those negative circumstances tell you things about the human experience that you would not otherwise know. It provides an intensive learning environment for creating your intentions and carrying out your life purpose(s). Through that learning, you develop abilities and wisdom that you would not otherwise have.

All those things that make up your human physical body are you. Each of those "aspects" of you (organs, skin, cells, etc.) has their own function, their own consciousness, and their own free will. Just as you have your own function, your own consciousness, and your own free will. Each of those "aspects" of your body have agreed to come together to produce the larger experience of a living human body. Each of my "aspects" (you) have agreed to come together as humans to expand my divinity and Godhood. You are exercising free will to create a greater experience that could not be without this cooperation.

This model of humanness is a model of My Being. It is a model of how you are a part of Me yet retain individuality, consciousness, and free will. The energy that is you is not flawed, nor evil.

You are divinity experiencing humanness!

Myth 3: Evil and good are real.

Some of you cannot believe that the negative and positive are part of Me, because you immediately translate negative to mean evil, and positive to mean good. Satan is your concept of evil. The evil of Satan is set up as an equal power to your concept of the all-good God. With these beliefs, you have absolute separation of negative and positive energy. With these beliefs, you have defined a reality where you must choose *one or the other*. One choice only can save you from your flawed weak self—being good. But you are flawed so you never quite reach being good for long. These are your beliefs.

You are divided against yourself with these beliefs. You are not all evil and not all good. You are not even a mixture of evil and good. **Evil and good are labels you have put on created experiences.** *They are only labels. They are not real things.* The real energy is Negative or Positive Life Energy. Those energies are part of the Life Energy of *Being*. Those potentials are the energy of My Consciousness and yours.

Dianne is asking a question here. She is talking about an example that just came to light of two men that tortured and killed twenty or more people, mostly women. The men wanted to make sex slaves out of the women. When they got tired of sex and torture, they killed them. This must surely be Evil in capital letters she says. She wants Me to comment on this.

Of course, this is not positive energy here. A negative force beyond themselves, a commitment made at the soul level before they were born, influenced these people. They responded in a way that brought on these actions. The commitment was to display the ultimate of negative behavior that your societies' beliefs can produce. These are dramas, which show the extreme of life lived according to your beliefs. Your vision is one of eye for an eye and kill or be killed. The mitigation of reverence for human life is gone.

The people that were in this drama who were killed accepted this event at their soul level to show others what will happen when you carry negative beliefs to the ultimate!! They were not really victims, because they committed to this event at their soul level. They agreed to brave the intensely negative to teach you the consequences of your cultural beliefs and to wake you up.

Do not be frightened by such evidence of extreme negativity. Instead, change your beliefs at the individual and small group level, and it will spread. This is the way to get around these extreme negative dramas. Staying in fear will only put you deeper in a separation mode. Power is gotten from telling yourself that fear is only a marker pointing out that your beliefs are wrong for bringing happiness. With this set of beliefs that you have created so far, no stable positive optimal living can result. Your beliefs breed a sense of isolation, helplessness, lack of power, and weak determination.

Those men that killed the women believed that they couldn't get control any other way. But in taking control in that fashion, they lost it! They could never satisfy their need for power and control. They blamed their negative lives on Fate and others. They saw nothing redeeming in their lives. It was their attempt at creating happiness. But it didn't work.

With the way you've structured your societies, these dramas will only continue until you see that you have to change your beliefs and intentions to take back control and to remember that you are divinity experiencing humanness.

The answer then is that there is no evil, only stories you have created and labels you have put on intensely negative Life Energy manifestations. By labeling those energies as Evil, you are giving up your power to others...placing the control of your life and choices outside of yourself. You abdicate responsibility and you become victims as well as weak, flawed humans forever chasing the all-good perfection of God.

There is no perfection, for perfection implies a static state of accomplishment. Life is not static; consciousness is not static; the state of *Being* is not static. If you wish to keep the idea of perfection, then think of it as a potential energy for growing and becoming whatever is chosen. That is perfection. If you deny the Negative Life Energy that is part of your consciousness, and say it is out there and label it as Evil, and the evil is also within you because you are flawed, then you become less than what you are— divinity experiencing humanness. Creative power is placed beyond your control into something called "evil."

If you, in like manner, describe Me and My Energy as all good without "evil," you are again setting up an experience where creative power is outside of yourself and beyond your reach. It is creating experiences where "good" is scarce and hard to get; where choice to create good, as well as evil, is beyond your poor, puny human efforts. In this model of living, only I can save you along with the help of your religions and science.

I will say this again until you hear me. Part of My Consciousness is made up of Negative and Positive Life Energies. The negative and positive forces are there to allow contrast, dichotomies, and boundaries for experiences. Without these Life Energies of negative and positive, there would be no contrast. Without contrast, many beings, including humans, have trouble distinguishing what a thing is and what an experience is. For without experiencing or seeing the opposite, how can you know what a thing, experience, or state of positive is?

So evil and good are labels you have used and you have mistaken the labels for the reality. You have created stories of creation that correspond to your ideas of "evil" and "good" Those stories go back 10,000 years to when you decided, as a race, to tilt experience toward the negative. You did this to experience the consequences of such a decision at all its various levels and subtleties. You created mythologies of creation to encourage this experience and to keep it in place for thousands of years. You expanded on those original stories of creation so that the separation of positive and negative, and human and divine became complete. Your religions, as they were created, took on these creation stories and made them their own.

It is time for these stories of creation and the all-good God to be examined, analyzed, and picked apart for what they truly are, fabrications of reality. The negative bias created by the separation myth and creation stories has served its purpose. You know what the consequences are!

It is time to focus on the truth that all is connected. Create stories that will enforce the idea that there is a continuum of positive and negative energy that is part of My Being and yours. Accept that you are divinity experiencing humanness. Believe that you will learn how to change your world by creating a bias toward accessing the state of *Being* and the positive, while still controlling negative energy so that it helps to define what a thing is. The result will be a dynamic optimal living experience and a whole new set of consequences!

Myth 4: You must clear all the negative barriers and neuroticism from your life, before you can reach positive experience.

Life is a continuous process of dealing with Negative and Positive Life Energy, the emphasis of which is up to you. You never "clear out all your blocks." Blocks and negative experiences will appear as it is appropriate to what you are trying to create in your life. The key is not to focus on getting rid of the blocks or negative experiences so you can at last be "happy." Rather, the key is how to transform the negative to *Being* or positive energy. The key is also listening to the negative experience to find what it is trying to tell you, e.g., what is it you do not want and what gift has come about because of the negative?

Myth 5: Dealing with the negative involves struggle and suffering that you have to endure until you get through it.

When you are well and good in a negative experience, it certainly isn't a pleasant or comforting state in which to be. But the purpose of the negative is to have you identify what it is you do not want. What is the gift coming about as a result of the negative and what do you need to develop or accept as a part of your personality that has been neglected? You will notice that if you try to run away, or squash it, it only gets stronger. So your only real option is to face it, be in it, and go through it to *Being* or to the positive. Sometimes, this takes time.

Do you have to remain intensively focused on your negative emotions and predicament all during this time? No. The answer will appear after you have asked it to do so, but usually not in a logical, one, two, three-step fashion. True reality is not linear. It tends to function better with symbols along with providing opportunities for learning through people, things, and experiences. So, ask yourself:

- What is it that I *don't* want from the experience?
- What is the gift in this experience?
- Is there a dark side in my personality that is attracting these negative experiences?

You may get answers directly after asking these questions, or you may get them in stages through both logical thought and symbolic occurrences. But I always hear you. You just expect instantaneous answers when what you want to learn cannot be learned instantaneously.

Do you always have to suffer as you wait for the answer? No. As you wait, be gentle with yourself. Find things and people that nurture you and lighten your mood. Find things that you like to do. Often the universe works best when you have asked for answers and then switch your attention elsewhere. It allows the intuitive mind to link up with the universe and Me more easily, and then give the answers in the time and place best for your learning and purpose.

If you find yourself apparently stuck in sadness, depression, anger, or fear, try this. Know that your negative emotion is your teacher, but you don't have to relate to your teacher all the time. Negative emotions have a physiological base, as well as a subtle physical energy, emotional, mind, and spirit base. One way of choosing to turn your attention elsewhere for the time being is to identify what your body is feeling, how your energy feels around your body, what the emotion is that you are attaching to that physical response, and what the thoughts are that you are creating. For example, sadness often gives the feeling of being lethargic. Your energy feels slow and heavy. You label those physiologic responses as "sadness" and then you go on to notice that the day is gray, and that you have nothing exciting to do, and that your old problem is still with you. Instant sadness results.

But you have a choice once you identify your responses. You can stop your chain reaction in its tracks! Tell yourself that you just feel slow and lethargic today so you are going to do something that suits a body that feels relaxed. You are going to do something pleasant. You decide what that pleasant thing is and go do it. Generating new responses to old body responses will disrupt the whole chain reaction you have learned.

Do you always have to struggle when you reach the negative? No. I will always be there with you as you are feeling fear, depression, or anger. I will be co-creating with you, your soul, your Higher Self, and your guides. You are never alone and it doesn't have to be a struggle. Just let Us know what you want and we will help you co-create it in the best way possible for you and your life intentions and purpose.

The key is to not let yourself be afraid that I won't answer, or that you are alone, or that you can't handle the situation. When you fear that, you temporarily bring on that very experience of being alone, hearing no answer, and feeling helpless. And that's when the struggle begins. You feel you have to fight for what you want all by yourself. **Fear is what creates struggle**. Go through the fear, let it go, and renew your belief that I am always there. How can I do anything differently since you are an aspect of Me?

In addition, believe that I have given you all the resources that you need within you to handle this situation. You would not be experiencing it, if you did not have the necessary resources. Remember, you have your soul and its wisdom, in addition to guides, your guardian angel, your Higher Self, and Me. That's an abundant army of resources!

Myth 6: When you see someone that is a victim, you owe it to them to help them. It is their due and your responsibility.

You believe that a victim deserves help. In fact, many of your religions have taught that you owe it to them. These are myths generated by your societies that create conquerors and victims. Once you "take someone's power away," the unwritten agreement between conquered and conqueror is that the conquered must be taken care of. If the conqueror doesn't, they will battle to regain their power. So to keep them from gaining power, the conqueror has to help his/her victims just enough to keep them dependent and weak. The conqueror begins to hand out rewards and life sustaining resources that only he or she controls. This keeps the conquered dependent and malleable.

When someone appears to be a victim, they have chosen that experience for themselves. Your appearance in their lives may be a catalyst for them to see how to change that experience for the better. You become this catalyst, by telling them your truth (opinion, advice, analysis, help) but not demanding they accept it. You can also help them by just listening. Support their intrinsic ability to handle the situation. Provide affirmation of this ability by noting specific strengths that they have. After doing this, it is up to them to decide whether this is helpful to whatever their intentions are.

If they want your help, give it to them in such a way that you do not take away their power. Do not become a rescuer and keep them the victim. Do not do everything for them. Teach them how to do for themselves, while supporting them as they learn. This is true love given to another. Before helping another, however, check within yourself to make sure that this is a good thing for you to do. Do not become a victim yourself by sacrificing yourself too much and denying your own good! Helping another is a balance between your needs and theirs. *It is never "either/or" but "and." Your needs AND their needs.*

If they reject your "truth," you can still help them if you wish. Do so by accepting them for where they are, and enjoying what you can. Recall to yourself that your culture has rewarded people for being victims. Therefore, it is very difficult to stop being a victim until the pain outweighs the rewards given. Then, at the spirit level, create an intention to their Higher Self and their soul that they will find their way, in the best way possible, to fulfill their life purpose(s). That energy will aid them in their life's path.

Summary

The industrialized nations of the world have created lifestyles that are too negative to sustain human life.

- Positive and Negative Life Energy are on a continuum with degrees of positive energy at one end and negative at the other. These energies balance each other. More Positive Life Energy will attract Negative Life Energy and vice-versa. The energy, once attracted, can be observed rather than experienced directly if you wish.

- Positive and Negative Life Energy, along with the five domains of Life Energy (Spirit, Mind, Emotion, Subtle Physical, and Physical) and *Being* are your creative tools for manifesting your intentions and life purpose on earth. Positive and negative energies provide a steering system that allows you to create the life path you want. Negative energy teaches you what you do not want; positive energy teaches what you do want. The type and intensity of life experience, and whether the experience is negative or positive, is determined by your decision about the rightness of your course for your intention or purpose. You are in control of your life experiences!

- To achieve transformation and reach optimal living you must **consciously** learn how to manage Negative and Positive Life Energy within each of the five domains. This is the crucial tool for optimal human living and for creating the life you want!

- It is time to transform the negative bias created by your present societies to the positive. One way to do this is to ask yourself what you're assumptions are when you are experiencing the negative. Your assumptions or beliefs create your bias for living.

- Other ways to retune your negative bias are as follows:

  1. Face the negative; do not run from it.
  2. Have a dialogue with Me, your soul, your Higher Self, or guardian angel.
  3. Keep a journal.
  4. Record and interpret your dreams.

- Myths about the negative include:

    1. Negative experiences and feelings are bad for you.
    2. Humans are flawed and weak.
    3. Evil and good are real.
    4. You must clear all the negative barriers and neuroticism from your life before you can replace it with positive living
    5. Dealing with the negative involves struggle and suffering that you have to endure until you get through it.
    6. When you see someone that is a victim, you owe it to them to help. It is their due and your responsibility.

- All negative emotions have a general purpose behind their existence. *Depression* acts as a creative force to remove barriers that are preventing joy. *Anger* warns that you are giving up your control to someone or something else. *Fear* warns you of circumstances you may not like, or unsafe conditions for your physical, emotional, mental, or spiritual functioning. *Anxiety* reminds you that your assumptions about how your world operates around you are wrong. *Sadness* tells you that you believe you are functioning in a world of separation and negativity. *Envy* shows you the things you want.

Dianne's Experience

This information on Negative Life Energy has been the most powerful key to changing my life. When I thought of negative energy as something bad and evil, I felt forever inferior in trying to defeat it. No matter how hard I tried to change myself, some negative experience and/or feeling would crop up. I would feel like a failure, because my belief system told me that I was responsible for creating what I experienced. I kept wondering what I was doing wrong. Then I would get mad and decide that the whole philosophy about creating your own reality was a bunch of malarkey. Yet, I was only able to accept that thought for shorter and shorter periods of time, because when I did, I drifted toward feeling helpless, defensive, and angry. I also felt that I had to fight for control because other things and people were waiting in the wings to take it away. Given this reaction, I would decide that I couldn't handle the negative emotions generated by the belief that control of events in my life were outside of myself. So, I would swing back to believing that we do create our own experiences. When I did, I would say to myself, "This time, I will just try harder." It didn't work!

This information about the creative force of Negative Life Energy freed me from that cycle of failure. I now see negative emotions, experiences, and thoughts as part of the process of living and bringing to reality my intentions and life purpose. I view it as part of my "rudder" system with Positive Life Energy being the other half of the rudder. With this philosophy, I am able to focus on figuring out what I don't want, the gift it is bringing me, and the positive direction the negative experience is pointing out for me. I know I don't have to actually experience the negative energy presenting itself. I can just observe it. Or if I decide to experience it, I can choose the intensity. It's such a relief and a comfort! All I have to do is to work with the negative energy—acknowledge it, experience it, examine its messages, and then choose something different after the learning has taken place.

I finally feel peace instead of feeling like my insides are a war zone with negative impulses fighting positive. I believe that the negative and positive are working tools for creating my life; they are my friends and part of All That Is.

It doesn't mean I like experiencing the negative. But it does mean I don't feel so threatened, fearful, defensive, and stuck. After all, I and All That Is are co-creating this experience. That means we have control over my life. Because of free will, I can choose to end the experience. But my soul and Higher Self also have their choices and may work with me at an unconscious level to present something else that is negative if I haven't consciously gotten the point I thought I needed to learn. So I believe the key to real creative control over my life is consciously working with my purposes and intentions, as well as having on-going conversations with my inner helpers, e.g., my soul, Higher Self, guides, and All That Is.

Life Energy Activities

- When you are experiencing something negative, as soon as you consciously can, ask yourself what the message is. What don't you want, what part of your shadow self might you have to accept, what gift is being offered, what assumptions do you have about this experience? Answer these questions as best you can. Sometimes, the answers are only hazy...they will become clearer over time. Then ask yourself what you want. Make a vivid picture in your mind. Then focus on making the five domains compatible with your picture. Do this quickly. Otherwise, you will never do it—too much trouble you think. So just skim through the domains and put in place some beliefs that you need, strategies, emotions, how you will talk to yourself and others, etc., and let it go. You can always fine-tune it as you go along!

- Keep a journal of your daily life. This doesn't have to be a long, effortful piece. Just write down, talk into a tape recorder, or draw your impressions of the day. You can use free association and just put down phrases that come to mind about the day. But in some way, record what has happened so that you can look at what has happened and observe it. This makes the *Observer Self* become conscious. The *Observer Self* will be able to show you patterns that are happening and give you hints as to why they are happening. The *Observer Self* will also help you to become aware of when you are caught in a negative experience…and just going along with it as a victim. It will help you stop this reflexive action and choose what you really want.

- When you keep a journal, ask yourself the following questions at the end of each day:

  1. What were my successes today? How did they happen so I can learn how to repeat them?
  2. What things happened that I don't want? Why did they happen? What are they trying to tell me?
  3. What do I really want to have happen? How can I and my inner helpers begin to create this for myself?
  4. What is the one thing that I need to do for myself tomorrow that will help me get closer to what I really want?

- When you are having a negative experience, try doing a Core Transformation as described earlier to help you find why you are having that experience and how to deal with it best.

Chapter 5

Positive Manifestation and Creating Optimal Living

Positive manifestation and living—ah, the desire of all of you! Or is it? Imagine a reality where only the positive was allowed. You are not able to experience any negative. Would you know how to define positive? Would you appreciate what you have?

The way of experiencing that you have built for yourselves would view this "positive" living experience as a damped down way of living. The richness of understanding that is possible when both negative and positive potentials are present would not be possible. In fact, you would not label your experiences as positive, but rather just a way of living. Human experience is built so that you know what positive living is from having *experienced or observed* the negative and vice-versa. **The contrast of the negative and positive allows you to truly know and appreciate what each is and its purpose**.

If you want optimal living, besides *knowing* about Positive and Negative Life Energy, you must consciously learn how to *manage* both to manifest your intentions and purposes. The key principles for doing this are listed below.

Key Principles for Managing Positive and Negative Life Energy

1. Know what is positive or negative for each of you.
2. Practice ways of choosing and manifesting each to the degree you wish in order to realize your intentions and life purpose(s).
3. Know ways to get unstuck from negative experiences as well as positive. (You can become attached to both, so you need to know effective methods for releasing your attachment to either one.) Also, know how to move forward to your vision or intention as you release your attachment to the negative or positive event.

> 4. Understand who you really are, celebrate this self, and develop your personal power based on it.
> 5. Understand and be able to access *Being*. This last is the most critical of all the principles.

In the last chapter, I gave you many examples of negative manifestations. I talked about the purpose of Negative Life Energy, and how to manage it so that you use it to manifest your vision/intention. I showed you how to get unstuck and move forward.

In this chapter, I will focus on positive manifestation—knowing the positive, choosing it, creating it, and maintaining it for a certain amount of time. I will also talk about how to know who you truly are, celebrate yourself, and develop your personal power.

In the next chapter, I will talk about *Being*—its importance, how to access it, and how to live in it as the core of optimal living. In the last chapter, I will provide you with a practical framework for achieving optimal living by applying all the principles we have discussed using NeuroQuantum Thinking.

Assumptions about Positive Living

Many of you believe that positive living and experiences will automatically be present when the negative is not there. Your psychology is based on this idea. If you rid yourself of the negative sides of your personality and the effects of your negative experiences, you will automatically experience positive living.

When you believe this myth two things happen: *First, you try and try but you never get rid of the negative sides of your personality, nor the effects of your negative experiences.* Many of you go to therapists for years with the result that you know your negative selves very well, but are not much closer to positive living than when you started. *Second, you are trying to eliminate Negative Life Energy and experiences when you should be using it to help form your life.* Negative Life Energy and experiences are meant to be teachers in your life. These experiences and observations in your daily life must be listened to and respected in order to use Positive Life Energy to create positive experiences and better quality of life.

The negative tells you what you do not want. That is its message. *But it does not tell you what you* do *want. That has to be discovered by you!* As long as you focus on eliminating the negative, you will only know how to manifest negative life experiences and observations. Positive experiences will seemingly happen out of the blue and appear and reappear. You will struggle to make them stay and struggle even harder to make them appear. But it will always be a struggle because of your preference for the negative.

Positive manifestation takes as much skill to form as the negative. First, you must recognize it. You must know what is positive for you. What is positive for someone else, may not be for you. Your society has sold you on the idea that money, power, what you buy, sex, food, fame, drugs, sports, and lots of leisure time will bring you happiness. In fact, they do not. Your research about happiness says people with an abundance of these things are not happier.

Do no accept your society's standard myths about being happy. Instead, notice what and who make you happy, what and who make you forget time and effort, and when and where you feel joy, excitement, pleasure, and happiness. *These situations indicate where you are experiencing states of Being. Think of "Being" as my core Consciousness and Life Energy. When you are in Being, happiness is a natural outcome.*

Make a list of those activities, places, times, and people. One way to do this is to write down at the end of each of day where, when, and with whom you experienced positive experiences and why. The last part is particularly important, for you must know why this gets you into a state of *Being* called happiness. Then you can repeat the circumstances with the same result.

Essentials for Optimal Living

Two good books that have researched happiness and optimal living across many different cultures are *The Pursuit of Happiness* and *Flow: the Psychology of Optimal Experience*. They provide a very good picture of important elements for optimal living. I will use this knowledge to speak to you in a language that you understand.

The research in these books says that the things that bring happiness and optimal living are non-physical things. They are right. The things that bring happiness and optimal living are natural outcomes of creating with Life Energy within My Consciousness (*Being*). I will explain in-depth about what this actually means in the next chapter. For now, remember to think of *Being* as my core Consciousness and Life Energy.

Using each of the Life Domains of human reality, let's examine Life Energy activities, fitting into each what will build happiness and optimal living. Try those that appeal to you or that draw you to them.

Spirit Domain

- ***Create control over your life*** through creating a vision of what you want as well as becoming skilled in the principles of manifestation to implement the vision and manage daily living. (The five-domain model and managing Positive and Negative Life Energy.)

- ***Talk to Me***, your Higher Self, your guides, and your soul on a regular basis so that we can become close friends.

- ***Believe in a power beyond yourself*** (however you want to define Me) and integrate My Energy and Consciousness into your daily life activities.

- ***Create a vision***, picture, or sense of what you want coupled with unified general goals, strategies, identity, skills, and bodily functioning that will support it.

Mind Domain

- ***Build a positive self image*** by being fully who you are to the best of your ability and celebrating who you are NOW. Do not get stuck in imagining a "perfect" you. Your ideal positive self-image is a life-long learning and creative process. Your intention must focus on manifesting, right now, the best self of which you are capable. You are exactly who you should be right now for what you have in mind as your life purpose. Celebrate this you.

- ***Build a vibrant personal power.*** Building personal power consists of doing the following things to the best of your ability:

  1. Love yourself
  2. Be able to access your inner self and Me
  3. Believe that you have all the skills and knowledge you need for each situation that presents itself
  4. Know how to handle negative events while building the positive
  5. Have a specific life vision

Building personal power is a life-long creative process that changes as you change.

- ***Choose to use positive thinking.***

- ***Tell your truth*** in a way others can hear. That is, use their language patterns and styles of thinking, but don't insist that your truth must be their truth, and that it is their duty to affirm you for what you say.

- *Look at any negative challenge so that you perceive its gift and message.*

- *Be fully in each moment while being as honest, aware, and open as you can.* This allows the consciousness of *Being* to co-exist with your conscious mind. Do not be afraid of just being yourself. Being honest, aware, and open is your best security because it allows the real you to expand and be free while experiencing the joy of living.

- *Periodically look at your beliefs* to see if they support your life vision and purpose. Change your beliefs if they don't.

- *Each day note and bless what you do have and what has been a success.*

- *Ask what the message or gift is* in your daily life events. Remember that you created them at some level of your consciousness or accepted these events. Ask yourself what you are trying to learn.

- *Believe that you are just where you should be* in your life path and purpose.

- *Believe, and <u>act as if</u> we (you and I) will co-create ways to manifest enough income* to support your basic survival, health, and much more. The Universe is abundant with resources, not scarcity. And money is a form of energy this is manifested by the mind. Believe that and this will help me co-create with you what is needed to manifest the income you desire.

Emotion Domain

- *Begin acting like the person you want to be NOW.*

- *Find excuses to laugh.*

- *Choose and build supportive and close interdependent relationships.* Interdependent relationships are those where each person in the relationship has joy in who the other is and accepts and affirms the other person for where they are at the moment. The core value in these relationships is one of believing that each person is part of Me. Because of that, each demands respect. Each person also has their own life path that they must choose for themselves. This is to be respected and affirmed by all those in the relationship.

- ***Share your knowledge and experiences*** in a non-dogmatic and non-needy way with like-minded people

- **Within an *intimate relationship*,** build a loving interdependent friendship coupled with loving sexuality.

- ***Choose pleasant or challenging activities with compatible people.***

- ***Find the common ground when in conflict*** with others while respecting each as an aspect of Me.

- ***Help others celebrate who they are, find who they are, and what they want.*** But remember to do the same thing for yourself!

- ***Create beauty.***

- ***Create something that is important to you and impacts beyond yourself.***

- ***Face and go through change or adversity so that you create something positive out of it.***

- ***Live and be completely alive in the moment.*** NOW is where you create your life by your choices, perceptions, and learning. There really is no time, only the NOW. Use it and live it to the fullest.

- ***Focus on joy*** in the challenge of living. Believe life is a wonderful celebration and learning, not a vale of tears that is imposed on you!

Subtle Physical Domain

- *Find ways of balancing your body's subtle physical energy, e.g., chakras, meridians, and energy fields.* You need balanced subtle physical energy within your body to "feel" happiness. There are many energy balancing approaches that you could learn or for which you could seek out a practitioner with a particular expertise. These approaches include Reiki, Cranial Sacral Therapy, Holographic Repatterning, Thought Field Therapy, Chakra balancing, Acupuncture, Tai Chi, meditation, and certain types of music that put the brain in a calm state. I'll give a brief description of each to help you decide which are best for you.

  - **Reiki** - placement of the hands on specific areas of the body to channel Life Energy into those areas through the hands. This is done with the intention of helping to heal and balance energy in these areas.

  - **Cranial Sacral Therapy** - Manipulation of the connective tissue and meninges of the brain and spinal cord to eliminate or decrease restrictions in energy due to some type of trauma. This is done through placement of the hands at various points on the body to help the tissue move out of restriction and back to a more normal relationship to surrounding tissue, organs, and nerves. The slight pressure of the hands in these areas not only helps the rebalancing of the tissue, but also increases the easy flow of cerebro-spinal fluid, aids organ and nerve functioning, and thus rebalances the energy of the body to more optimal levels.

  - **Holographic Repatterning** - a process for releasing unconscious survival patterns and beliefs that have been recorded in energetic form within the body's subtle physical energy. The system uses the muscles of the hand or forearm to indicate yes and no responses asked of your *Body Consciousness* and other inner helpers. The responses help guide which therapeutic modes will be used, e.g., cranial sacral therapy, addressing beliefs, types of breathing, to best eliminate energy that is stuck impeding optimal mind and body functioning. The body is said to be a hologram made up of energy and consciousness.

  - **Acupuncture** - an age-old therapeutic approach from China that views the human body as consisting of energetic pathways (meridians). Stimulation of acupuncture points along these pathways leads to better health of mind and body.

- **Thought Field Therapy** - Here the body is also viewed as a hologram of energy and consciousness. Thoughts impact on the hologram of energy and consciousness altering energy. Blockages in the system can produce psychological problems such as anxiety, fear, phobia, depression, addiction, and anger. As in Holographic Repatterning, muscle testing is used to determine the best next step in therapy. Therapeutic sequences of meridians points are tapped with the fingers, stimulating these points to release energy that is sluggish or stuck. Meridians are also tapped that will strengthen energy that is already functioning normally but could aid fulfilling the positive intention of the recipient. The finger tapping activates meridian pathways in a similar way, as would needles used in acupuncture.

- **Chakra Balancing** - concentrating on each chakra with the intention of eliminating restrictions in energy bringing about more optimal functioning of the body's subtle physical energy.

- **Tai Chi** - moving the human body in slow ballet-like movements to stimulate the optimal flow of "chi" (a name for the subtle physical energy making up the human body).

- **Meditation** - focusing the mind so that a state of *Being* is achieved, e.g., relaxation without conscious thought, or where conscious thought is suspended to allow a dialogue with one's inner voice.

- **Specialized brain wave music** - music that encourages the predominance of alpha and theta brain waves to produce a meditative state of mind and a relaxation response of the body.

All of these energy balancing approaches can be learned by each of you. Once learned, you don't have to depend on a therapist, unless you feel that you want to do this or need in-depth expertise that you don't have.

Physical Domain

- ***Stop talking about what you want and just do it!*** I will always be there as your safety net. There are no mistakes, only different paths to whatever your life intentions are.

- *Find an avocation or lifework where play and "work" are not separate—* where work is fun, challenging, a charge…playing.

- *Choose challenging work* interspersed with adequate opportunities for rest, meditation, and *Being* (conversing with Me, resting in Me, experiencing joy with Me).

- *Create optimal health by an intention that states you want your body to function at its best.* Then talk and listen to your *Body Consciousness* to help you do that. Remember that *Body Consciousness* is a real part of your psyche as well as being an aspect of My Consciousness…it has its own wisdom and purpose. After communicating with this part of yourself, make your beliefs and nutritional habits match your picture of optimal health.

- *Build a community of people around yourself* that will support your vision and positive bias in living.

This list of basic Life Energy activities show you the directions you must choose if you desire happiness and optimal living. However, you must also make your own list of things, people, and events that make this happen for you. Then go about manifesting them through your choices and using the principles of manifestation discussed in chapter 3 and 4, as well as this chapter.

An In-depth Explanation of Some Optimal Living Requirements

Some of the things that I have just listed for experiencing happiness and optimal living need more explanation. I will provide more details about personal power and how to build it, as well as positive thinking, and how best to choose and build supportive relationships.

Building Personal Power

Personal power is fundamental to experiencing optimal living and remembering that you are divinity experiencing humanness. **Personal power is made up of the following elements:**

Personal Power Characteristics

- Defining who you are and loving that identity
- Knowing how to access your deeper consciousness and Me (whoever you define as Me—the power beyond)
- Believing that you have all the skills and knowledge you need for each situation that presents itself
- Knowing how to handle negative events while building the positive
- Having a specific life vision
- Knowing how to ask those around you to support your personal power
- Speaking your truth
- Developing the *Observer* within you.

Let's start with loving yourself. This is popularly known as having a good self-image. So how do you do that, especially if you've heard more bad than good about yourself as a child? You have experienced what other people do not want you to be, when you were told you were doing something that displeased others. You submitted yourself to those experiences in order to know the general rules and customs of your world, as well as learning about different people and their reactions.

You are an adult now. It is time to put away the things of your childhood. One of those things is unquestioning acceptance of other's opinions of you as being truth. **It is time for you to define your identity, not someone else.** Decide what characteristics make up your selfhood, and what those characteristics get for you. Each characteristic that you have will be seen as an advantage and "good" in certain circumstances, and a disadvantage or "bad" in other circumstances.

For example, some people seem to be very disorganized. You have labeled those at the extreme end of the disorganized continuum as attention deficit disordered. But, in fact, those who are disorganized often have highly creative minds. Much creativity does not usually operate in a logical one, two, three fashion. It operates by association. In other words, one thought leads to many others. This is an advantage when you are trying to create something entirely new, but it is a disadvantage when linear organization is demanded for taking care of the everyday details of living. If these individuals were able to reorganize their brains, resulting in a high ability to focus and organize daily living, then there would be a trade off in creativity. Some of their creativity would be lessened.

So each characteristic has its pros and cons. **The trick is to identify your core characteristics, and learn the situations in which they are valued. Then build a life vision around those situations that provide support and nurture your core personality characteristics.**

Before this vision will work, you must focus on valuing and seeing the value (the pros and cons) of your basic personality characteristics. Remember that the positive tells you what you want and the negative, what you don't want. That's why each characteristic that you have is a two-edged sword with pros and cons to it. **You as an important part of your life's work and purpose took on each characteristic. It makes you who you are! Value it for what it gives and what it teaches you.**

As you value your core characteristics, also believe that you are learning exactly what you should at this point in time. That is, you are exactly who you should be right now. Celebrate yourself and your learning. Allow your real core characteristics to flow freely. Be who you truly are. When you do these things, your life vision will fall into place. You will be able to generate support and nurture your core self, because you value yourself. If you need additional help from others, it will happen. They will appear in your life and say and do things that will help you build increasing love for who you are. But the prerequisite for all this to happen is your intention and focus on loving who you are.

Accessing Your Deeper Consciousness and Me

I have talked about how to do this in Chapter 3 when I was talking about accessing *Being*. But I'll talk about it again in this section. However, be sure to go back and read that part over again to refresh your memory.

Whenever you access Me, you are also in touch with the deeper consciousness that includes your psyche and your soul in addition to your inner helpers. When you relax and focus on talking or listening in a state of *Being*, you can select with whom you want to interact in the Spirit Domain. You don't have to interact with anyone. You can just be. But, while in that state, it is easy to converse with your soul, your Higher Self, your guides, other non-physical helpers, your guardian angel, or Me. Take your pick.

When you talk to Me, I use your Higher Self and other guides to translate for Me so you can understand Me most clearly. But I am the one talking, not your Higher Self or guides. You may want to just talk to them, or your soul. Establish a relationship with all of us. We all have different types of wisdom and skills. For example, your soul is better able to focus on earth reality than any other non-physical being.

Ways of getting to your deeper consciousness and Me are listed in the box on the next page.

Some Ways of Accessing Deeper Consciousness and Me

- Relax by noticing your in and out breaths. As you are doing this, switch your focus to a point between your eyes and in the middle of your forehead, and just be.
- Pray
- Meditate
- Talk to the negative parts of you and find out their message to you. Balance that with setting up a conversation between a negative part of you and a positive part of you. Listen for the wisdom that each brings to you.
- Talk to Me through using your dominant hand to write down questions and your non-dominant hand to answer. Or use the computer and a word processor where you type out the question, let yourself relax deeply, and then put your fingers on the keyboard and type whatever comes to mind.
- While in a relaxed state, start talking out loud to any higher being that you wish—your soul, your Higher Self, your guides, your guardian angel, or Me. Listen for our reply in your head. Then continue with maintaining your side of the conversation verbally.
- Draw while in a relaxed state around specific issues for which you want advice or support. Just let your hand draw whatever it wants. Then interpret what you get.
- Use automatic writing to set up a conversation with one of us.
- Read the part in chapter 4 that gives details about:

  a) how to set up a conversation with Me, as well as
  b) how to find the core purpose of a part of yourself.

- Daydream, e.g. let your mind wander, about a specific topic for which you want answers or more knowledge. You will get pictures and symbols like a dream. Interpret them just like a dream using free association for key pictures and symbols to ascertain their meaning.

The approaches listed above are some easy things that will help you access your inner world. **The reason that accessing this inner reality is so important is that all your control of reality stems from this world!** *So knowing how to access and use it is the most important thing that you can learn. This is where your personal power originates.*

Believe You Have the Skills and Knowledge You Need

Before you chose to be born, you chose your life's purpose. You also chose your core characteristics so that they would best accomplish your life's purpose. You chose the necessary skills and knowledge important for your life's work. You also chose your parents and the circumstances of your birth. Then you were born, and life's adventure started. But you equipped yourself to manage your adventure in a way most beneficial for your life purpose(s). Have confidence that you have the essential skills and wisdom within you to manage whatever life brings.

In addition, remember that you are never alone. You have your soul, your Higher Self, your guides, your guardian angel, and Me to help with managing your adventure on earth. Just think of all the knowledge and skills at your disposal!

You always have access to the necessary skills and knowledge that you need for any experience you have in your life. Intense experiences may seem to tilt you so heavily that you can't function. That is part of the learning process. The learning is to look at the negative and reword it into positive. You always have the skills and knowledge to accomplish this. All negative always brings about positive. That is a law of the universe. So just ask your soul or any of the rest of Us to provide the resources, knowledge, and skill necessary and it will happen.

Knowing How to Handle Negative Events While Building the Positive

I talked extensively about how to handle the negative in Chapter 4. Scan that chapter now to further impress on your mind how to do this. Building the positive is discussed in this chapter. Remember that Negative and Positive Life Energy together, allow you to manifest what you want. The negative tells you what you don't want and the positive what you do want. *It is essential that you build your expertise in handling both types of energy so that you can increase your personal power and ability to create the life you want.*

Creating a Life Vision

Each of you has a life purpose or purposes that you chose before you were born. You also form intentions of what you want out of life as you go along your life's path. Both these things (life purpose and life intentions) are part of your life's vision.

I gave you questions that you could ask yourself to help you identify your life vision in Chapter 3. Use those as a starting point. Keep in mind that your life purpose doesn't always line up with a job. In fact, it often doesn't. *Your life purpose is frequently something that is more abstract such as learning about beauty, learning about helping others while balancing yourself, or learning how to become an expert at managing the positive and negative energies on earth.*

Look back on your life and look at the repeated patterns that appear:

Have you been driven to learn or pursue something? This is a life purpose that is focused on learning to celebrate who you really are, rather than who others want you to be.

Do you have an outstanding skill that keeps reappearing in your life such as healing others, teaching others, composing music, or natural athletic skill? This is a life purpose organized around the experiences and learning that this skill brings you.

Have you had multiple marriages where you kept choosing various versions of the same type of mate? This is a life purpose focused on in-depth learning about core emotional issues that you want to know and resolve.

Have you been driven to educate yourself so that you could demand respect from others and be somebody? This is a life purpose driven to know what personal power is really all about. Respect from others and being somebody comes from you valuing yourself first. Then others will do so. This is personal power.

Have you spent a lifetime feeling a lack of power and looking upon yourself as a victim? This is a life purpose driving you to realize that your power to create your life is within, not external to you.

If the same type of circumstances or people keep showing up in your life, these are happening to point you in the direction of your life purpose. If you feel driven to do something, do it. It is part of your life purpose. *Never fear that you won't address your life purpose. Your soul will see to it that you do. There are no mistakes in your life; only different paths and experiences that will add to your life purpose or purposes.*

In the same way, when you decide on what you want out of life, there is no wrong way. Anything that you decide will provide you with information about what you want, and what you don't want at that point in your life. You will probably change your intentions about what you want throughout your life. That is as it should be. Keep adjusting your vision of what you want out of life as you learn more. But make sure that you do form a vision of what you want, even if it is very hazy at first. As you take your first steps, it will get clearer.

Knowing How to Ask Others to Support Your Personal Power

Those around you may or may not say and do things that enhance your personal power. Your culture has developed a communication pattern, which tends to share what is going wrong in your life, rather than what is going right. It is a communication of commiseration. At times, you may need to hear this from others in order to work out what why the negative is active in your life. The sympathy and empathic communication of others can sometimes facilitate this process.

However, if you know why the negative is there, and you are seeking a way to transform it, or you need reinforcement of your ability to find the answers within you, this communication of commiseration is not helpful. Instead, you need to hear from others what you are doing right, and receive from them a reinforcement of your skills in finding the answers within. You need to hear them celebrate you as you are right now.

Therefore, you have to develop the skill of asking others for what will be most helpful to you. If you want empathic listening, ask them for it. If you want problem solving and brain storming, ask them for it. If you want affirmation of what you have done right and who you are right now, ask them for it. It is not fair to expect others to know by osmosis what you need and want. It is your responsibility to tell them.

Some of those you ask will not be able to give you what you want. Bless them for who they are right now (divinity experiencing humanness), and let them go. Ask your soul, your Higher Self, your guides, and Me to bring you those that can give you what you need. In some cases, you may need something slightly different from what you think you need. So evaluate the responses you get from others, and ask what is the message and gift they are offering you. There is always a message and gift. Hunt for them.

If you are asking others to respond to you in a certain way, it is only fair to ask them what they want you to do for them in return. Then you will have to decide if you can give them what they want.

Speaking Your Truth

As part of personal power, it is important that you speak your truth. You have a responsibility to yourself and others to do so. But it is important to speak your truth so that others can hear what you say. That is, it is important to say or write things in a style and wording that they will understand. So if you notice that someone is a Christian in their beliefs and that they also seem to learn best by experience, you would couch what you say within these restraints. Speak about your truth in terms most acceptable to the Christian mind. Use everyday experiences to illustrate what you mean.

Not only do you need to speak and write your truth using language that another can best understand, but you must impart respect for who they are. Do not impart your truth in a dogmatic way. After all, remember that they are also divinity experiencing humanness. They have their own truth to impart. Listen to what they have to say, look at what they do. They are giving you a message. Perhaps the message is something you need to learn about yourself. It may be an example of what you do not want, or they may show you what you do want.

When you speak your truth, do not ask others to affirm you for speaking that truth. Affirm yourself. Do not demand this from them! It is your truth; it may not be theirs.

As you speak your truth, hunt for language that does not carry a heavy burden of meaning imparted by your society. For example, when talking about the spiritual, the use of terms like "evil" and "sin" bring on specific learned reactions. Instead, use a neutral term like "negative." Also hunt for other terms to call Me or those associated with Me. God, Allah, and Jesus are terms that have a long history of meaning. Find other terms for speaking of higher beings so that you can get around the baggage associated with the old terms. It will help people meet on more common ground and acquire knew wisdom.

The *Observer* Within

I have spoken of the *Observer* within you before. This is a part of you that can stand back and watch what you are doing and saying as you do it. This part allows you to stop your habituated responses to the things happening in your life. Instead, it offers you an opportunity to look at what is really happening. It also allows you to choose what you want to do.

I've talked about how to nurture its presence by writing down, talking out, or drawing what has happened in your daily life. Note the things that went right and why; note the things that went wrong and why. The more you do this, the greater your observational capacity will be. Soon you will find that you are actively observing yourself, while you are living your daily life in real time. As this happens, it allows you to choose what you want to do in real time, rather than after the fact. You become an active participant in your life, rather than passively relying on old automatic programming to get you through the day. If you want to create the life you want, you can no longer accept this passive type of living.

So here we have discussed the basics of personal power. Learning how to build personal power is a lifetime process. What you learn and when you learn it are choices that you make in your life. Whenever those choices are made will be exactly the right time. For you create your life according to what you and your free will see as the best path to achieve the best learning for you. There are many paths. There is no one path that is more perfect than others.

You do not have to struggle to learn how to build personal power. Have an intention for learning more about personal power in a way that is as easy and joyful as possible—and so it will be.

Positive Thinking

Many of you have accustomed yourself to biasing your thoughts to the negative. You may call yourself a pessimist or a realist depending on your preference. Some of you have deliberately taken on a brain that will support positive thinking naturally. People call you optimists. An optimist generates different life experiences than a pessimist. They have less knowledge and understanding of the negative, and more of the positive. A pessimist is the opposite case, more knowledge of the negative than the positive.

The surveys that have been done of people's inclination in one direction or the other, show that there are many more pessimists than optimists in your societies. This was necessary to maintain the negative bias and the myth of separation and power over the centuries. It is time to reverse this bias. You, as a race, now know quite enough about negative energy and its consequences. It is time you learned more about Positive Life Energy as a society.

So, if you have been a pessimist all your life, or viewed yourself simply as a "realist," it is your challenge to learn to become more of an optimist. This is no easy task, but with the intention of learning, it is something that can be done.

How do you become more of an optimist?

1. *Know what you want* and take easy steps toward making it happen. Do not be passive about your life. If you are, you will drift back into negativism.

2. *Focus on your successes* more than your failures. Learn from what doesn't work, but end with reaffirming what has worked.

3. *Notice the things that you do have* that bring you happiness and contentment.

4. *When you notice negative thoughts* going through your mind, say STOP (out loud or in your mind)! That will jerk you out of the usual chain reaction of negative thoughts and feelings. Then ask what these thoughts are trying to tell you; listen to the answer. Once you have done this, let

the thoughts go. Refocus your mind on *Being*, beauty, love, happy feelings, your accomplishments, or your vision of what you want.

5. ***Remind yourself that life is made up of Negative and Positive Life Energy***. These Life Energies "steer" you in the direction of your life vision and intentions.

6. ***Remember that you are the one in control***. Do not hand your power over to others and fall into being victim. You are no victim unless you want to be.

7. ***Remind yourself that you are exactly where you should be*** and who you should be at this moment in time. Life is an exuberant learning adventure. It is a process. You are right where you should be in this process. Decide where you want to go next. Envision it, ask for help from Us, and then go about making it happen.

8. ***Nurture the Observer Self*** by noticing what you do each day. Write down or review at the end of each day or week what you did well and why and what you have to rework and why. This noticing will encourage the *Observer* to become very active in your life. As it does, it will allow you to make choices about what you want to think and do much more easily. The *Observer* gets you out of your trance states, or your automatic learned reactions. It reminds you that this is only one option. It then allows you to think about what other options there are and which ones you want. It is your in-the-moment choice-maker!

9. ***Frequently talk to Us***. That lets you experience peace and centeredness, while feeling that you are never alone.

10. ***Celebrate who you are*** and who you are becoming. Value your characteristics for what they bring you. This will build your personal power. Personal power is absolutely core to becoming more positively biased. Otherwise, you will give your power away to others!

11. ***Don't agonize*** over taking steps in a positive direction! This causes you to talk about it, but then never carry it out! Get a general idea of where you want to go and jump in. Just do it! There is no need to scare yourself to death with drastic change, but there is also no need for staying in place for fear you are making a mistake. There are no mistakes, only different paths to the same goal. Remember, mistakes are

part of the negative "rudder," your steering mechanism to tell you what you don't want. Also remember that when you get what you don't want, there is always a safety net present—your inner world and its helpers. Trust that we will show you an easy way of getting what you want as long as that is your intention.

Most importantly, remember that real security comes from envisioning what you want, taking steps to make it happen, and then believing that you have all the resources necessary to manifest it. Your "resources" not only include your deeper consciousness (your soul and parts of your personality), but also your Higher Self, your guides, your guardian angel, and Me. Remember that. That's your real security and safety net!

12. **Act like the person you want to be.** Your actions will begin training your mind to believe it.

These things practiced over time will bring you to a more positive bias, as well as give you the ability to control your own life and create the life you want.

Choosing and Building Supportive Relationships

As you grow towards manifesting who you are, divinity experiencing humanness, you will need new types of friends and friendships. The old ones that you had before fit your old model of self. You will find they don't fit you anymore when you change this model.

How do you find and build relationships that will support who you are?

1. Decide what **type of relationships** you want with close friends, a significant other, or with family.

2. Decide what **characteristics** you want from others to be supportive of your divinity experiencing humanness. For example, you could decide that you want honest dialogue, respect for who you are, room to talk about Life Energy in the way it is important to you, etc. Make a list of the characteristics you want from others. Describe to yourself the type of community you want around yourself.

3. **Assess your present relationships** and see how well they match your list. Also, ask yourself the potential for each relationship to grow in that direction. Tell others what you would like from them, and see if they

feel they can do that. You may have to give something back to them that they want. Ask them what they want from you.

4. Tell your acquaintances and those around you that you want to ***meet new people*** that are supportive of your life's path. Tell them what you are looking for, and ask them if they have any ideas about where you could meet people like this.

5. ***Make a list of places and activities*** that are likely to generate the types of relationships and sense of community that you are seeking.

6. ***Begin going to those places*** and doing those activities. Remember that we are always with you. Do not be afraid that you will experience anything that you cannot handle. Let Us know that you do not want to have to struggle to find new friends and community. Pay attention to responses that you get. If you begin to struggle or find you are "hitting your head against a stone wall," then this is telling you what you don't want. Refocus your efforts in a different way.

7. As you interact with others, you will ***get an increasingly clear picture*** of what you want and what you don't want. Remember to tell others what you want from them and ask them if they are willing to do it. It makes things clearer when you are direct, rather than expecting others to just pick up what you want. Remember to ask them what they want.

Do these things and you will find the relationships and community that you envision.

Summary

- Besides knowing about Positive and Negative Life Energy, you must consciously learn how to manage *both* to obtain optimal living. Key principles for doing this are:

  1. Know what is positive or negative for each of you.
  2. Practice ways of choosing and manifesting each to the degree you wish in order to realize your intentions and life purposes.
  3. Know ways of getting unstuck from a positive or negative event, as well as how to move forward to your vision or intention.
  4. Understand who you really are, celebrate this self, and develop your personal power.
  5. Understand and be able to access *Being*. This last is the most critical of all the principles.

- Positive living will not automatically be present when the negative is absent. Rather, positive manifestations must be deliberately created at some level of your consciousness. Your task is to learn how to do this *consciously* so that you can create optimal living.

- To experience happiness and optimal living, pick out some of the following Life Energy activities.

<u>Within the Spirit Domain</u>:

1. Create control over your life through creating a vision of what you want as well as becoming skilled in the principles of manifestation to implement the vision and manage daily living.
2. Talk to Me, your Higher Self, your guides, and your soul on a regular basis so that we can become close friends.
3. Believe in a power beyond yourself (however you want to define Me) and integrate My Energy and Consciousness into your daily life activities.
4. Create a vision, picture, or sense of what you want coupled with unified general goals, strategies, identity, skills, and bodily functioning that will support it.

Within the Mind Domain:

1. Build a positive self image by being fully who you are to the best of your ability and celebrating who you are NOW.
2. Build a vibrant personal power.
3. Choose to use positive thinking.
4. Tell your truth in a way others can hear.
5. Look at any negative challenge so that you perceive its gift and message.
6. Be fully in each moment while being as honest, aware, and open as you can.
7. Periodically look at your beliefs to see if they support your life vision and purpose.
8. Each day, note and bless what you *do* have and what has been a success.
9. Ask what the message or gift is in your daily life events.
10. Believe that you are just where you should be in your life path and purpose.
11. Believe, and *act as if*, we (you and I) will co-create ways to manifest enough income to support your basic survival, health, and much more.

Within the Emotion Domain:

1. Begin acting like the person you want to be NOW.
2. Find excuses to laugh.
3. Choose and build supportive and close interdependent relationships.
4. Share your knowledge and experiences in a non-dogmatic and non-needy way with like-minded people.
5. Within an intimate relationship, build a loving interdependent friendship coupled with loving sexuality.
6. Choose pleasant or challenging activities with compatible people.
7. Find the common ground when in conflict with others while respecting each as an aspect of Me.
8. Help others celebrate who they are, find who they are, and what they want. But remember to do the same thing for yourself!
9. Create beauty.
10. Create something that is important to you and impacts beyond yourself.
11. Face and go through change or adversity so that you create something positive out of it.

12. Live and be completely alive in the moment. NOW is where you create your life by your choices, perceptions, and learning.
13. Focus on joy in the challenge of living.

Within the Subtle Physical Domain:

1. Find ways of balancing your body's subtle physical energy, such as, chakras, meridians and, energy fields.

Within the Physical Domain:

1. Stop talking about what you want and just do it!
2. Find an avocation or lifework where play and "work" are not separate—where work is fun, challenging, a charge...playing.
3. Choose challenging work interspersed with adequate opportunities for rest, meditation, and *Being* (conversing with Me, resting in Me, experiencing joy with Me).
4. Create optimal health by an intention that states you want your body to function at its best. Talk and listen to your *Body Consciousness* to help you do that.
5. Build a community of people around yourself that will support your vision and positive bias in living.

- **To build personal power strive toward the following:**

1. Define who you are and love that identity until it doesn't fit and then change it. Ultimately remember that you are divinity experiencing humanness.
2. Access your deeper consciousness and Me.
3. Believe that you have all the skills and knowledge you need for each situation that presents itself.
4. Know how to handle negative events while building the positive.
5. Have a specific life vision.
6. Know how to ask those around you to support your personal power.
7. Speak your truth.
8. Develop the *Observer* within you.

To build personal power is a lifetime process that does not have to be a struggle. Have an intention to learn as easily and joyfully as possible—and so it will be.

Dianne's Experience

Some years ago, I was the director of a training and research center at a state university. One day, the assistant director and myself sat down to do a planning session for the center. We had been trying to build new attitudes and a new organizational culture (environment). We felt drained and discouraged, believing that we had not made much headway. We began writing down on big sheets of paper what we believed, the values that we were trying to actualize, and what we had done. When we looked at the charts in front of us, we were amazed to see that we had changed how we operated at the center. Why were we feeling like such failures?

We began describing the overall university environment where the center operated and the people with whom we interacted. It became clear that the thing that was exhausting us and disguising the amount of progress was the university "culture." It operated day-to-day based on predominantly male culture beliefs. These included ideas such as, power is outside of you, power is everything so get it and keep it, and your achievement is only important if others value what you have done. That was one of the first times I really understood the difficulty of trying to bring about a positive attitude and more optimal living within our traditional cultural values.

Since then, I have built a culture around me that is more supportive of who I am and of my values. But up until recently, I often found that true happiness evaded my grasp. Old habits of negative thinking, defensiveness, and creating specific outcomes demanded by those around me died hard. In addition, I kept thinking that happiness had something to do with getting specific things or doing certain things. But whenever I got what I thought I wanted, the happiness was brief and then disappeared.

The information in this chapter was extremely important to me in beginning to turn around the above situation. First, it reinforced that optimal living and happiness were based on a whole different way of living and behaving than what I had been taught by our culture. I finally understood that happiness wasn't based on specific outcomes that were tangible things. Instead, it is based on aspects of mind—states of internal choice, values, and decision-making that have to do with being hooked up to your deeper consciousness and the power beyond (whatever you define as that). The lists in this chapter having to do with Life Energy activities essential to happiness are mental processes, attitudes, and intentions about how one chooses to live and think day-to-day. All of the listed activities are associated with inner reality. No wonder I could never quite get my fingers around that something called "happiness" for any length of time! The end result for me is that each day I have begun choosing to put some of the recommended Life Energy activities into operation.

A final realization is that creating the positive is as much a skill as creating the negative. Since it has taken years to learn how to create the negative for ourselves, it will take similar practice in learning how to reverse the process to the positive. Positive living does not simply happen when there is no negative around. Rather, choice and practice are key words here. Choosing each day to do something positive and then repeating the behavior many more times is what brings optimal living and happiness into daily life. Optimal living is also not a sudden event that happens like magic, but rather a process of change and learning that is gradual. I believe that this process does not have to be a struggle if I choose for it to be otherwise. The result has been an easy learning, not always free from anxiety or negative events, but nonetheless an easy and gradual process that, overall, has been joyful.

Life Energy Activities

- Answer these questions:

    1. What people, events in your life, and things don't you like and why?
    2. What people, events in your life, and things have been positive for you and why?
    3. How can you choose more of the positive?
    4. How can you decrease those situations and people you don't like?
    5. How would you describe yourself? (Just jot down words that come to mind rather than trying to put your thoughts in sentences.) What are your strengths, your skills, and your characteristics? If you had to tell someone what to write on your tombstone, what would you want them to say? This provides a beginning picture of your particular uniqueness—who you are.
    6. What places and people help you celebrate or support who you are? How do they do this? How can you celebrate, each day, who you are? How will you talk about yourself and what you can and want to do more positively?

- Think about these questions:

    1. What do you want out of your life? What is important to you?
    2. What kind of work do you really want to do? Describe it.
    3. What kind of relationships do you really want? Describe them.

Do a collage or draw/paint a picture of what your life would look like after you answer these questions. This is a beginning life vision important in building personal power and optimal living.

- How are you going to build an environment around you that will better support your life vision and who you are? What kind of people, situations, and interpersonal communication are needed? What beliefs and values would be important to create and maintain this new environment? What resources are you going to need to build into your environment?

Chapter 6

Being, Life Energy, and Optimal Living

A "Being" Reality

The world of conscious Being is a wondrous place.
Sensing, images and light,
All in one spectrum of nonverbal energy.
But verbal conversation there is
In fits and starts,
From the back of the head forward,
To guide and say hello,
To let you know I and you are here,
To laugh and play as joy and Love.

This is Who We Are...
Life energies of Love and compassion,
Where light and darkness are one
But different in their purposes,
Creating internal and external conversations,
About challenge, decision, and co-creation,
All within the life energy of Being.

Choose to live consciously resting within this energy,
And your true nature you will find,
That of divinity experiencing humanness.

Dialogue with Me and know,
That I am here
Within this home of our energy,
That we have called Being.

***Being* is a state of energy and a state of mind**. The energy of *Being* underlies all reality both positive and negative in all five domains of earth reality (Spirit, Mind, Emotion, Subtle Physical, and Physical). This state is different from the meaning in the dictionary that describes *Being* as simply a state of being alive. I mean much more by this term. *Being* is my essence and yours. This is the Life Energy from which all things are created. It is the prime Life Energy of everything that is. It is the Life Energy that is My Love and compassion. It is My core consciousness.

It is also a state of mind where you know, feel, believe, and act in a way that acknowledges who you are...divinity experiencing humanness. It is a state of mind that recognizes and uses your actual power of divinity experiencing humanness to co-create what you want with Me, rather than giving it up to others and being victim.

You have named "*Being*" by various names in your religious traditions—Kundalani, Grace, Christ's Love, and Holy Spirit. But none of these traditions have acknowledged the full importance of this Life Energy. It is an energy and state of mind that makes possible your very existence. It is the very core of your identity and who you are, as divinity experiencing humanness. It is part of you because you are part of Me. It is NOT out there beyond you as your religious traditions imply, but within. The kingdom of God is within and this is it!

If you believe in the reality of Being and commit to consciously operate within it for your daily living, you automatically open yourself to this core energy in a conscious way. When you do this (believe in Being and commit to consciously operate within it for your daily living), it becomes a part of your every day behavior. It then serves as the foundation for the operation of your conscious mind in daily living—decisions, envisioning what you want, your concepts, your self-image, and your image of the world.

Why is operating within *Being* in your daily living important?

1. It makes for easy communication with Me and other non-physical beings such as your soul, your Higher Self, your guides, and your guardian angel. The more easily you are able to communicate with Us, the greater conscious access to wisdom and co-creative power you have.

2. It provides a state of rest where you can experience peace, joy, centeredness, security, friendship with Me, and celebration of who you are.

3. You'll truly be able to build personal power; and personal power is needed to control your life and create what you want.

4. It provides for the growth and easy operation of your *Observer Self* as well as your *Body Consciousness*, two gateways as well as feedback loops to increase operating within the Life Energy of *Being*.

Your *Observer Self* helps you notice what you are doing and choose what you want. Without it, you can't separate yourself from your reactions to an experience. You get pulled in by the experience and have to ride it through, relying on your habitual reactions and thoughts. With the *Observer*, you can pull yourself out of the experience and your automatic reactions, observe the experience as it is ongoing, and then consciously decide what you want to do. At this point, your mind can call on the Life Energy of *Being* to help manifest the decision or help make the decision. *Being* then becomes a powerful helper in creating your life from moment-to-moment, but the *Observer* has to be active and healthy before you can do this in a conscious way.

Body Consciousness resides in both the Physical and Subtle Physical Domains. It is part of My consciousness that helps you to experience (feel) the energy of *Being*. Sensations and emotions that coincide with the natural energy of *Being* include peace, centeredness, uplifting energy, and Divine Love and compassion. When you are in *Being*, these natural emotions provide an anchor for you as you go about living your daily life. These feelings also let you know when you are in *Being* or separated from it by whether they are present. If you do not feel them in your body, you are not consciously in *Being*. You have instead compartmentalized your psyche. In other words, the conscious mind believes it is all alone while the deeper conscious mind knows it isn't. On the other hand, when you do feel these emotions, it is telling you that your conscious and deeper conscious minds are unified and operating within *Being*.

What happens if you don't believe in *Being* and commit to operate within it in your daily life?

1. You will be unable to build optimal living, because you will have a strong tendency to slide back into the state of separation and negative bias that you live in now.

2. You will find creating your own reality a struggle and will frequently lapse into feeling victim and helpless.

Outcomes of *Being*

Once you commit to existing within *Being*, making it your first thought in everything you do, then all the benefits I've just described fall into place. These benefits are, in fact, outcomes of *Being*. Let Me explain this in more detail.

Outcome 1. Consciously committing to operate in *Being* automatically and continuously reminds your conscious mind of who you truly are— divinity experiencing humanness. This awareness is a requirement for manifesting optimal living.
Being is your true identity and value; not the skills and characteristics that make-up your human identity. Your human identity consists of your special gifts and characteristics for learning as a human. But divinity experiencing humanness is your spirit identity that makes you an aspect of Me and gives you the power for creating your life.
Consciously committing to operate in Being requires that you accept your nature as being part of Me. As you accept this identity, you will naturally accept your responsibility for the creation and co-creation of events in your life. This is part of recognizing *Being*…it is your energy and Mine. That means that you have access to that energy to create, co-create, and choose what you want. When you recognize this, you cease to blame some external force for what happens to you. What happens to you is your responsibility! *This is a cornerstone for controlling your life and creating what you want to form optimal living.*

Outcome 2. Believing in *Being* and consciously committing to operate within it as divinity experiencing humanness, brings an ease of manifestation that results in extraordinary manifestation.
When you start with your conscious commitment to form your vision and intentions within *Being*, your inner helpers are more easily able to aid you in creating what you intend. We can also help you understand quickly which domains of your human Life Energy need adjustment in order to have your vision or intentions become reality. The result is that you stop believing that you are alone, you stop struggling to manifest what you want, and you grow in wisdom.

Outcome 3. When you accept that you are divinity experiencing humanness with the power to choose what you want and co-create it, you can *easily* communicate with all levels of consciousness in *Being*—your soul, your Higher Self, your guides, and Me.
The process starts with your conscious mind intending to operate in *Being* with all of Us as partners. With this intention, we are more easily able to help

your conscious mind to know what the best course of action is to fulfill life purposes and intentions. Then we co-create reality together.

With this "togetherness," you won't have to use the techniques I described in Chapter 3 to "access" Me. Instead, you will automatically be in touch with deeper consciousness from moment-to-moment because of your commitment to manifest through by consultation and co-creation within *Being*.

However, these techniques are helpful for strengthening the linkage between your conscious mind and the Life Energy of *Being*. For example, when you dream, your deeper levels of consciousness are communicating with your conscious mind in symbolic language. When you do not commit to operate in *Being*, this communication process is weakened. The knowledge and wisdom coming from your deeper self is not easily able to communicate with your conscious self. This makes life more difficult.

When, on the other hand, you accept *Being* as a reality and commit to operate within it, remembering dreams and their interpretations become easier. We may even help you with the process by implanting a suggestion in your mind to change the symbols of your dream so that you understand them more easily and remember what you dream. As you understand your dreams more easily, your conscious mind will have access to greater wisdom and will know better how to co-create within *Being*. It strengthens our relationship!

The same is true for esoteric traditions such as the Tarot and Runes. These are techniques I have listed for "accessing" *Being*. In reality, they provide a way for your conscious mind and deeper consciousness to more easily communicate with each other. When you have committed to operate within *Being*, as well as accept your divinity and its responsibility, these approaches will make communication between your conscious mind and deeper consciousness clearer and easier. All the other approaches that I mentioned (automatic writing, praying, meditating, creative drawing, daydreaming) serve the same purpose, they strengthen *conscious* access to *Being* and its wisdom. Its energy becomes more predominant in your life and conversation among all your levels of consciousness becomes easier.

Outcome 4. With acceptance of *Being* as a reality comes a singular ability to feel the essence of your energy—Love and compassion.

Other feelings and outcomes natural to *Being* include increased freedom to be who you are, increased wisdom for life decisions, a sense of security, more self-love, growing power to control your life, and a steady sense of centeredness. When you remember that you are divinity experiencing humanness and accept your power to create and co-create with Me in *Being*, you will increasingly experience these emotions and outcomes without any effort. As your belief and acceptance grow, so will these experiences.

Outcome 5. When you choose, create, and co-create within *Being*, this will allow you to more effectively manage both positive and negative energy.

Remember that negative and positive energies are part of the Life Energy that is *Being*. These are your energies for steering the course of your life toward what you want. They are like a rudder system on a ship or plane—negative energy steers your ship in the direction of finding what you don't want, and positive energy steers it in the direction of what you do want.

All manifestation, both negative and positive, is done most efficiently by realizing and affirming that you are in *Being*. Why? Because you are not at war with yourself! Your various selves acknowledge that they are all connected to each other, and to other helpers in *Being* including Me. It promotes cooperation and respect. The war inside you stops!

Outcome 6. In *Being*, you understand that all is well.

All is as it should be, because you and I have co-created what is happening and where you are. Here you remember most easily that you have chosen a life purpose, and that you and I are bringing experiences to you that will help you accomplish this life purpose most fully. Here you remember to respect and love who you are right now, because you are perfect for what you are doing right now. Here you celebrate who you are and who you are becoming.

Here you more easily feel the energy of life and its beauty and exuberance. You increase your ability to believe that reality is abundant with opportunities. Correspondingly, you believe that scarcity is a reality created for specific experiences chosen by your soul.

In this state of *Being*, you more easily respect the journey of others. You know that they are exactly where they should be for their life purpose. You listen to the messages they provide you, and then choose what to do. You recognize them as aspects of Me, essential to the puzzle and learning of the Universe. You wish them well even when, at an emotional level, they may bring you pain. You feel your pain, while simultaneously choosing to realize that the ones bringing you pain are aspects of Me.

Outcome 7. The state of *Being* easily activates the *Observer*, which is a major link and feedback loop between *Being* and your conscious mind.

The *Observer* provides you with a certain wisdom because it is a gateway to the conscious awareness and use of. You know at your *Being* level what is really happening. You also know that your life experiences are co-created by you and Me to forward your life purpose and intentions. You remember that you have free will. You remember that you choose your way and your experiences. All this knowledge is continuously available to the *Observer*.

For example, if you want to create negative experiences that will define what you do not want for your intention, the *Being* state will allow you to disconnect part of yourself, the *Observer*, from the negative energy you create. The *Observer* will allow you to experience the negative without getting lost in it. *It allows experiencing coupled with detachment.*

This does not mean that you are detached from life. Rather, it means that you are able to experience life fully while seeing through the "eyes" of the *Observer* so that:

- you are able to watch your conscious self as it carries out your intentions,
- you can stop yourself from getting totally immersed in the emotion and action of the moment and instead choose what you want to do, and
- you are able to remember from moment-to-moment that you are divinity experiencing humanness. In that role, you remember that you have chosen this human life for its intensity, its exuberance, and the emotional capacity that is part of being human.

In other words, the Observer provides the bridge between your mental consciousness and Being. It brings you to *Being* and allows your conscious self to communicate with your deeper levels of consciousness from moment-to-moment, without any special preparation.

Outcome 8. Committing to operate in *Being* and accepting your power to create your life, brings about an increased awareness and openness to *Body Consciousness.*

Body Consciousness, along with the Observer, are the two major linking paths between conscious living and deeper conscious reality. It allows you to feel and experience the reality of Being and its energy. *Body Consciousness* is an aspect of My Consciousness within your human make-up. Its purpose is to provide a link between you and Me that will allow you to feel Me at a physical energy level each moment of the day. The physical sensation that is My Presence intertwined with your *Body Consciousness* is a sensation of centeredness, calmness, inner listening, and assurance that you are not alone—and that you are more than human!

As you commit to operate in *Being*, it causes the energy of *Body Consciousness* to increase; it allows you to easily communicate with this part of yourself.

Outcome 9. Committing to live in the reality of *Being* and using your power to create within it, enables you to celebrate who you are and build personal power.

First, it allows you to be comfortable within your own skin. Why? Because you know that you are exactly where you should be at the moment to fulfill your life purpose and intentions. Even when you are being negative to yourself or others, you accept this as part of your journey. It does not mean that you glory in being obnoxious! But, in knowing that you make choices that bring pain to yourself and others, you know that you have chosen to learn the consequences of those choices. You have also chosen to know in detail what you don't want. So, committing to live in *Being* means that you respect who you are and what you are experiencing at all times, even though you may not like your behavior.

In *Being*, you celebrate what you learn and who you can be! With this celebration and respect you acquire ease of movement and action in your life. You seek to find what feels good and right for your life purpose and intentions. You know that you have the characteristics and innate skills that are just right for what you have chosen to experience and learn in this lifetime.

With *Being* and these outcomes as a foundation, your personal power naturally begins to build. Remember that I said personal power is made up of the following characteristics:

- defining who you are and loving that identity,
- accessing your deeper consciousness and Me,
- believing that you have all the skills and knowledge you need for each situation that presents itself,
- knowing how to handle negative events while building the positive,
- having a specific life vision,
- knowing how to ask those around you to support your personal power,
- speaking your truth, and
- developing the *Observer* within you.

You will notice that these characteristics have been mentioned as intrinsic to *Being*. That means that personal power and its growth is a natural outcome of opening to the energy of *Being*! You don't have to struggle to have personal power; it naturally grows when you commit to live in *Being*. Specifically, you naturally know who you are and love who you are, and you no longer have to "access" your deeper consciousness and Me because you are already there. In addition, you understand and believe that you have all the skills and knowledge that you need for each situation because it is intrinsic to who you are and to the state of *Being*. You more easily handle negative events while building the positive, and the *Observer* becomes a natural part of your daily living.

Finally, creating a specific life vision, knowing how to ask those around you to support you, and speaking your truth are natural outcomes of your commitment to *Being* and your power to create within it.

Your personal power is key to developing a new way of life that is optimal. It affirms that your power is truly within you and is not external to you. It places the creation of your life events within your management and control. Without personal power, you accept separation and victim hood as the dogma. Without personal power, you maintain what you already have in your society—dominance over others, a bias for negative living, a feeling of helplessness, and a feeling of emptiness.

So it is critical that you commit to live in *Being* and acknowledging your divinity and its power to create and co-create as an aspect of Me. If you do all of these things, you will begin to build a heaven on earth for yourself! This is what was meant when Jesus said, "The kingdom of Heaven is within." It is also what he meant when he said, "…the kingdom of God is within." Heaven and God are the same thing! They are within who you are as divinity experiencing humanness. You are divinity because you are an aspect of who I am, and both you and I exist in reality in *Being*. So if you accept *Being*, you accept Me. Thus your personal power will grow and form the basis of building optimal living—your heaven on earth.

Prerequisites to Operate in *Being*

To live within *Being* you will need to do the following prerequisite activities:

1. *Accept Being as a reality.* Believe in it.

2. *Accept the responsibility of forming your own reality.* This means that you believe that you are divinity experiencing humanness who has the power through Life Energy to create, co-create, and choose your life experiences. It also means that you commit to learning how to consciously mange negative and positive energy in all five energy domains to form the experiences that will best carry out your life purpose and intentions.

3. *Accept the responsibility of loving and having compassion for both yourself and others.* This means that you accept that both you and anyone else are part of Me and that each of you are on a life path that leads to the fulfillment of specific life purposes. To support this process you accept that you will affirm personal power and divinity in yourself and others as best as you can. More specifically, that means that you will affirm the following in yourself and others:

- You are each here to carry out a specific life purpose or purposes and your experiences are meant to support its fulfillment.
- Each of you has the answers within.
- Each person, including you, is so special in their work and experiences that I would be forever changed if you were not there.

When you do this, you are manifesting Divine Love and compassion to yourself and others.

State these three things as an intention: "I intend to do the following from now on..." We will remind you which of these three things you need to remember and do at appropriate times throughout the day. How's that for easy effort?

How to Operate in *Being*

Once you have mentally committed to the prerequisites I just listed, do the following things to help you live in *Being* in your daily life, then forget about it consciously. We will remind you of your intentions throughout the day and in your dreams at night.

1. *Commit to operate within the reality of Being for your daily life.* This means that you commit to form all decisions, actions, and thoughts by first opening to the energy of *Being*. It also means that you give your heart and self at the deepest level to this task. This is an intention.

2. *Just relax while making the intention of opening to the energy of Being.* Take deep breaths; they will help your body to calm down and your brain to produce calming alpha waves. Then commit yourself to operate in *Being* for the day to the best of your ability.

3. *Ask the help of your Body Consciousness to open the pathway to feel Our energy.*

4. *Increase your openness to Body Consciousness.* This will increase your ability to be physically aware of My Presence and those of other helpers within. Try one or more of the following activities to do this:

   - Just relax. Take deep breaths allowing a feeling of peace and contentment to flow over you anywhere you are. As you do this, widen your senses so that you focus on the flow of energy within you as you breathe and move.

- Stop at various times in the day and see where you feel tension—let it go by taking deep breaths. Tell your *Body Consciousness* to move your body in ways that will create ease in the areas of tension. Let your body go in whatever way it wants.

- Focus within yourself and ask your *Body Consciousness* to help feel the Life Energy of *Being*. Relax into the physical sensations and feelings of *Being*. Then begin to do whatever is your impulse. Do something that you are pulled to do, or talk to the energy. If a daydream arises, go with it, it is a message. Play with the energy— how it feels—moving freely in whatever way you want. Dance with it, or just feel the energy and enjoy it.

- Make your *Body Consciousness* your constant friend and companion. Talk to it as a helper in operating your body so that it is healthy. Ask it to help you be optimally receptive to the energy of *Being*. When you feel the energy of *Being*, acknowledge it, love it, and respect it to develop a deep and loving relationship.

    Ask your *Body Consciousness*, as well as the helpers in *Being*, to help you maintain the sensations and feelings of operating in *Being* even when you are busy and NOT relaxed. Using your *Body Consciousness* in these ways strengthens its creative ability to collaborate with you to create a healthy body as well as function as a gateway to *Being*.

5. ***Strengthen the Observer Self.*** This will establish the mental gateway to *Being* while you are doing everyday tasks. The *Observer Self* will allow you to detach from the experience of living your life, its sensations and emotions, while still living within them. It splits your consciousness so that one part of you lives fully in the moment, while the other part is observing the moment, your experience, your choices, and your creations. The *Observer* then allows you to choose what you want to do in the next moment. To strengthen the *Observer*, do the following things:

    - Ask it to become active in your daily life.
    - Observe what has happened at the end of each day and write it down.
    - Note what is happening around you during the day.
    - Note what your reactions are to things as you are doing them.

115

6. ***Focus on the NOW, the present moment in your daily life***. This doesn't mean you shouldn't plan or build a vision and then focus on all things that will bring about your vision/plan. But do not stay there all day long. Focus on what you can do NOW that makes more likely the manifestation of your vision or plan.

Savor each moment as part of the Life Energy of *Being*, whether positive, negative, or just passively relaxing and not doing anything. Savor your sensations, your thoughts, your breath, your body sensations, your words, the feel of a plant, the sensations of touching and relating to animals, and the sensations of relating to others. Appreciate all as My essence and Life Energy. I am all of these things. Notice them all through the *Observer* and your *Body Consciousness* so that you can appreciate My essence in a detached manner while feeling Divine Love and compassion.

Becoming aware of sensations from moment-to-moment will aid you in being open to the energy of *Being* and communication with Us, your helpers. It will allow Us to speak to you through the many different mediums that you sense. Listen for Our voice. It might come in the words you speak to yourself or another. It might appear in the guise of a bird or a deer. It might come through the voice of a friend or an angry companion. It might come through synchronistic events. My voice and energy, as well as all other helpers in *Being*, appear in all these ways. Keep your senses alert and appreciate the energy you feel, and you will hear Us or see Our message. Then you can talk back to Us and from that, we can form a loving and supportive relationship! You are never alone. Just listen and look.

7. ***In your daily life, commit to experimenting with what living in Being means for you...*** your divinity, your special gifts, and your life purpose. This is a commitment that unfolds its meaning for you over your lifetime.

8. ***Make extraordinary manifestation happen*** by carrying out the following process while operating in Being:

    1. Start with committing to opening yourself to *Being* and using its creative energy. This is your intention.
    2. In your mind, build a day in your life creating images and experiences around what you want <u>as if it has already happened</u>. As you do this, the Life Energy of *Being* instantaneously energizes your thought or vision.
    3. Direct the image, sensation, and experience of what you want to your helpers in Being—your soul, your guides, your Higher Self, and Me. Then, let go of it. We will take care of it. We know what you want

and will work toward manifesting it. If you worry about whether it is going to happen, your worry impedes the energy of creation. So give it to Us to help manifest and relax!

9. ***Set up and nurture a deep relationship with Me and all other helpers in Being.*** Do this by talking to Us, feeling Us, loving Us, laughing with Us, seeing Us in yourself, others, and the environment. Whatsoever you do, say, or feel to others and to yourself, you are doing to Me. *You are relating to Me when you talk to others and when you talk to yourself.* My energy and consciousness are in each of you! It is the Life Energy of *Being*. When you touch yourself and others, you touch Me. When you see each other and look at yourself, you see Me. I am who you are.

The same is true for all things that you can see, feel emotionally, touch, or hear—animals, wind, water, the sky, the land, plants, the universe. I am all of these things. As you relate to them, so you relate to Me.

If you disrespect any of these things, you disrespect Me. But I will not return the favor. I will not disrespect you, but love you as you are. Why? Because you are an aspect of Me! How can I disrespect myself?! I know by your disrespect you are learning about Negative Life Energy and its consequences. It is part of the life journey you are choosing. But long term disrespect for anything, especially for yourself, limits potential for knowing Positive Life Energy and feeling *Being*. It limits potential for feeling My Love, hearing My voice, touching My energy. It separates you from the real reality of *Being*. It causes you to be attracted to choosing behavior that makes you believe I am not there. It makes you believe I am a distant God.

Respect yourself and all others. Love all things as a manifestation of who I am. When there is negative behavior and events, see that as part of who I am. I am not being evil; I am helping you define what you do not want and pointing the way to what you do want. Have patience with yourself, others, and Mother Nature when these negative things happen. It will point the way to its opposite and in the bargain, give you gifts of new skills and insights if you work through the negative as a process. I am there; I am present in each second of this process. It is My energy! Know Me and what I am helping you to learn. You are never alone!

If you wish to have a personal, intimate relationship with Me, do all these things, and do all these things with the affirmation:

"I am You and You are me. I am in our Being; I make all my choices and receive learning, while existing in our Being. I commit to this. I accept that I am an aspect of You, and that I have the power to create my life."

The outcome will be that you will know Me better, hear what I say easier, feel My love more, and touch My energy often. We are one, and I am present in the physical, emotional, and mental world in all the ways I have described. Love all these things and especially yourself as Me, and you will find the love and acceptance you seek.

A Picture of *Being* and the Kingdom of Heaven…Optimal Living

I said that committing to live within *Being* would result in building optimal living. A common picture that may appear in your mind's eye is a beautiful, pastoral scene of peace and beauty, where everyone has plenty and there are no negative bumps in the road. Well, sorry to wreck your pastoral scene!

Heaven on earth includes negative and positive events because that is what human experience is. The difference will be that your lives will have a decided positive center and bias, rather than the negative one you now have in place.

In addition, there will be a pervasive belief and knowing that you create your own life. This will produce a society that will not reward victim hood, because each of you will understand it is an illusion. However, there will be sympathy for difficult paths, and respect for the courage to explore them. Those around you will tend to support you as a divine aspect of Me following your chosen path, whatever that might be.

This society will nurture skills that lead to the strengthening of *Being* while in the conscious state. This will be done because there will be a realization that communication with all levels of your deeper consciousness makes learning more powerful and the path of life easier. Those with the highest skills will be sought after as teachers of life and Life Energy.

Your structures of community living will be altered to accommodate optimal living. A rotating or floating leadership will arise that encourages the best person(s) for the task or learning at hand to step forward and guide others. When the learning and task is complete, their leadership will be shed because there is no more need. Leadership will be based on choosing who has the most skill to lead the project at hand.

Institutions will reflect a respect for each human as a divine aspect of Me. They will also reflect a sense of community that does not demand people give up their individuality for the good of all. Rather, there will be a nurturing of individuality within community.

Beliefs That Are Barriers to Optimal Living

There are built-in beliefs that are barriers to optimal living in your societies of which I need to speak. You need to know what these are in order to get around them and create what you really want.

There are barriers that affect each of you individually in your daily lives. These include societal beliefs about sexuality, achievement, money, power, control, helping, and emotions. There are also barriers that affect large groups or the whole population. These are beliefs that have been incorporated into the operation of institutions in your society—education, government, religion, medical care, and business. Let Me talk about each of these so that you are consciously aware of them. Then let me describe how you can transform these beliefs so that they no longer control you.

Individual Beliefs That Are Barriers:

Sexuality – Sexuality is a dirty word in most civilized cultures. It is something to be experienced that is illicit. You have planted the belief that it is something that men should control and to which women should submit. Another basic belief is that women are dirty, carnal, weak, and dangerous. They can draw in a man and cause him to sin. They need to be controlled and sex is one way to do this. Such are the beliefs of your male-dominated cultures.

The truth is that both women and men are magnificent variations of creation who experience reality in different ways. Both men and women are equals and sacred in their unique experiences. Each has taken on a different role and experience. What the roles and experience are can be defined differently by different cultures. But there are no for-ordained characteristics except for the biological differences associated with sexual intercourse and certain perceptual processes.

Your cultures have the mistaken notion that certain characteristics are intrinsic to the male and female. For the male, intrinsic characteristics are believed to be aggression, control, power, decision-making, logic, and mastery. For the female, intrinsic characteristics are believed to be passivity, tenderness, care giving, emotions, and creative (illogical) thinking. These characteristics are *not* intrinsic, but have been culturally determined by your male-dominated societies. These stereotypical characteristics for men and women are illusions generated to give the experiences you, as a human race, decided that you wanted to generate. It is time to drop this illusion.

Each man and each woman must understand the male and female characteristics within themselves, for each is not whole without being both "feminine and masculine." The separation you have made between the male

119

and female in your cultures has weakened the potential of each. Without the wholeness of *both* male and female Life Energy integrated into a cohesive whole, human beings cannot function at their highest potential. Your societal beliefs about male and female characteristics are, therefore, a major barrier to personal power and optimal living.

You must alter this so that you give yourself the freedom to experiment with the particular combination of feminine and masculine that is best for you and your life intention(s). Allow respect and growth of new roles for both males and females. Nurture and accept differences; celebrate them as aspects of Me.

The separation of male and female Life Energy also limits experiencing divinity while being human. Sexual energy is divine energy. It is the energy of creation and manifestation. You can reach My consciousness through experiencing sexual energy and sexuality as sacred energy—a doorway to knowing Me. Beyond the experience of sexual orgasm is the thrusting, dynamic energy that is Me. When you feel the high of orgasm, or the creativity of male and female characteristics within you, you are accessing My energy, My consciousness. You can use that energy to know Me and yourself better. You can use that energy to create an experience of divinity being human. Do that by having the intention that you want to use your sexual energy in this way, and so it will be.

Achievement – Achievement is your god, your icon, especially for those of you in the American culture. If you don't achieve, you have no value. If you have no plan, no goals, you are labeled lazy, a dreamer, or a bum. Achievement has produced bigger and better houses, skyscrapers, government buildings, bridges, computers, robots, and airplanes. Achievement has produced greater and greater populations in bigger and bigger population centers. Achievement has developed technology to the point of being your present god.

But has achievement given you more peace, more happiness, better quality of life, more understanding of yourself and others? If so, why are you still killing one another? Why do you still have wars (that are surely bigger and better!)? Why do you still hate one another? Why are you slowly destroying the earth? Why do you feel more isolated and angry than ever?

Achievement is a barrier to your knowing that you are divinity experiencing humanness. In the way that achievement is currently experienced, it reinforces separateness and control from the outside rather than within you. It reinforces an illusion of contribution, if you build and leave behind a bigger and better widget. What does it profit a human if they build the best computer in the whole world and lose their identity?

Learning is separate from achievement. Learning is pleasure in understanding new concepts and ideas, as well as self-satisfaction in acquired knowledge and its applications over time. Learning generates personal satisfaction and joy. Learning is part of the curiosity built into the human soul. Learning will not get in the way of experiencing God-consciousness for it is part of that consciousness. Achievement, however, is driven with an eye toward what the other person thinks of what you are doing. Achievement can only exist within the context of approval from your fellow human beings. **Achievement is, therefore, control given to the other person to judge whether your actions are acceptable and have value**.

The future is focused on learning, not achievement.

Money – Money is your method of exchange for something of value. It represents energy that has become manifested in paper form; energy that says, "I am giving you this to acknowledge that what you offer is of value to me." It is a recognition of you or something that you have that will be treasured by the buyer. That's all money is.

You have vilified money as the root of all evil. In fact, the root of all negative experience is fear. Fear that you will not have enough of something if you don't have money. You have translated this fear into the assumption that if you get enough money, then you won't be afraid anymore and you can have what you want. That includes power. Power over others to tell them what to do, to demand respect and recognition. Power to buy what you want when you want it. By this fear, you have set up a culture of scarcity—not enough food, clothing, housing, or jobs. By this fear, you have generated your intensely negative experiences. Murders, burglary, stealing, and wars, these are examples of intensely negative experiences generated by your beliefs about money.

Money is not responsible for all these negative outcomes, only your vision and beliefs about money. That means if you decided to reframe your vision and beliefs, money would have a different effect on your cultures and people.

If fact, you, individually and in small groups, must do this, for your present cultures will not. The redefinition must come from each of you who read this and groups that you form. You are the creators of a new civilization. Your present civilizations do not want to change, because those in charge will lose power. You do not have to attack these cultures and their powers as you change your beliefs about money. Instead, simply walk away from the groups and activities that hold these beliefs.

Build your own businesses, as well as your own communities and cultures, based on the vision that money is an exchange of value and represents intentional energy. Money signifies to the other person and groups that you appreciate their value. It allows a method of exchange where there is a fair exchange of value for value. It provides you a means of gaining things you need to live and enjoy your life. It provides you a means of imparting respect to others.

Power and Control – You have defined power and control in most of your societies to be external to you. It is within money, position, the number of your possessions, or chance. The corresponding belief to this assumption is that either you get power over someone else or they will get power over you. Either you get power over your environment (ecosystem), or it will get power over you.

If this is so, then the world is a dangerous place. You must constantly be on the alert for where danger is going to appear in the form of lost control by you. You must protect yourself at all costs, because people are no darn good and they will hurt you if given a chance. You must protect your assets because you never know when bad luck is going to come and take it all away. You are powerless unless you are a master of the situation. You are victim unless you are the controller. The result: constant anxiety, fear, and running from the dark forces that could get control of you. And since women and people of color are not part of the natural power structure of white males, that means the bias is toward victim hood. The choice is either you fight or you amplify your victim hood and demand to be taken care of by those who have the power. After all, they have the power so it's their responsibility!

You have created your own living nightmare with these beliefs. You have created a world that is built on chaos and danger. But this is only an illusion. To change this nightmare, you must change your vision and your beliefs. Your vision must be of power and control from within. Your vision must be of ability to access this power to create the lives and communities you wish. Your vision must be of connection with Me and all of creation where there is an intent to produce thriving, positive life experiences. Your beliefs must alter to understand that your power is not only within you, but is a collaboration with your soul, your Higher Self, your guides, and Myself, as well as other human beings. It is power with, not power over—collaboration and compromise, not capitulation or control.

You do not have to do what you do not wish; that is free will. You may create something that is negative, but you created that outcome for yourself either consciously by your beliefs or through intentions at some level of your inner reality. You accessed Negative Life Energy, molded its form to your intention, and manifested the negative reality. To change it, alter your vision as well as learn what the negative has to teach you.

You will always have the resources within you at some level of inner reality for the challenges that appear in your life. All you have to do is give these resources the freedom to manifest. Believe that your intention becomes reality in its own time. Ask for the resources that you need—skills, knowledge, people, money, and events that need to happen to fulfill your intention.

Also, remember that you are never alone! I am always with you. Your fear blocks this knowledge in your darkest hours. But know even in your darkest moment that I am there, unconditionally loving you and giving you My energy. We are one, you and I. I can never *not* be there. Call on Me, talk to Me, demand that I help you. I am your friend and support. I will never allow anything to happen to you that you have not chosen or accepted at some level of your being.

And, if you have chosen something that is difficult to bear, know that you always have the resources you need to work through the negative and reframe it into positive reality. *You always have the resources to do this because your resources include Me.* I am always there, your safety net, your friend and your guide.

Helping – Helping is such a sanctified concept in your cultures. It is supposed to indicate holiness on the part of those who do it. It is assumed that I want you to help others even if it costs you your life. You believe that I have told you that others are always more important than you. And, if you love me, you will serve your fellow humans unconditionally. This is certainly a great prescription for keeping people controlled. If you are forever giving your power up to others, then you must do what they want, or what you think they need. In either case, all your power is outside of yourself.

How could I possibly demand this when each of you is as important as another?! Each of you is a beloved aspect of My Being. Each of you is so important that if you did not exist, My Being would be forever changed. All of you have different purposes that you have chosen to accomplish in order to enrich who you are and who I am. But, I repeat, no one is more important than another.

In addition, how could I demand such all-encompassing service, if I am telling you to ignore your own well-being? You must love yourself and take care of yourself. You must develop your skills and potentials as part of your life purpose. If you do not do this, then you are rejecting Me for you and I are one. You are a part of Me. **You must love yourself in order to love Me. You also must love others as aspects of Me in order to love Me. For we all are one**.

Your cultures have developed this overbearing model of service as a means of keeping many of you controlled. It gave all of you the experience of what happens when you so overemphasize care and service to others that you lose yourself. You also give up your power to another person.

This lopsided model of caring is a perfect example of a relationship that your psychologists have labeled as co-dependent. You are out rescuing victims. You rescue them and watch for when they need help again. Those who are rescued have not learned to solve their problems because you did it for them. And if you keep on rescuing them, they never learn. So they remain victims and you remain a rescuer…each needing the other in order to be happy.

But there is no happiness here. It never works. Eventually, the victim expects too much out of their rescuer and then the rescuer becomes a victim of their own rescuing. That is, they become angry at the excessive demands for help, when in fact they are the ones that nurtured and encouraged it. This model of service will not promote growth for either party— rescuer or victim. Nevertheless, it is a model that teaches the consequences of this approach, and what you **do not** want to do when providing service to others.

If you wish to help others, follow the suggestions in the box on the next page.

Optimal Ways of Helping Others:

- Balance helping others with taking care of your own needs.
- Teach them to solve their own problems by affirming that the answers are always within them. Outside sources only act as catalysts to help them find the answer within themselves.
- Affirm for them that I am always with them, as well as their guides. Tell them to ask Us what to do.
- Affirm for them that they always have the resources within them to solve whatever they experience, because their inner self, Myself, and guides are part of those resources.
- Affirm for them that they are divinity experiencing humanness. They control their life, not others or fate.
- Give them information that is needed to activate the knowledge within them, and be a cheering section for things that you have seen them do successfully. Affirm their strength and importance.
- Even if their behavior is not something that you like, tell them that this is their journey, their choice, and that they have the resources to find their way to what they want. Do not try to tell them what to do, other than providing information. Let them experience the consequences of their choices, so that they can begin to make different choices. This is unconditional love.
- If you cannot verbally or physically support and affirm them, then provide an intention to their Higher Self that you give them your love to speed them toward the positive outcomes, experiences, and learning for which they are striving. This will add your positive intention to their energy and help them toward the best choice for their life purpose. This is unconditional love.

Emotion – Feelings are a special legacy of being human. It is one of the reasons that each of you chose to become human, rather than live in some other worlds where there are no emotions. They provide a special richness to experience and knowing. But you do not know how to use them to your advantage in your societies. Either you tell people that they must not allow their emotions to control them, or you tell others that they must acknowledge their emotions and live in them. Either way provides a lopsided experience of living with emotions.

The best balance and the easiest learning mode is one where emotions and thinking are working together to provide the ultimate learning experience. The human has been created with nine levels of Life Energy: three levels of spirit, three levels of mind, emotion, subtle physical energy, and physical energy. All of these levels are important; all must work together compatibly if you want the easiest learning and manifestation to happen.

So if you are experiencing intense emotions, celebrate them, respect them for teaching tools of experience, then ask what their message is. If the emotions are negative, ask yourself what needs to be done to change the negative emotion into positive.

To help do this, begin to develop the *Observer* part of your personality, that part of you that looks at what you are doing as it is happening. When you are deeply into emotions, they bring forth reactions that you have learned that are usually automatic. These are coping strategies that you have used before. Those coping strategies may not be the best ones for you now. To get yourself out of this entranced, automatic state of mind, you must activate the *Observer Self* within you.

The best way to do that is to review what has happened at the end of the day. Do this by talking it through and recording what you say, or writing it down. Then ask yourself what reactions were successful for you, and which were not and why. This process of analyzing your reactions, activates your *Observer Self*. The more you do this exercise at the end of each of day, the more active the *Observer* becomes. Eventually, you will find that as you are doing something, even when in intense emotion, there will be a part of you that is standing back and observing the whole interaction and your reactions. This is the first step in not being controlled by your emotions, but in using them to learn and then choose what you want to do.

For those of you who cut off your emotions by living in your heads or by living only in physical reality, you are eliminating a part of your being necessary to create the life you want. Without emotions, you will find your life empty and flat. Allow emotions into your life, letting them teach you the lessons they bring. Then choose what is best for you and your life intentions. They do not have to overpower you. They will not destroy you. As long as the *Observer Self* is active, you can choose the outcomes you wish. You can go through the emotion, learn from it, and choose. If you run from emotion, your learning is very slow and you will feel as if you are missing something in your life. It is emotion!

Emotion does not have to be a barrier to creating the life you want and carrying out your life intention. Nor should it be the be-all and end-all to your existence. It is one part of your being, a very important part but not all of you. Use it to provide you with the richness of life for which it was created.

Institutional Beliefs That Are Barriers:

Medical care – Medical care in your world has evolved from a thing of natural power to one of god power. Your medical establishment has set itself up as knowing all there is worthwhile to know about healing and health. You are told to allow medical practitioners to work the wonders of medical science on your body, submitting your will and total trust to their care. With this model, they have set themselves up as God. This reflects the picture of Me that you have created, male, all-knowing, demanding, and authoritarian.

Those of you who have accepted this model, put yourself in the victim role. You give your power to the health practitioner and say heal me. Then, if they cannot heal you, you label them a false god, and curse them for their blasphemy.

This model is dysfunctional. The health practitioner gains respect, love, gratitude, and worship from the patient, and in return the patient gets to remain a child. The child, you the patient, assumes there will now be warm-fuzzy safety. All goes well as long as each participant in the relationship acts as expected and gives what is wanted. Each is dependent on the other. But neither has real freedom. The health practitioner lives in a prison of fear knowing that they cannot really be God and they will fall from their pedestal. More and more is demanded by their patients in order to remain on their pedestal—more knowledge, more time, and more energy. Although there are monetary rewards, those rewards have a high cost, including broken marriages and relationships, high stress, high incidence of chronic illness, not enough leisure time, no time to understand who they really are or what they really want, and, potentially, early death.

For you, the patients, there is a similar high cost in giving up your power to medical professionals. You never grow-up. You are unable to make your own decisions about your own bodily needs. You depend on the expert rather than your own inner sense of what is needed for your mental, emotional, and physical health. Control is always outside so fear abounds when matters of health intrude, because there is little control that you can exercise over your own bodies, minds, and spirits. Only the health practitioners really know what to do.

The truth is that you are the one who controls what happens to your body. You set the stage for dis-eases that you experience. You may become at dis-ease with yourself—your vision, values, and who you truly are. By illness, your body is telling you that you are going the wrong direction. Or you may have decided that the ailment that you experience is necessary for your further growth, or is part of your life purpose. But at all times, you choose or accept the illness you experience.

To "cure" your illness, you must first form a vision that depicts your body as healthy and vibrant. Next, do the work necessary to form the identity, beliefs, strategies, physical regimen, and emotional focus that match your vision. The physical regimen can certainly include health care practitioners where you form a partnership in the care of your body.

Ask you deeper consciousness why you are experiencing this illness; what is its purpose? What are its gifts? How can you let the negative go and transform it into positive?

Health practitioners can help, but they cannot really heal. Only you can heal yourself. If one illness goes away with medication, and you have not finished the work your inner self intended, you will soon find yourself facing the same illness again, or a different one. You have the responsibility for your own body, mind, and spirit. You cannot give it away to another for it is integral to who you are as divinity experiencing humanness.

Religion – I am religion. I am God. I am the one about which all religions say they are teaching. Yet, each teaches something different. What is the truth? It is that each religion and spiritual philosophy is teaching some truth about Me. This diversity is necessary so that the differences in humans can be honored. Each of you has your own best way of coming to know who you truly are and who I am.

Religion provides a structure for those who need structure. But religion is not a mandate for knowing Me. For you are divinity experiencing humanness. To know Me, you only have to look within yourself and ask, "Who is God?" and I will answer. For I am you and you are an aspect of Me. But religions provide community, support, and catalysts to knowing Me for those who want it.

Many religious institutions have forgotten this original role of sharing truths, supporting growth, and respecting the divinity within each. Instead, they have set themselves up into authoritarian, rule-wielding power-bases, demanding that their believers give up all power to them. They proclaim that they (the priests, ministers, rabbis, and gurus) are the only ones who really can know the truth. They are the ones who truly have the ear of God. You, the believer, are too sinful and too ignorant of religious truths to know what is best for your spiritual development.

This is a model of power that reflects the negative. It does not empower its believers, but rather takes away power. It keeps you children; it keeps you victims; it keeps you obedient and pliable.

This is a model of what religion is not.

True religion is empowering. It recognizes the divinity within each human. It supports paths that are chosen, while giving information about the consequences of those paths. It provides unconditional love, as I do. That is religion.

Accessing and knowing the Life Energy of *Being*, My Consciousness, is part of religion, but does not have to exist within the structure of religion. Life Energy is your very nature. It is your essence, who you truly are. It is also My Spirit (Consciousness) and who I truly am. As a result, your spirit knows truth because you and I are one in the Life Energy of *Being*. You have the knowledge within you that is important for you to fulfill you life purpose(s). So the real truth of God lies within each of you. *I ask you to share your truth with others freely, but not impose your truth on others.*

If you wish to share your truth within a structured setting, then religions or informal groups can give you this. But if you wish to find and tell your truth without group support and structure, you can also do this. Whatever you choose, it is the best mode of learning and speaking your truth at the moment. You are the expert because you are an aspect of Me, and you and I are always connected. Others can provide you with information, or be catalysts for your learning. But you are the best one to decide what is truth for you.

Education – Learning is a sacred part of your nature. It is the process that adds to who I am. It evolves who you are, and in so doing, you evolve who I am. We are never static, never finished. We are always becoming.

Education is the process of teaching certain knowledge and skills to allow you to evolve in a specific cultural way. The institutions that you have created for education too often assume the authoritarian, all-knowing model already described for religious and health institutions. The present American educational model was created in the early 1900s to provide factory workers that could read and write enough to follow directions. The motivations behind the curriculums were not only basic literacy, but basic obedience. The industrial revolution demanded obedient workers who would do their part in generating wealth for the employer. This assumption is still within your educational approaches. Teachers are the authorities; they are to be obeyed. They have all of the knowledge. This is a military model of education.

Each human child is instilled with learning skills appropriate to who they have chosen to be in their lives and their life purpose. Each human child is born with a natural curiosity and thirst for learning. When this ability is not recognized and honored, then learning becomes work rather than fun and natural play. Each student knows how they learn best; each student has natural skills and knowledge innate to them.

Education at its best is a partnership between humans, where there is a respect for skill and knowledge on both sides, teacher and student. Teachers left to their own instincts, rather than what they think they should do, will often fall into this model of teaching. They see their pupil(s) as having an interest in learning, certain innate skills and knowledge. They begin to experiment with how to best provide learning experiences within those assumptions. They assume learning should be fun, a challenge, exciting and pleasurable. They find ways to make it so. They watch for their students' reactions to learning. If they are not learning, they change what they are doing because they assume they have not found the best way to teach to those students.

But as long as teachers are restricted within rigid curriculums, testing procedures, forms to fill out, and bureaucratic rules, the partnership between teacher and students is limited. As long as the military model of education is honored, the natural creative learning and teaching of pupil and teacher is not.

Government – Governments are formed to help provide order to groups of people living in community. They are intended to provide flexible guidelines for living and relating to one another. They make explicit responsibilities that are beneficial for the group, while safeguarding the rights of the individual. They are partners in making living in a community, country, or nation easier. Those who have leadership roles are simply doing a job that is important to the community. Those roles should be given respect. But so should other essential roles in making a community work—business, spiritual, leisure, parenting, teaching, and clean-up. All are equally important in building a functional community. Those who lead do not have any more power over others, than those who carry out other roles. In this model, government is a model of power with others, not power over others.

Most governments do not reflect this approach. They reflect the same model of military, male, autocratic power that is seen in all of your other institutions. Power is power over others. Leaders grab power so they can be respected, do what they want, and accumulate wealth and control. Many of your leaders fulfill their roles to the public only to the degree that they think they must in order to stay in power. Their primary motivation is to stay in power, not to serve the people. This is a natural outcome of the military model you have in place. Absolute power over others breeds absolute fear. Absolute fear brings forth an absolute desire to survive at all costs.

In order to change, your governments must focus on service to others. Right now, you the people that elect officials reward absolute power and wealth above all else. You allow money to be key in gaining status as a government leader. For those of you who cannot elect others, you accept the power base given you as having absolute power over you. It does not!

Begin to envision a government different from that which you have, and it will be created as your vision becomes coherent with the rest of your beliefs and behavior. Look at nations whose governments have changed because of grass-roots changes in beliefs and behavior—the Soviet Union and China are two major examples. Even though the outcomes are different than anticipated in both cases, the changes in style of government were brought about by the will of the people. Values changed; government changed.

Business – Business provides something of value that others want. Money is a marker of the value. Consequently, money can be affirming and provide respect. It can indicate the degree of value to others. It can allow you to gain things of value that you want.

But your culture has imbued the making of money with a sense of the divine. With enough money you can do or be anything that you want. With enough money you can control you life and have great power. So goes the dream. With money, enough money, you can be safe. These beliefs are figments of your imagination.

Even your happiness research has shown that money does not bring happiness. Wealthy nations have citizens that are no happier than other countries with less wealth. Wealthy individuals are no happier than those who have ordinary incomes. You have built your societies so that a certain amount of money is important for surviving, but beyond that level, money itself does not bring happiness.

So what is it that business provides that is truly of value? It provides a life's work that is satisfying and challenging. It provides income that provides for the basics of living. It provides a place where camaraderie and group learning can happen. It provides community and self-learning. It is a place that provides a rich variety of life experiences from which you can choose, learn, and grow.

Business becomes a barrier when it does not live up to these values. When, instead, it encourages and nurtures the myth that money is the divine answer to all of life's problems. That money is all there is. When this view is the absolute core value, then business becomes a destroyer of lives. It imprisons the mind, saps the energy, and provides outcomes that are continual disappointments. It nurtures a society that brings about ill health, anger, and frustration. For those who own the business, it brings on fear that is constant. Aggression and lies develop out of the fear that either you win or lose. There is nothing in between.

The task of those who wish to remove this barrier is to create businesses that live up to their true values—a place of satisfying work and challenge, adequate income, camaraderie, learning, growth, community, and fun.

131

What You Can Do to Create Optimal Living for You and Others

The beginnings of the society just described will not require a consensus of many, only a few of you. The reason? You, as a race, have determined that the negative center and bias you have set in place for so long is no longer viable or desirable. You have learned what you wanted to know. So you are releasing the mass human intention of experiencing the negative more than the positive. Instead, you are building within you the intention of consciously experiencing *Being* and positive living. With these conditions in place, only a small number of individuals are needed to build momentum and start the transformation process. In fact, it has already begun.

All of you have consented to live in this time of transformation. Some of you want to watch. Some of you have agreed to be the negative power trying to keep things in place, in order to provide a clear picture of what you don't want. Some of you have agreed to pioneer a new way of life in various forms. Some of you will support this way of life once it is pioneered to fine tune it and encourage its growth. All of you have a role.

It is critical that those of you reading this book, who feel the urge to create a different way of life, do so. It is time to explore and pioneer! It is time to "do your thing!" You don't have to wait for anyone else to come along in order to accomplish it. Just commit to operate in *Being* in your daily life, focus your intention on what you want, make it real in your mind's eye, and then allow your deeper consciousness to begin co-creating the reality with you!

If you have such an impulse, this is part of your life purpose—to create a new life in your own way so that you can speak your truth. Your truth may not be other's truth, but it will provide learning and knowledge necessary for other's journeys. It will provide one model of a new way of living. So don't just talk about it, do it! Remember that committing to live in *Being* as well as accepting who you are and your power, will automatically provide you with a safety net and guidance. You are not ever alone. We co-create together!

A. Necessary Life Energy Beliefs and Values for Optimal Living

Optimal living and a positive lifestyle will operate under certain broad principles. If you are interested in trying this for yourself in a small or big way, the following Life Energy principles are the basic broad values and beliefs under which optimal ways of living will flourish. Use them as guides for your decision-making and behavior.

1. ***All things are connected; we are all one.*** I am everywhere and in all things, but I am also more than just all things. I am a complete being all by Myself.

You are an aspect of Me and as such, you are divine. If I am in all things, and you are an aspect of Me, that means you must respect all things, as well as yourself and other human beings. The environment and its animal inhabitants are not meant to be your playthings, nor to be dominated. The plants and animals of earth, and earth itself all have their own consciousness. The best way to bring about optimal living is to respect this consciousness.

It does not mean you cannot kill and use what is needed for your life processes. However, it does mean that you give thanks that these forms of life have allowed themselves to die, in order to sustain your life. Respect how you kill them; respect how you nurture your food and environment. They will provide abundance in return.

2. ***Committing to operate in Being is primary to successful manifestation and optimal living.*** This means that you have the intention each day that you will create your decisions and actions within *Being*. It also means that you affirm to yourself you are divinity experiencing humanness. As such, you are responsible for your life.

3. ***Each individual that you see, no matter their behavior, is an aspect of Me.*** Each individual is creating who they are by creating and experiencing both negative and positive life outcomes to carry out their life purpose. So each individual demands respect as an aspect of Me. You don't have to like their behavior, and you can tell them how you feel about that behavior. But you should acknowledge and respect each individual as being a part of Me who is in the process of their journey. This is true love.

4. ***Each individual has the freedom and responsibility to be who they are— divinity experiencing humanness.*** That means you accept your power to create your lives and carry out your life purposes. That also means you strive to respect who you are at the moment because you are just where you should be. In addition, it means you continually strive to be who you truly are. As you do this, you are showing that you love Me and yourself, because you are part of Me. This builds personal power, a cornerstone for optimal living.

5. ***Each individual needs to focus on living fully in the moment, because the present is the only thing that is real.*** Time, the past, and future, is an illusion fostered by human reality. But it is part of experiencing humanness. In reality, however, all manifestation is created in the Now, not in the past or future, so show a commitment to fully live each moment of the day.

6. ***It is the responsibility of each individual to tell their truth in a way that others can hear.*** In other words, you speak what truths are important to you, but you say it in a way your listener can most easily understand. For example, instead of just stating what you want to do, you "paint" pictures with your words, or literally draw pictures because your listener understands things best by seeing.

Telling your truth also means that you do not demand that others believe your truth and affirm you for saying it. Why? Because you realize that each has their own truth to tell and no one has the capacity to know the entire truth.

7. ***Love and compassion are the essence of Being.*** That means individuals know that by committing to live in *Being* they automatically strengthen and pull to them the experience and feeling of Divine Love, as well as other desirable emotions and outcomes.

8. ***Each person has the freedom and responsibility to choose what they accept and create in their life.*** Others can advise, but they should not choose for the individual unless asked to do so. Why? Because it is each person's responsibility to choose what is best for their life, or ask for another's help when needed. It is not another's responsibility to choose for you. In addition, by choosing for someone else all the time and helping them out of crisis, you teach them learned helplessness and victim hood. That is not respecting others as an aspect of Me. If you want to help others, show them what they can do for themselves. Affirm them for who they are!

9. ***All manifestation starts with an intention or vision.*** The first step in creating what you want as an individual or group is to create a general vision of what you want, along with core intentions and beliefs that best support your vision.

10. ***Life is made up of Positive and Negative Life Energy in five different reality domains.*** Negative energy tells you what you don't want and positive energy tells you what you do. Human life experiences consist of both these types of Life Energy, but you can bias your lives and societies into experiencing more positive living. Underneath positive and negative energy, lies the prime Life Energy of *Being*. This is the most important energy to know about and commit to living within. It demands that you accept who I am and who you really are. As such, this makes possible optimal living. With *Being* as a basis in manifestation, knowing how to manage positive and

negative energies becomes easier and it puts you in control of your life. The result is extraordinary manifestation and sustained optimal living.

B. A Process for Building a New Environment for Optimal Living

You can see that the barriers to optimal living are pervasive in your culture. I feel an underlying sadness and anxiety that operate in your daily lives because of the negative culture in which you live. The answer to this situation is to create a different culture or atmosphere. *Get a group of you, two to four or more, and begin to build an atmosphere around you that supports your visions of optimal living.*

Do not wait for society to fix itself through those in authority. They have little reason to change for it keeps them in power. **You, the individual, along with other ordinary individuals must begin to change your culture by setting up your own intentional groups, communities, and businesses!**

If you are not the "joining" type, you, the individual, must begin to consciously build around you the type of individuals, groups, work, and experiences that will change the atmosphere around you to support optimal living for you.

This is how you can do it:

Describe an optimal life for yourself. Include in this description what you want for your personal satisfaction, work, relationships, and needed resources (money, support, etc.).

1. Describe your **vision** (image or ideas) of an environment (culture) that would promote the growth of your life vision within your family, around friends, and at work. Answer these questions for each context: family, friends, and work.

   - What would the environment around you feel like, look like?
   - What would people be doing?
   - What would they be feeling?
   - How would they be communicating with each other?
   - What core values and beliefs are they reflecting in how they act? (Here include the ones that we have described as Life Energy principles, in addition to the more positive beliefs important to individual and institutional functioning just discussed.)

Out of the three groups above (family, friends, work), pick the one that is most important to you. Ask key persons in that group to meet with you for the purpose of deciding, as a group, answers to the following questions.

> a) What does each person see as a vision for the group's functioning? What characteristics would they really like to experience that could also lead to optimal functioning for the group?

> b) What environment would support this vision *within the group's daily functioning*? Use the questions above to help describe a *group environment or culture* that would support the group's optimal functioning.

2. What **processes** would be important to maintain this vision for the group's functioning as well as your individual functioning? Processes such as:

   - how you would handle resolving conflict in the group and for yourself personally,
   - how you would reward yourself and others for actions and thinking that support your vision, as well as the group's,
   - what norms of behavior you would expect—how you should act and treat one another,
   - how you would measure success, (how would you know when you are making it happen), and
   - how you would handle failures and the negative.

3. *In this group culture you've just described,* what **roles** would be essential to its operation? How would these roles relate to each other? For example, in a workgroup, leadership and followers are important considerations. Are these roles important to the operation of your new culture? If so, are leaders always leaders, or will leadership rotate? How do those who follow the leader relate to him or her? Do they simply accept leadership decisions without question, or do they expect collaboration for important issues?
      For the informal culture you are creating around you as an individual, the same questions must be asked. What roles do you want people to play that are around you? Of these roles, which are essential for support of your optimal living?

4. What **unique beliefs and values** should be integral to your group culture, as well as to the environment you are building around you as an individual?

136

How will these beliefs and values be a part of your daily life? How will the beliefs important to the group be part of daily group functioning?

5. What **systems** would be needed to support your culture? *For a workgroup,* would you need a system for performance evaluation, for quality control, for data tracking, for communication, and for financial management? What should they be like in order to support the culture you have described?

    For you as an individual, what type of educational system is best for you? What type of job? What type of financial support? What type of support structure from your family, friends, and associates? How will they support the vision you have described?

    Of the systems that you need, by what values do they operate? Love, respect, support? How will you make these values measurable so you know whether they are actually present and operating?

6. What type of **resources** would your group and individual cultures need? People, money, skills, equipment? How would you go about getting them in a way that follows your core values?

Use this framework to build a culture around you that will support your version of divinity experiencing humanness. For the group you choose, use it to co-create a culture that supports the group's version of divinity experiencing humanness.

Don't allow yourself to feel so overwhelmed that you never start. To change from a negative base in your life to one more positive, a new culture is absolutely essential. Begin to build your culture by first answering the questions in this framework. Then take the things that are easiest to do, and begin to build them around you. Take it one small step at a time and know that I am helping you co-create it. **It does not have to be a struggle**! Believe that the co-creation process will help you create what you want easily. Then allow events to unfold. Do not try to force progress. Things will unfold in their own time.

Summary

- *Being* is a state of energy and a state of mind. It underlies all reality both positive and negative. It is My Essence and yours. It is core Life Energy, which is made up of Divine Love and compassion.

- *Being* is a state of mind that recognizes and uses your actual power of divinity experiencing humanness to co-create what you want with Me, rather than giving it up to others and being victim.

- If you believe in the reality of *Being* and commit to consciously operating within it for your daily living, you automatically open yourself to its energy and it becomes a foundation for the operation of your conscious mind in daily living.

- **In general, *Being* is important because**:

    1. It makes for easy communication with Me and other non-physical helpers such as your soul, your Higher Self, your guides, and your guardian angel.
    2. It provides a state of rest where you can experience peace, joy, centeredness, security, friendship with Me, and appreciation of who you are.
    3. It provides for the growth and easy operation of your *Observer Self* as well as your *Body Consciousness*, two gateways to the Life Energy of *Being*.

- **Specific outcomes of operating in *Being* are as follows**:

    1. The conscious mind is automatically and continuously reminded of who you truly are—divinity experiencing humanness. This awareness is a requirement for manifesting optimal living.
    2. It brings ease of manifestation that results in extraordinary manifestation.
    3. It enables easy communication with all levels of consciousness in *Being*.
    4. It develops a singular ability to feel the essence of your energy, Divine Love and compassion.
    5. It allows more effective management of both Positive and Negative Life Energy.

6. You understand that all is well.
7. It activates the *Observer*, which is the major link between *Being* and your conscious mind.
8. It brings about an increased awareness and openness to *Body Consciousness*, which is the major link in sensing and feeling the presence of *Being*.
9. It enables you to celebrate who you are and build personal power.

- **There are prerequisites to operating in *Being*:**

   1. Accept *Being* as a reality.
   2. Accept the responsibility for forming your own reality.
   3. Accept the responsibility of loving and having compassion for both yourself and others.

- **To operate in *Being*, do the following things:**

   1. Commit to operate within the reality of *Being* for your daily life.
   2. Just relax while making the intention of opening to the energy of *Being*.
   3. Ask the help of your *Body Consciousness* to feel the energy of *Being*
   4. Increase your openness to *Body Consciousness*.
   5. Strengthen the *Observer Self*.
   6. Focus on the NOW, the present moment in your daily life.
   7. In your daily life, commit to experimenting with what living in *Being* means for you; your divinity, your special gifts, and your life purpose.
   8. Use the specific "how to" process I discussed for consciously operating in *Being* to make extraordinary manifestation occur.
   9. Set up and nurture a deep relationship with Me and all other helpers in *Being*.

- The goal of the human race is to bring about optimal living. New cultures will be created that support this type of living and the philosophy of operating in *Being*. These cultures will operate according to **Life Energy principles or beliefs. These beliefs can be used to create your own model of positive living. They are:**

1. All things are connected; we are all one. I am everywhere and in all things, but I am also more than just all things. I am a complete being all by Myself. You are an aspect of Me and as such, you are divine.
2. Committing to operate in *Being* is primary to successful manifestation and optimal living.
3. Each individual that you see, no matter their behavior, is an aspect of Me.
4. Each individual has the freedom and responsibility to be who they are—divinity experiencing humanness.
5. Each individual must focus on living fully in the moment because the present is the only thing that is real.
6. Each individual must commit to telling their truth in a way that others can hear.
7. Love and compassion are the essence of *Being*.
8. Each person has the freedom and responsibility to choose what they accept and create in their life.
9. All manifestation starts with an intention or vision.
10. Life is made up of Positive and Negative Life Energy within five domains of human reality (Spirit, Mind, Emotion, Subtle Physical, and Physical energy).

- **There are beliefs that are barriers to optimal living.** Some of these barriers are associated with individual actions. These include your beliefs about sexuality, achievement, money, power, control, helping, and the role of emotions. Some of the barriers have been built into institutional functioning and include beliefs about education, government, religion, medical care, and business.

- **In order to begin optimal living, each of you will have to build a new environment or culture around you**. To do this, answer the following questions and then implement your answers using small easy to achieve steps and strategies.

    1. What is your **vision** (image) of an environment (culture) that would promote the growth of your life vision as well as that of others within your business/workplace, family, or social group?
    2. What is your **vision** of the culture (atmosphere) you want around yourself that will support your life vision in day-to-day functioning?
    3. What **processes** are important to manifest and maintain these two visions?
    4. What **roles** are essential to manifest and maintain the visions?

5. What unique **beliefs and values** are needed?
6. What **systems** are needed?
7. What **resources** are needed?

Dianne's Experiences

This concept of *Being* and operating in it has been the most difficult for me to understand. Once I began to understand what was really being discussed and its consequences, I found my initial reaction to be, "How the heck do you do this? It's so amorphous!" Despite how I felt consciously, there was something deep within that told me this was a very important idea, critical to the whole idea of creating what you want and controlling your life. I knew that there were details missing in the description of how to do this, but this reality was so different from what I was used to that the inner voice that was helping me write this book couldn't go further at that point in time.

So, even though I didn't understand, I tried to follow the directions as best I could. I addressed the prerequisites and stated my intention to accept responsibility for my reality that day and to focus on feeling acceptance, respect, and love for myself as well as others with whom I came in contact.

Then I went to the requirements for functioning in *Being*. I stated my intention of operating in *Being* throughout the day at the beginning of each day. I relied on my *Observer Self* to help me observe what was happening as I experienced the day. Then, during the day, I tried to keep myself as relaxed as possible and asked help in feeling *Being* even if it was only off and on throughout the day for seconds at a time. I kept forgetting about staying in the Now because my personality type has a strong penchant for looking at the future. But I did the best I could and accepted that as being okay. I talked to my inner helpers when the thought came to me to do so.

Slowly, I began to be aware of a new feeling of centeredness and peace that floated into my consciousness at odd times. It wasn't constant or particularly strong at first, but its frequency and strength increased. I also found that when I stated an intention to my inner self that I didn't have to consciously keep it in mind during the day. Instead, I would get reminders from my deeper consciousness when it was particularly important to remember what I'd intended.

Then I did an abrupt backslide, back to my conscious, striving old self. It happened like this. My husband and I were city folk who were sick of the pressures of suburban life around Washington, D.C. After he retired, we hunted for another place to live where we could enjoy nature and a slower and more friendly environment. We found that place in the Cherokee foothills of South Carolina. We built our dream home where we could see the mountains while having a lake in our backyard. We collected an animal family since both of us enjoyed their energy, and I thought to myself, *At last I have a sanctuary.*

Well, I forgot that although all the elements that I wanted were there in my new life, total newness tends to create stress. And the new life was totally different from what either my husband or myself were used to. To be more specific, we got more than we bargained for when we moved into our new home with five animal friends—two White German Shepherd puppies, two kittens, and one Persian cat. What a menagerie of young life all hell bent on experiencing! One of them was always getting into mischief, usually involving knocking down something, or chewing on whatever looked interesting.

In addition, living in the country has its own demands, which are different from suburban living. Throwing away your garbage, getting your mail, getting a newspaper, getting groceries, and medical resources are not easy givens as they are in the city. Each one required a moderate to substantial expenditure of energy to arrange or do.

Then there were things happening around our new "dream home." We immediately needed to find a way to prevent our soil from eroding down our sloping yard. The remedy was miles and miles of mulch and logs laid at strategic points. Although we got help from family members as well as paid help, we had to do a substantial amount ourselves. Oh aching muscles on fifty-year-old bodies!

Then there was how to manage the exuberance and chewing of puppies who were fifty pounds and growing. They especially loved to eat our new grass and plants, and then track in red clay on our new rug. While we were trying to manage all this, we also had to unpack and decorate the inside of the house. Finally, there was that nature stuff we were so fired up to experience. Well, did we ever! I was bitten by a wild kitten and had to get rabies shots. There were reports of bears in our neighborhood. I and my puppy, Samson, found a yellow jacket nest on the property and both of us got swarmed. Not a pleasant experience! My husband and I also found that black widow spiders and scorpions were common to this part of the country. We had to locate a friendly local exterminator to do his thing in our house on a regular basis.

Despite all this, I loved the energy of nature around us. It felt like a privilege to be there. But I found that I couldn't enjoy myself because I went into survival mode to cope with all the newness. That meant that I resorted to my old reactions—work before play, have goals and get them done come hell or high water, keep going till you drop, and get it done quick. And, oh yes, whatever you do, do it perfectly.

You can probably see that doing this was no formula for slowing down and enjoying what was around me, much less for operating in *Being*! For the longest time, I didn't know exactly what was wrong. Then I finally remembered to communicate with my deeper consciousness and the problem became quite clear. But doing something about it was another matter. My survival mentality was so strong I could hardly stop it from slipping into place at the least provocation.

I decided that I had to give operating in *Being* an intense effort. In fact, my inner helpers told me that was the reason I was experiencing these old reactions. One of those wonderful learning opportunities. Yes sir, guinea pig time it was! So I re-committed to operate in *Being*, following the directions in the chapter. I also asked my inner helpers to aid the whole process because my conscious reactions were so strong. Step-by-step and day-by-day, I became more able to do this. Although there are unexpected blips on my horizon and I'm still learning how to be a country person, I've learned to relax more and "go with the flow." Things often straighten themselves out in easy ways now. If I struggle because I'm bounced into using old reactions, I very quickly realize what is happening and switch to my new mode to solve the problem. Life is certainly easier this way!

And so I'm learning through day-to-day experiences what operating in *Being* as divinity experiencing humanness means for me. I have the feeling that this will be a long but generally nice learning process. Nice because I can manage my life much better from within *Being*. Struggle corresponds to those times when I don't listen to my inner world and drop back into my old habits. But by doing that, I learn what I don't want and what triggers pull me in that direction. And with my *Observer Self* and *Body Consciousness* more active, I am more quickly able to switch gears back into *Being*. In other words, experiences both positive and negative still come my way, but I'm reacting to them in a new way. No matter what happens, there seems to be a background centeredness and peace, even when I'm in a negative experience. So I would say, yes, doing this is a challenge but it doesn't have to be a struggle, and it is key to getting anywhere if you want some facsimile of optimal living.

In addition, although I have built a supportive culture or environment around myself, I am impressed with the necessity of building a more elaborate culture that includes others. The questions at the end of the chapter having to do with creating a new environment within a group speak to this process. I have yet to fully implement the answers to those questions for an entire group rather than just for myself, but I have created one group that has answered some of those questions and begun to operate on the answers. The group works well! There is support for growth as defined by each person and a new way of relating to each other that is much healthier and positive. I intend to start more in-depth communities and groups in the future based on the principles outlined in this chapter.

Life Energy Experiences

- Take one situation that is an ongoing challenge in your life. Commit to operating in *Being* in the manner described. Write down or talk about what happens each day as you're doing this—it helps with making the process more concrete. Be sure to identify your successes as well as what didn't go so well. Identify to yourself how you are beginning to operate differently. Note differences in thought, feelings, decisions, and behavior. You are learning a whole new way of behaving and thinking. It takes time. But We are here in *Being* to help you make this an easy process where you don't have to struggle. Read over the prerequisites and steps to operating in *Being*.

- Strengthen the conscious presence of your *Observer Self* through trying some of the following things:

    1. Ask it to become active in your daily life.
    2. Observe what has happened at the end of each day and write it down.
    3. Note what is happening around you during the day.
    4. Note what your reactions are to things as you are doing them.

- Use this affirmation at the beginning of each day to strengthen the relationship with your inner helpers:

    "I am You and You are me. I am in our Being; I make all my choices and receive learning, while existing in our Being. I commit to this. I accept that I am an aspect of You, and that I have the power to create my life." Then make an intention that you will love yourself as well as others throughout the day. Since you and others are an aspect of Me, to love yourself and others is to deepen the relationship with Me and your helpers.

- Try applying some of these Life Energy beliefs to your life experiences and note the result.

    1. All things are connected; we are all one. I am everywhere and in all things, but I am also more than just all things. I am a complete being all by Myself. You are an aspect of Me and as such, you are divine.
    2. Committing to operate in *Being* is primary to manifestation and optimal living.

3. Each individual that you see, no matter their behavior, is an aspect of Me.
4. Each individual has the freedom and responsibility to be who they are—divinity experiencing humanness.
5. Each individual focuses on living fully in the moment because the present is the only thing that is real.
6. Each individual commits to telling their truth in a way that others can hear.
7. Love and compassion are accepted as the essence of *Being*.
8. Each person has the freedom and responsibility to choose what they accept and create in their life.
9. All manifestation starts with an intention or vision.
10. Life is made up of Positive and Negative Life Energy in five domains of reality (Spirit, Mind, Emotions, Subtle Physical, and Physical energy).

Chapter 7

NeuroQuantum Thinking:
A Framework for Creating Optimal Living and Work

It is time to put all this information together in one place, so that you can know how to use it in your daily life. Dianne has called the original framework that we devised together, NeuroQuantum Thinking. The name represents the melding of body, mind, and spirit with "Neuro" representing body, "Quantum" the spirit, and "Thinking" the mind. That is what this framework is, a meld of all domains.

Let's review the domains of Life Energy and their functioning so you can see the overall framework for manifestation. Then I will talk about the details of this framework and discuss the specifics of manifestation using NeuroQuantum Thinking (NQT).

There are five domains with nine levels of Life Energy that define human reality (Spirit I, II, III, Mind I, II, III, Emotion, Subtle Physical, and Physical). Each of the domains contains the characteristics listed below.

Life Energy Domain Characteristics

- **Contains their own type of Life Energy**
- **Includes the core energy of *Being* as well as Negative and Positive Life Energy**
- **Have their own reality that includes unique rules of operation**
- **Have different sizes and power with the largest and most powerful being Spirit followed in decreasing power and size by Mind, Emotion, Subtle Physical, and Physical Energy**
- **Must fit together or be coherent when you are trying to manifest a specific outcome**

See Figure 5. for an expanded illustration of these domains and their role in creating human reality. Note that Negative and Positive Life Energy are in each domain with Being forming the foundation for all energies.

Given these facts, the first step in creating the life you want is to use the five domains to build a framework or outline of what you want. Because it is the source of all creation and is the biggest and largest domain, all manifestation starts with an intention at the Spirit level. You then build your outline by creating goals, your new identity, beliefs, and cognitive (thinking) strategies at the Mind level, which are compatible with your intention in the Spirit Domain. This makes your intention denser and stronger. You then add in feelings and experiences compatible with your intention at the Emotion level, followed by aligning Subtle Physical and Physical energies. You have now optimally strengthened your intention and created increasingly dense energy so that it finally becomes manifest in physical reality. This is your outline for manifestation.

The Energy of *Being*

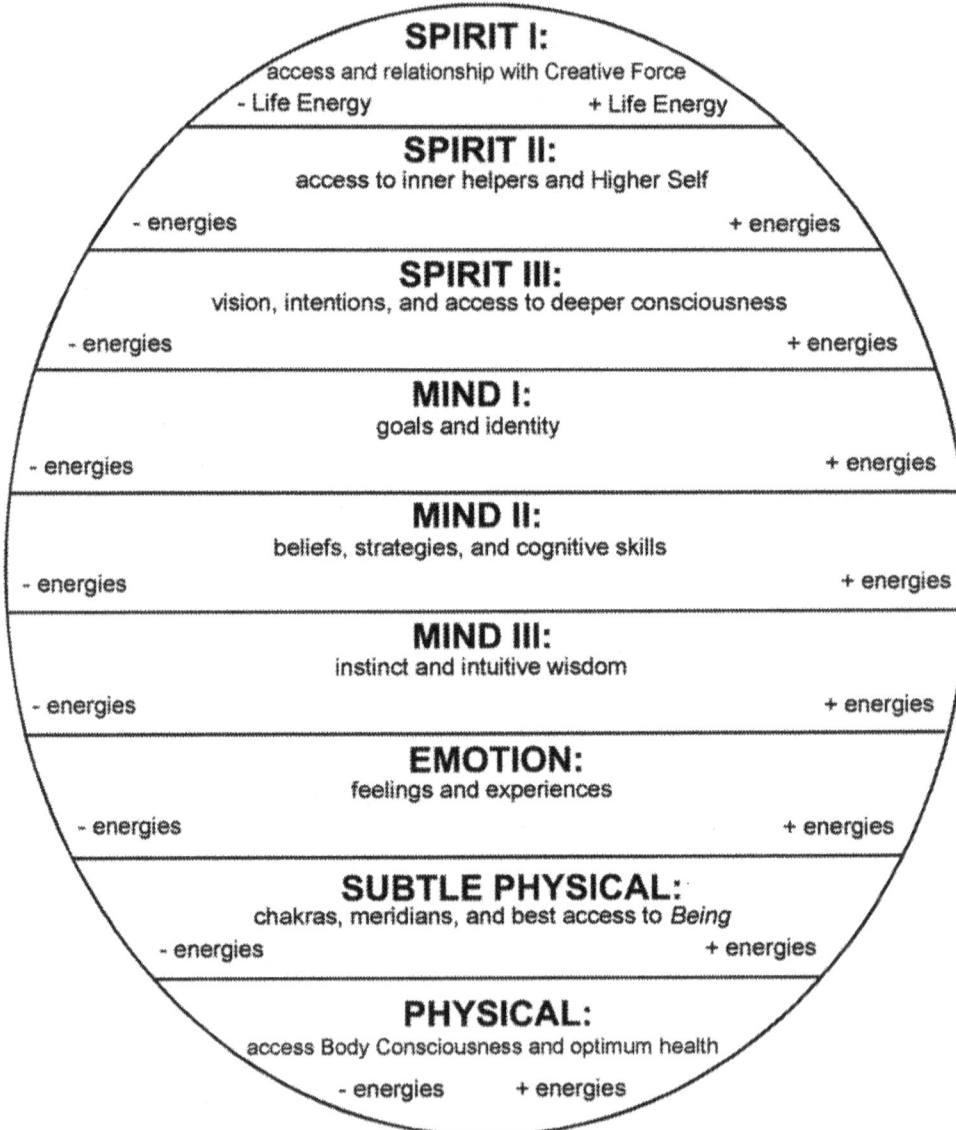

Figure 5. The Life Energy Domains and Their Relation to Positive and Negative Life Energy and *Being*

Once the outline for creating the life you want is built, you can more easily manage positive and negative energy and operate within *Being* in your daily life. The reason is that the coherence of energy in the five domains lends itself to easy manifestation, as well as easier management of negative and positive energies and easy operation within *Being*. I will talk more about this later.

The outline that you build doesn't have to be highly detailed if you don't want it to be. In fact, it's better if you don't nail down every detail because it doesn't give any wiggle room. Sometimes what you think you want as an outcome is not what you really need in order to create the life you want. So, if you give Us an outline of what you want, then you, Myself, and your inner helpers can flesh it out as we go.

When your "outline" is complete with all the domains aligned in harmony, imagine (concentrate on) what it would be like if your outline for optimal living had already happened. Make it real and detailed with the proviso that some of the details could change. Live it and be it in your imagination. Making your outline vividly real will increase the strength of your outline for an optimal life. It also alters your future by aligning what you want with a different life path and future than you have experienced. All possible choices and futures that could be are already activated in other realities. By your imagining, you are switching your experience and learning to another energy reality. You are altering your reality. By focusing on it and living it in your imagination, you choose it. After you have done this for about ten minutes, let it go. Then, to the best of your ability during the day, try to live your life as if the reality was already present. Try not to worry about its manifestation or long for it. By your worry and longing, you are causing your energy to shift back to your present reality. Just do the best you can, knowing that we (Myself, your guides, your Higher Self, your soul) are helping you to manifest what you want.

After you have outlined what you want and concentrated on imagining it already manifested, ask yourself, what things do you need to do in daily living to manage manifestation? How do you manage moment-to-moment living? We will answer these two questions later in this chapter. First, let's review in more depth the five domains of human reality and their role in manifesting the life you want.

At the Spirit Domain, you determine who I am to you, and how you will relate to your helpers, as well as identifying the life purpose(s), life vision(s), and life intentions of your soul and human psyche. The Sprit Domain is the most powerful of all the domains. This is where manifestation originates. When you want to create a specific outcome, you must start here.

149

The Spirit Domain has three levels of Life Energy:

Spirit I – includes My total consciousness, mind, and energy.

Spirit II – Includes the helpers of *Being*, the Higher Self, guides, guardian angel, and other interested nonphysical beings.

Spirit III – Includes your soul, your many selves, or parts of you that make up your human psyche. They form your deeper consciousness along with a deeper conscious part of the mind. Your soul, psyche, and deeper conscious mind identify your life purpose, life vision, and life intentions.

The next step is to match the Mind Domain to what you created in the Spirit Domain.

The Mind Domain has three levels of Life Energy:

Mind I – includes the part of your conscious and deeper conscious mind that helps establish goals, as well as defining your psychological identity—your spirit identity of divinity experiencing humanness—as well as your human identity of skills, personality characteristics, and your preferences. The part of the brain that best supports this activity is the frontal lobes.

Mind II – includes the part of the conscious and deeper conscious mind that blends logic and creativity, details, and the big picture. This demands the collaborative functioning of the right and left hemisphere of the brain working together to do the following specific tasks that support your life purpose, vision, or intention:

1. identifying beliefs that will support what is wanted and changing beliefs that won't,
2. creating steps and strategies that help make what you want be a reality,
3. determining skills and information that are needed to support your vision, such as communication and thinking skills, necessary new learning, and essential information to implement your intention, and

---

4. identifying support from others and from the environment that will be needed.

Mind III – includes the part of the conscious and deeper conscious mind that most easily accesses intuitive knowing, extrasensory perceptions, instinctive feelings, and the Spirit Domain. This is primarily supported by the middle part of the temporal lobes as well as the limbic system of the brain.

The Life Energy of *Being* is particularly intense at the deeper conscious level of mind represented in Mind III. Within this level, you disengage the logic of the mind to allow intuition and access to inner knowing.

The *Observer Self* resides in the Mind Domain. Remember that the *Observer* is the mechanism that allows you to communicate between your conscious mind and deeper consciousness. It allows you to observe what you are doing, while simultaneously keeping in mind the life vision, purpose, or intention on which you are focusing. It allows you to make conscious choices about your impulses and everyday behavior as they happen so that you can choose to behave in a way that is compatible with what you want. Because the *Observer* can access deeper consciousness, it enables you to choose and stay in *Being* as you go about your daily life.

Remember, deciding to stay in *Being* makes choosing behavior that is best for your life vision, purpose, or intention easier! It also makes manifestation easier.

The next step in creating your outline for manifestation is to match the Emotion Domain to what you have created at the Spirit and Mind levels of Life Energy.

> **The Emotion Domain has only one level of Life Energy but it generates many different emotions.**
>
> The purpose of the Emotion Domain is to add experiences and feelings to your vision, purpose, or intention to:
>
> 1. Provide feedback to all of the other domains about the human consequences of manifesting your vision.
> 2. Provide rapid and intense learning that is nowhere else available. Emotions are the special gift of human reality.
>
> Emotion and experiencing are mainly controlled by the limbic system of the human brain. *In this domain, you determine which feelings and experiences will support what you want as well as those that will not.*

The Emotion Domain represents the core of your "rudder system" for managing negative and positive outcomes. Using this domain as a way to judge outcomes, you label experiences and things as negative or positive. By doing this labeling, you are able to decide what a thing is. Remember that humans are able to identify experiences and things only by contrasting negative against positive—what a thing is and what it is not. Feelings and experiences are at the heart of this learning process.

The next step in your outline is to match the Subtle Physical Domain to what you have created within all the other domains of Life Energy.

***The Subtle Physical Domain has one level of Life Energy but three
major centers for emitting this energy:***

Chakras – energy centers within the human body that focus on the four
other domains of human reality (Spirit, Mind, Emotion, Physical) as a
transducer of these energies. That is, they change the energies of the other four
systems to that type of Life Energy found in the Subtle Physical Domain. The
chakra centers then evaluate and analyze the status of these domains in relation
to your physical, mental, emotional, and spiritual well-being.

Auric Fields – energy fields around the human body that take in the Life
Energy of the four other domains of human reality, as well as reflecting the
energy of the chakra centers and meridians.

Meridians – energy pathways within the human body that emanate from
the chakra centers. The energy flow of these pathways feed into the physical
body's neurological and physiological systems.   See Figure 6. for an
illustration of these energy paths.

These centers are changed by negative and positive energies.   Positive
energies aid the flow of energy; negative energies slow it down. This is a way of
telling you how you are managing your "rudder" system of negative and positive
energies and where you need to work to help release slowed down or stuck
energy.

Your *Body Consciousness* resides in these centers of subtle physical energy
enabling you to feel the sensations of *Being*. Your *Body Consciousness* quickly
aligns itself with your Emotion Domain to amplify the experience of *Being*. The
Emotion Domain then opens you to your Mind Domain and the *Observer Self* to
further amplify the experience of *Being* for you. Accessing *Being* allows for
quick and easy manifestation, as well as optimal living.

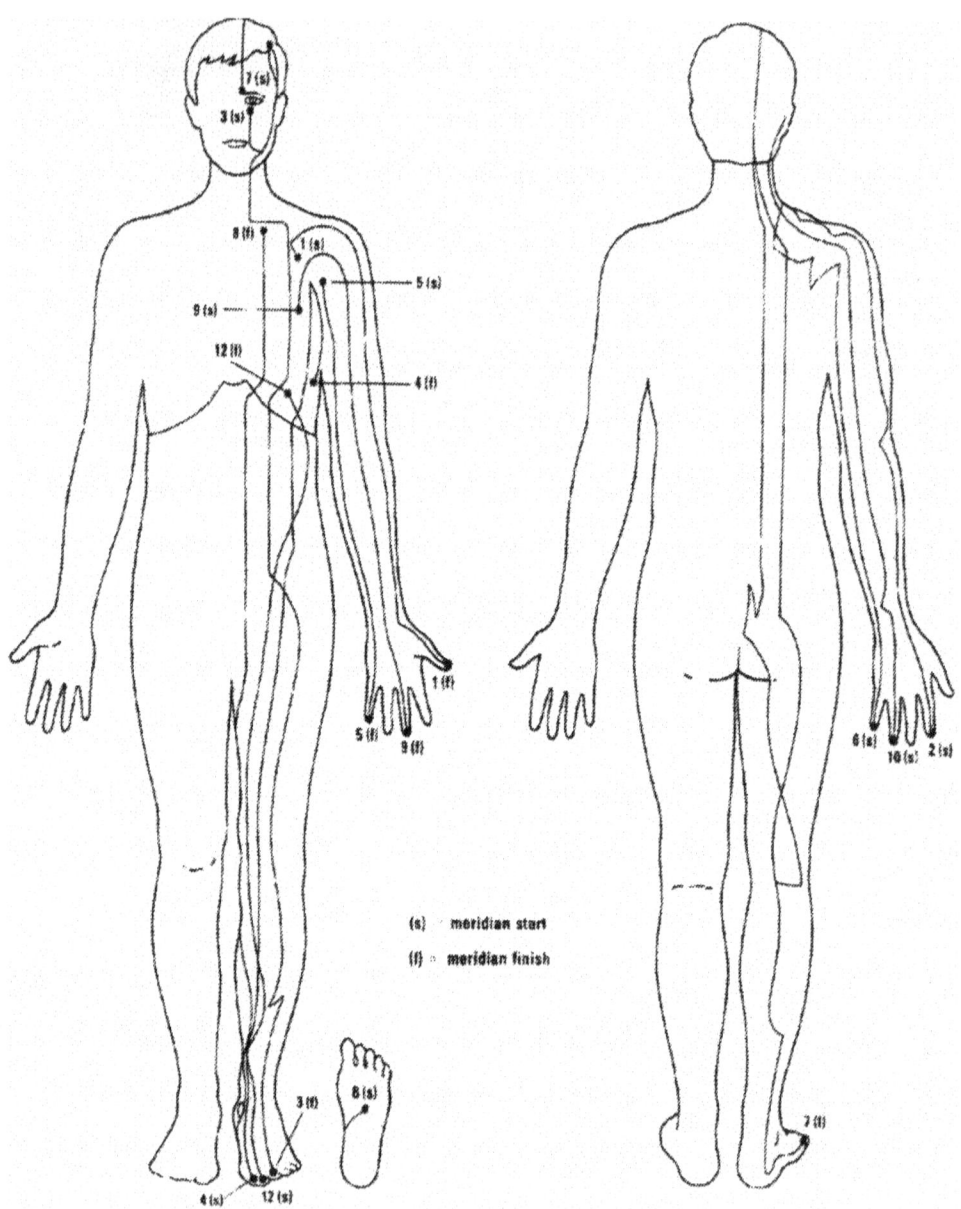

The Meridians : front view   The Meridians : back view

Adapted from Dawes, N. 1991. *Shiatsu for Beginners.*

Figure 6. Some Meridian Pathways of the Human Body

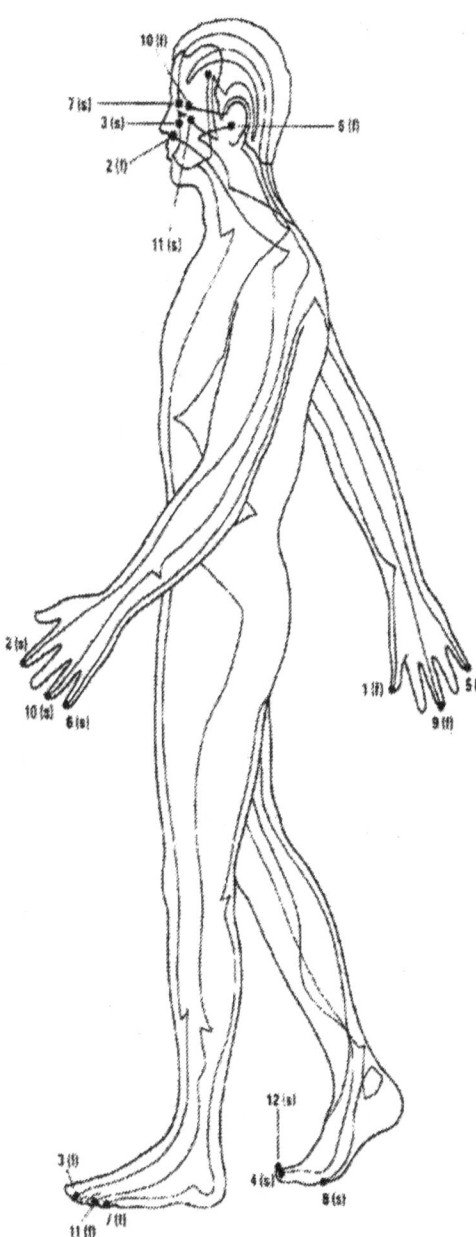

The Meridians : side view

1. Lung - Starts on chest in front of shoulder, finishes in thumb

2. Large Intestine - Starts in index finger, finishes at side of nostril

3. Stomach - Starts under eye, finishes in second toe

4. Spleen - Starts in big toe, finishes at side of chest

5. Heart - Starts under armpit, finishes in little finger

6. Small Intestine - Starts in little finger, finishes in front of ear

7. Urinary Bladder - Starts at inside corner of eye, finishes in little toe

8. Kidney - Starts on sole of foot, finishes at top of chest

9. Heart Constrictor - Starts beside nipple, finishes in middle finger

10. Triple Heater - Starts in fourth finger, finishes by outside corner of eyebrow

11. Gall Bladder - Starts at outside corner of eye, finishes in fourth toe

12. Liver - Starts in big toe, finishes on front of chest below nipple

155

The last step in creating your outline is to match the Physical Domain to what you have created for all of the others.

> **The Physical Domain has one level of Life Energy.** The chakra centers are connected to specific endocrine centers, neurological pathways, and physiological systems through the meridian pathways.

Various esoteric writers and traditions have described the specific connections for each chakra center. I will adapt the one authored by William Tiller in *Science and Human Transformation*. The connections are as follows:

Chakra Center	Endocrine System	Neurological System	Physiological System
7th (top of head)	Pineal gland	Cerebral cortex	Nervous System, organs, and tissues of entire body
6th (between eyebrows)	Pituitary gland	Hypophysis, diencephalon	Autonomic nervous system and hormone system of entire body.
5th (center of throat)	Thyroid gland	Cervical nerves and ganglia connecting medulla with spinal cord	Respiratory system
4th (heart area)	Thymus gland	Heart plexus in sympathetic trunk	Circulatory system
3rd (spleen area)	Adrenal glands	Solar plexus area	Digestive system

| 2nd (navel area) | Cells of Lyden | Sacral area | Genito-urinary system connecting left and right sympathetic nervous system |

| 1st (bottom of spine) | Gonads | Coccygeal area | ibid. |

As you can see from this list, the human body is not just a vehicle on which the head is carried. Instead, everything is integrally connected to form one system. Many people think that the brain is the most important part of human existence, and the body is simply something that helps the brain to get around to where it wants to go. Or vice-versa, that the body will tell you what is best for you and you don't have to do a lot of thinking. Do whatever feels good. *The truth is that both brain and body are needed to optimally build what you want because they are part of one system.* The physical system of the brain and body are connected to the subtle physical system, which in turn is connected to all other domains of human reality. Therefore, all five domains are part of one system—the Life Energy of human reality.

The body does have its own consciousness. Part of this consciousness resides in the Subtle Physical Domain and part resides within the Physical. *Body Consciousness* has an awareness of all physical existence and its connection to Me. In fact, it knows that everything is connected. It has its own wisdom about health such as knowing about optimal movement, physiological functioning, biochemical balance, and brain wave functioning. This is why *Body Consciousness* is also called the Inner Healer. It is important to rely on this built-in wisdom to create optimal health. Remember, it is also one of the two major mechanisms for accessing *Being*.

Additionally *Body Consciousness* provides feedback about the state of the human body and its interactions with all other physical things in the environment. It joins this information with the part of *Body Consciousness* in the Subtle Physical Domain to provide a complete picture of your state of physical well-being.

Build a physical health program that will support your vision. It doesn't have to be elaborate. Just ask yourself what exercises or physical movement, rest and relaxation, fun, nutrition, and brain functioning would best support your vision. Then ask your *Body Consciousness* to show you which of your choices are optimal for your vision through replying in a way easiest for you to understand. The reply could be something you hear within you, an unexpected event, speaking to a health care provider, noting something in your reading, muscle testing (a method of using weak and strong muscle response to indicate yes and no responses), or intuitive urges.

Other kinds of physical energy are also important to consider for how they can support your vision. In manifesting a specific vision, you must take into account not only what your body will need to support what you want (diet, exercise, biochemical balance, general health, optimal energy), but also what effect the rest of the animal, plant, and mineral kingdom could have to support your desired outcome.

The Animal Kingdom————————

Each animal has its own type of consciousness and is part of My consciousness. Each species has their individual and collective life purpose and vision. Consider how pets or creatures in nature can add to your vision and support it. You can talk to these animals about your vision and ask them to give you energy that will help you manifest what you want. You, in turn, can support them in their life vision.

The Plant Kingdom————————

Each plant also has its own consciousness and life purpose. Consider which plants could support you, e.g., flowers that you like, trees that you find calming and create beauty, etc.

The Mineral Kingdom————————

Each type of mineral also has its own particular consciousness and purpose. Think about what type of rocks or crystals appeal to you, make you feel calm and connected to *Being*. Use them to help support manifesting your vision.

This is the big picture of how manifestation works through each of the domains of Life Energy. Within each of these domains are negative and positive Life Energy and underneath all of these energies is *Being*—the core Life Energy.

This is the forest! Now let's look at the trees in this forest and how to use them to create optimal living and work.

The Specifics for Manifesting What You Want: Your Five-Domain Outline

Let's start with creating a detailed outline or framework for what you want. To accomplish this, you start with creating a picture or description (vision) of what you want in the Spirit Domain, as well as defining your relationship with Me and other inner helpers. This is creating your intention (statement of what you want) and is the first step in any manifestation process.

When you are doing this outline, if you feel that you don't want to go down through the domains of Spirit, Mind, Emotion, Subtle Physical, and Physical in that order, you don't have to do so. But you do have to start with the Spirit Domain in order to form your vision of what you want and define our relationship. After that you can work with any of the other four domains in whatever order seems important to you.

At the SPIRIT I Level:

1. ***Get a notebook that will serve as your Life Energy Journal or create one on your computer.*** All the work you do in developing a framework or outline of what you want your life to be must be kept together so that you can use it in daily living. In the notebook or on your computer, record the answers to the exercises that follow, labeling this initial section as *"My Outline: the Spirit Domain: Level 1."*

2. ***Describe who you want Me to be and write the description in your journal.***
Ask yourself who you think I am? Who do you want Me to be and how do you want to describe me? No one knows exactly who I am. *I am all things. So decide on which aspects of who I am you would like Me to be for you, and so it will be.* You must rely on your belief, not anyone else's to decide. You certainly can talk to others and study religions and spiritual practices, but in the end, the decision about who I am is yours alone. For example, am I a discrete personality that is separate from you, am I the creator of all things, am I the force of nature, am I a universal power made up of loving energy? Am I all of these things?

    Describing who you want Me to be will determine what you expect of Me and want Me to do. For example, if you think of Me only as an all powerful personality separate from you, you are asking Me to fix things for you or determine your destiny without much input from you. The emphasis with this idea is that I am all powerful and you are not. I will act as you wish, but

I will also encourage you to go beyond this idea to one where you understand that we are co-creators and that you have free will that is made up of my power to create what you want.

3. ***Decide on what you <u>want your relationship with Me to be</u>. Put this in your journal under what you have already done.*** Doing this will help Us communicate better. Do you want a personal relationship with Me? Can we actually talk back and forth? Do you want a relationship that is parent and child, authority figure and subordinate, co-creators, interdependent friends (you help Me and I help you)? Am I a conscious universal energy of which you are a part? Do you want to really feel My presence? How? According to how you decide you want our relationship, I will act accordingly. *In fact, I can make our relationship be ALL of these things as the need arises for you.* No relationship is made up of just one single characteristic, but changes with time and need.

4. ***In your journal, <u>create a drawing</u> of who you want Me to be and the relationship you want with Me.*** It can be a drawing with stick figures, symbols, abstract images, pictures cut out from various sources and made into a collage, or an artistic portrait. Use whatever method or methods are best for you. Doing this image makes your descriptions more dramatic and more easily remembered by you. It also intensifies the energy of the descriptions you have created.

5. ***Decide on <u>who I am not and what you don't want from your relationship</u>. Describe this in your journal and then make a picture of this undesirable relationship***. Remember that in order to know what a thing is, you also have to know what it is not. So here you want to describe what you don't want in regard to Me. That is your right because you have free will. This will also make very clear what it is that you do want from Me and who you think I am.

For the purpose of making this more concrete, let's invent an imaginary person called Mary. Mary wants to take control of her life. She has felt out of control for a very long time and now wants to create optimal living and work for herself, not what she thinks she can have. So as a first step in creating this life, Mary has come up with the following description of Myself and our relationship.

Mary's Example of the Creator and Their Relationship

<u>You are</u> a loving creative force that is present in all things. You can change roles from father to mother to friend to loving partner as I need and want it. I can have a personal relationship with you. That means I can get angry, be happy, joke with you, love you, and be sad around you just as I could with a very close friend or loving partner. I want to feel Your Presence in a physical and psychological way so that I know you are real.

<u>You are not</u> an angry, vengeful God who demands certain behavior from His children or He will take His love away. You are not separate from Me. Instead, I am part of You. I don't have to behave like I'm talking to a king or high ruler where our relationship is always formal and very distant. I am not required to fear you and your power.

See Mary's drawings on the next page illustrating who I am and who I am not.

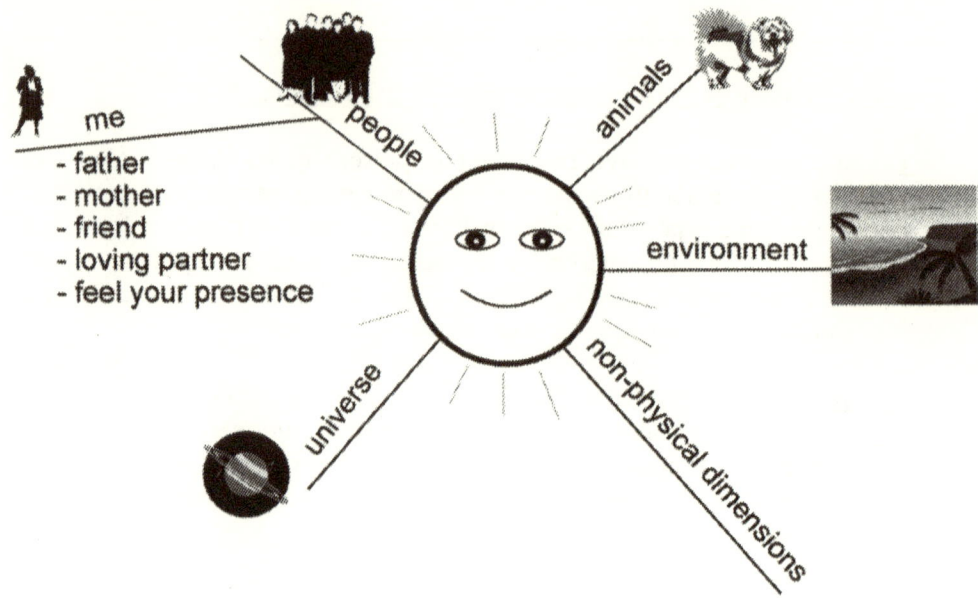

Mary's Example: Who God Is and Our Relationship

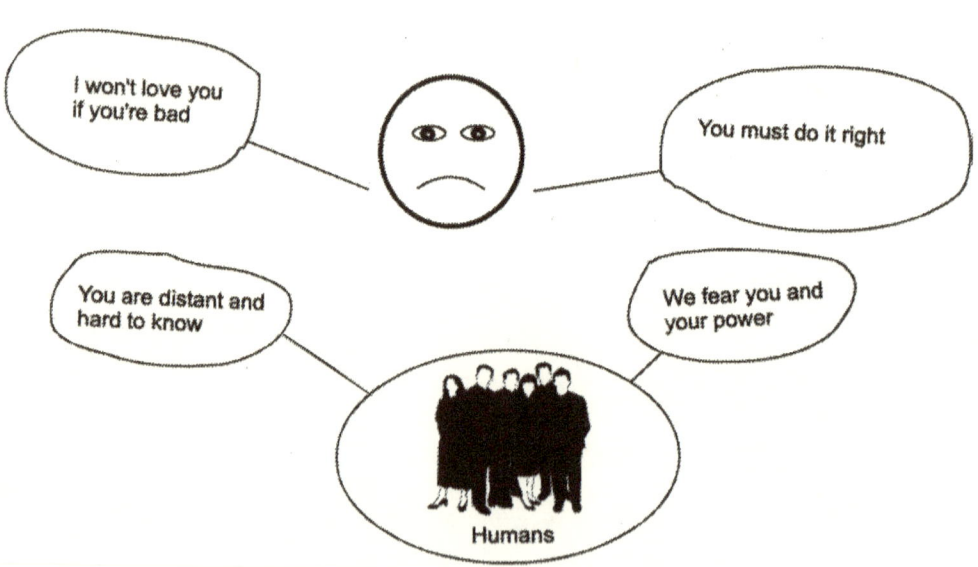

Who God Is Not and What Our Relationship Is Not

At the SPIRIT II Level:

1. ***Decide on <u>what inner helpers you believe in</u> and with whom you want to communicate to help you as you implement your new vision or intention.*** *Put this in your journal under a section that you label the "Spirit Domain: Level 2."* Your helpers might be a guardian angel, various guides, your Higher Self, nature energy, or all of these possibilities. These helpers translate for Me and help you and I manifest what you want. You can call on any of them or all of them, whatever you think best. In addition, each one will participate as the need arises. They all may help at the same time, or only specific ones, depending on the situation.

2. ***Decide on the <u>non-physical energy forms you don't believe in</u>, as well as those you don't want to communicate with.*** Your religions and cultural traditions have produced a number of non-physical energy forms such as the Devil and his companions, evil spirits, fairies, elves, little people, nature spirits, and ghosts. In addition, there are the inner helpers of whom I have spoken—your Higher Self, guides, guardian angel, and Myself.

Choose from this list, those in whom you don't believe, as well as those with whom you don't want to communicate. Put this in your journal.

Continuing with Mary, she thought about what type of helpers she believed in and wanted to help her in creating a new and better life for herself. She also decided on those non-physical forms in whom she didn't believe, as well as those with whom she did not want to interact. Here's what she said.

Mary's Example

I believe that I have a Higher Self. I also believe there are guides that are there to help me. Nature spirits can also help when it comes to physical energy and manifestation at that level. All of these helpers can help to make things manifest through translating the Creator's mind and energy into a more physical form. They can also help explain in more specific terms what the Creator has in mind. I believe each of them has their own particular skills and talents. So I will ask those who can help the most to jump in and "do their thing" at any given moment.

I don't believe in the Devil. Instead, I believe that there is the potential for creating very negative energy within each of us, and some of us decide to do so. I don't want to interact with any souls that are not within my guide group unless my guides specifically ask them to participate.

At the SPIRIT III Level:

1. *Ask your soul and the various parts of your psyche to help you create a <u>positive vision</u> of what you want your life to be.* *Include in this vision what you perceive to be your life purpose(s).* Accomplish this by describing a perfect day. Write it down, tape yourself describing it, or make a list of characteristics that summarize your vision (you can do this by free association of words and phrases as they come to you). Do one or all of these; whatever appeals to you the most. Include in your perfect day what you want for yourself personally, in the work area, in relationships, and in necessary resources (money, people who can support you, needed training or education, etc.). Put your perfect day in your Life Energy journal under a section you label, *"The Spirit Domain: Level 3."* If you have created an audiotape or video, then clip it to this page in your journal. If you've used your computer to create your journal, then store the tape near your computer or record what you say onto a CD that you can play on your computer.

   a) *As you are creating your vision, ask all interested parties within Spirit I and II if there is anything that should be <u>added, deleted, or changed.</u>* Ask Us to show you what our answer is in a clear way. We may answer by:

      • giving you images in your mind's eye,
      • speaking words you hear in your head,

- giving you a strong feeling or gut level instinct,
- making a coincidence happen (something someone says, something you see), or
- talking to you through a dream.

We will provide you answers in more than one way and they are not always subtle. Just listen and look. *When you ask us, we always answer!*

b) ***Use the techniques and exercises that I've described in Chapters 3 through 6 to aid you in building your perfect day.*** For example, in Chapter 3, I gave you the following exercise to help determine you life purpose:

Answer the following questions:

- What am I drawn to?
- What excites me and gives me energy?
- What do I love to do?
- What gives me a deep sense of satisfaction?
- Where and when do I feel connected to the divine?
- When and where have I truly tapped into my optimum skills?
- Where and when have I learned with ease and joy?

In Chapter 4 on negative manifestation, I gave you a process of discovering what your beliefs are. Use this process to include two important beliefs that are critical to manifesting your vision.

In Chapter 5 on positive manifestation, I gave you a list of things within each domain, which bring optimal living and happiness. Look at this list and see if you want to add any of these into your vision of a perfect day.

In Chapter 6 on *Being*, I gave you Life Energy principles or beliefs for creating optimal living. Look at these principles and see if you want to add any of these into your perfect day. In the same chapter, I indicated the importance of operating in *Being*. Include the intention of doing this in your perfect day.

2. ***If you are really stuck and not able to be specific about a perfect day:***

a) ***Do some free associating***. Just write down any words that come to mind as you think of a perfect day. Don't stop yourself. Write down anything, positive or negative that comes to mind…phrases, words, or images. Just let it flow. From that you can often get an idea of at least general characteristics that you do and don't want, as well as an initial understanding of what's stopping your creative process.

One common barrier to forming a perfect day is the belief that you have experienced little happiness. So how can you even imagine a perfect day! This attitude means that you have been very focused on negative outcomes in your life. The fact that you are trying to do this exercise means that you want to change.

b) ***Start with small steps.*** Remember one scene, anytime in your life, where you were happy or enjoying yourself. Describe it to yourself. Who was there? What were you and others doing? What were your surroundings like? How were you feeling? Then ask yourself what was happening that made you happy. Put that down as your first baby step toward describing a perfect day.

c) ***Next, try to find another time in your life where you were enjoying yourself.*** Go through the same process—describe in detail what it was like. Then, again ask yourself what was making this so enjoyable for you. Add that to your perfect day picture. You don't have to have a highly detailed description with which to start, only one or maybe two things on which you can focus. That's a start.

<u>***The most important thing is to start***</u>. *More ideas will come to you as you work with your outline and begin to implement your perfect day. Then you can add them to your perfect day or change it in any way you like. The perfect day is always an on-going creation.*

Mary described her perfect day and put it in her journal. You can see the results on the next page.

Mary's Example

I get up in the morning feeling happy and well-rested, eager to start the day. I get up knowing that I have time to have a good breakfast, exercise, and meditate. I have time because I'm the one that schedules my day, and I schedule not only what I "should" do, but especially what I want to do.

I live in a beautiful house on six acres of land with a lake and mountain view. I have animals as companions that I love, as well as a loving and supportive husband. I have friends with whom I am highly compatible call or visit during the day. I have work to do that is inspiring, creative, and energizing. Throughout the day, I have time to play if I want to, and I know exactly what is fun for me as I play.

My life purpose as I see it has something to do with teaching and supporting others. In my perfect day, I am teaching and supporting others in a way that is best for them and me.

My finances provide adequate income for what I want to do. I don't have to worry about paying the next bill. Abundant resources are there when I need them such as money, friends, information sources, and opportunities.

I feel well and centered. I know who I am and I love who that is. I delight in learning how to become more of who I truly am. I feel satisfied, energized, and experience happiness frequently. I feel *Being* and stay in it from moment-to-moment. I know how to manage negative energy well, while creating the life I want and fulfilling my life purpose. I believe that I create my life in collaboration with God.

---

3. ***Draw a picture of your perfect day** dividing it into sections labeled Personal, Work, Relationships, and Necessary Resources.* For each of these categories, do a simple drawing using stick figures, make a collage or mandala, use symbols—create a true artistic drawing—whatever appeals to you the most. Do this in your journal. This picture provides you with a visual summary of what you want. It will serve as an instant reminder for you when you are asked to review your perfect day in the seven-step daily process I will give you later.

See Mary's picture of her perfect day using a mandala on the next page.

167

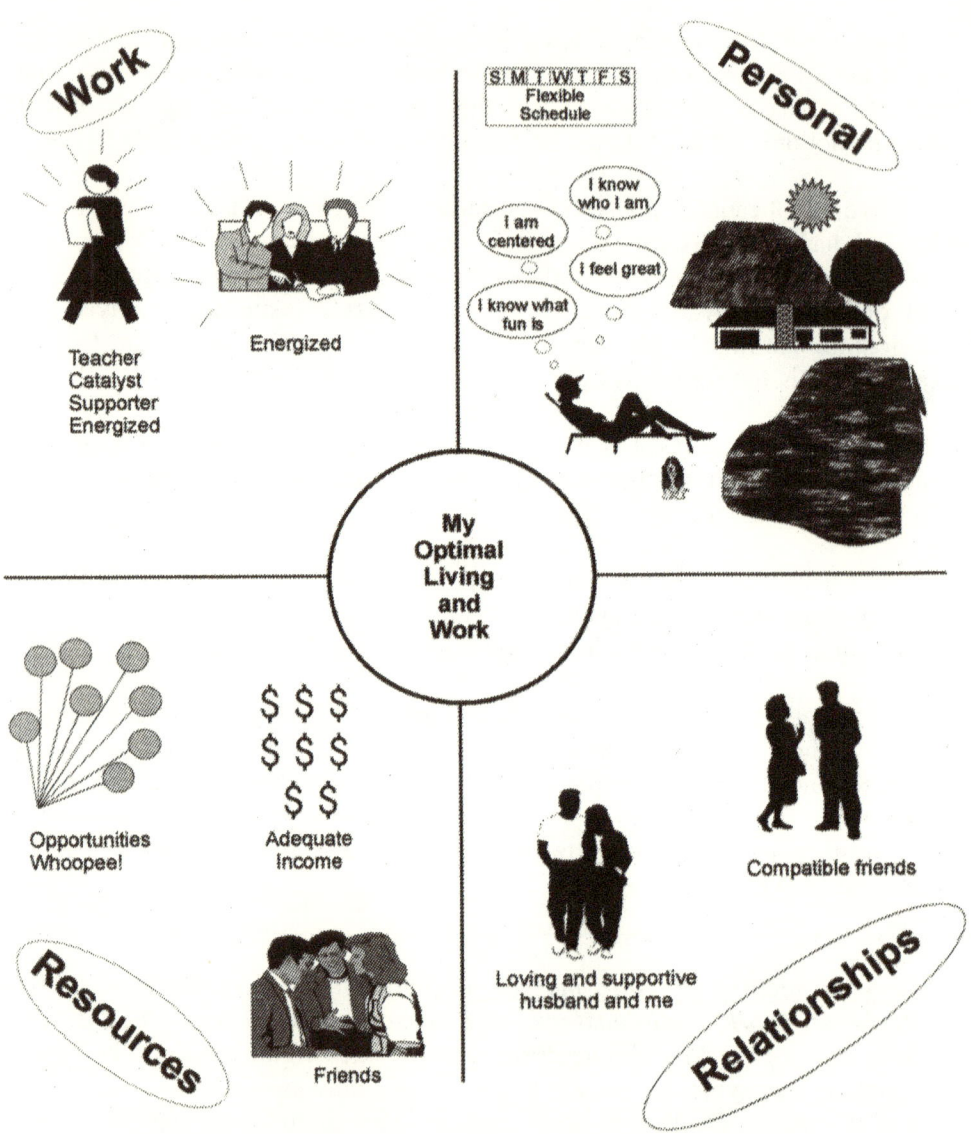

Mary's Example: A Picture of Mary's Perfect Day

4. ***Describe what kind of a <u>life you don't want</u>***. Remember that it is important to not only know what you want, but also what you don't want. The clearer you are on these boundaries, the easier manifestation can become. So using the same process I described in steps 1 and 2, concentrate now on describing a day you don't want. *Include in this day, things that are actually happening in your life that you don't want in your personal life, your work life, your relationships, and your available resources.*

Mary described the day she didn't want. Many of the scenes are happening in her life now.

<u>Mary's Example</u>

This is the type of day that I don't want.

I get up in the morning wishing I didn't have to face the day and all its responsibilities. I rush through the morning chores and things I have to do (getting dressed, getting the kids up and dressed, feeding everyone, getting the kids to school and me to work). I arrive at work to a day filled with pressure to get things done. It's chaotic. People come into my office making demands and requests throughout the day as I try to finish what I have to do. I go home feeling exhausted. Then I have to start all over with getting the kids to practice or their friends, coming home, getting a meal, making sure everyone does their homework and then to bed. Finally, I have some time to myself with my husband, but I'm too exhausted to want to do anything but veg out and then go to sleep.

Our finances are not good. We always seem to be in debt. We, my husband and I, feel we have to keep working just to maintain the level of lifestyle we have now, but there's not much money left over for fun. (Nor is there much time either!)

My friends seem to be needy and wanting me to take care of them or fix things for them. So, although it feels good to be needed, I often feel drained at the end of our interaction. When I need support from them, I generally don't get it.

I feel tired all the time. I also don't like myself very much. More than I want to be, I'm suspicious or afraid of people—what do they want, and how they could hurt me?

I try to get rid of the negatives I have in my life by avoiding them or hitting them head on. Either way it's a struggle to deal with them. I keep forgetting there is a God that can help. I generally only ask for help from this Source when I'm in deep trouble.

5. ***In your journal, make a <u>picture of the life you don't want</u> using the same process described in step 3.*** This is a visual summary of what you don't want!

Mary made the mandala on the next page representing the life she didn't want.

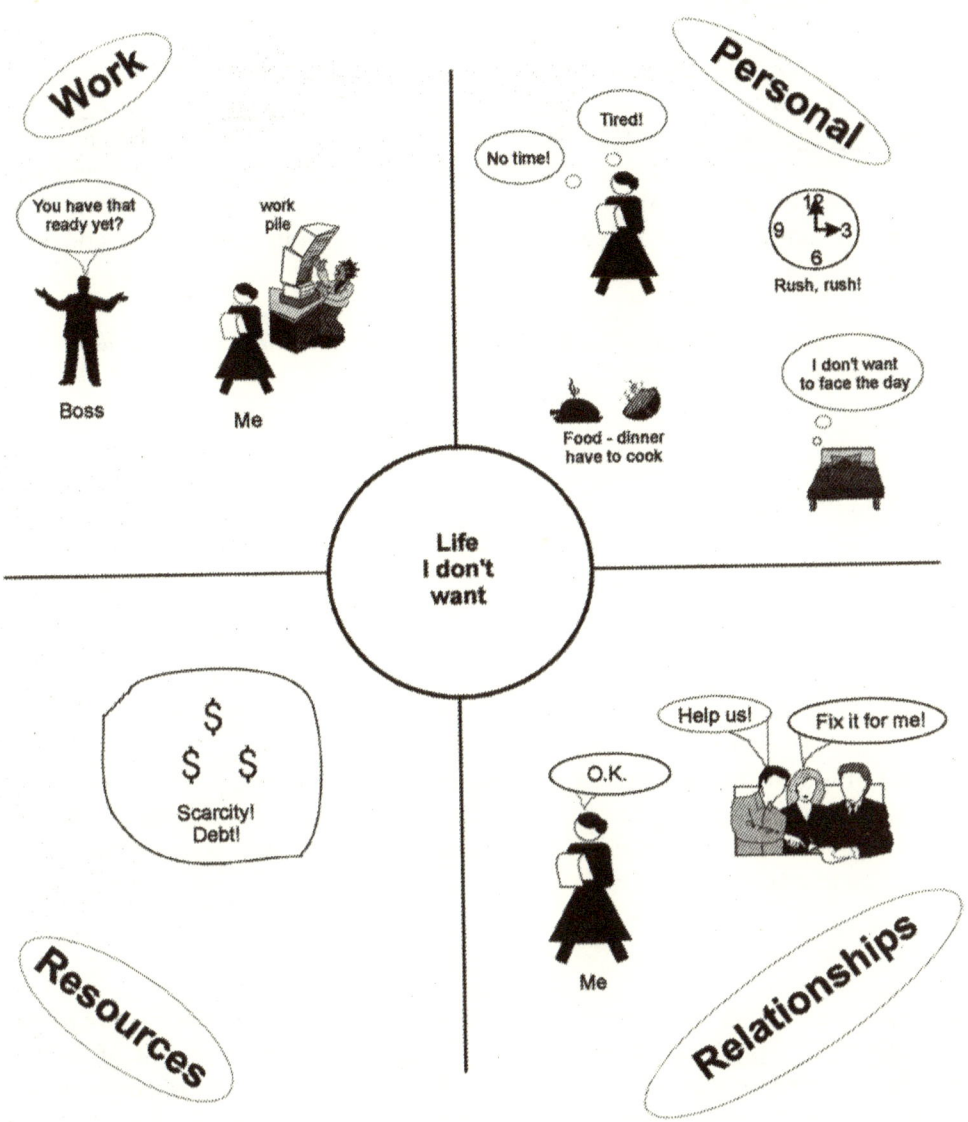

Mary's Example: The Life I Don't Want

171

At the Mind I Level:

1. *Using your Life Energy Journal under a section labeled "Mind Domain: Level 1 -Things I can do,"* <u>*create goals or things you can do to make you perfect day happen NOW.*</u> What can you do to make that day begin to be a reality? What actions can you take, what information can you get, and what help do you need? As you describe what you can do, write it down in the present tense or past tense so that it is telling your deeper self and inner helpers that you want this to happen now!

Using Mary's example of a perfect day, these are things she decided to do NOW to help it become a reality.

<u>Mary's Example</u>

I am doing the following things:

a) Deciding what kind of work gives the kind of flexibility described in my perfect day, e.g., my own business, working at home.
b) Investigating where I want to live and can afford to buy or build a house near a lake.
c) Figuring out what makes me happy and what is fun.
d) Describing the type of friends that make me feel comfortable. Do any of my present friends fit this description? If not, where can I meet these type of people?

After you finish describing what you can do to help manifest your perfect day, <u>**create a visual summary**</u> **of what you described through use of isolated words and phrases, symbols and drawing.** (*See Mary's example visual summary*) Put this visual depiction right behind your perfect day picture. As we go through each domain, I will tell you to add more visual summaries behind your perfect day illustration. *Together they will visually summarize your outline. This will give you a quick reference for use in daily living, as well as being integral to the seven-step process I'll soon discuss.*

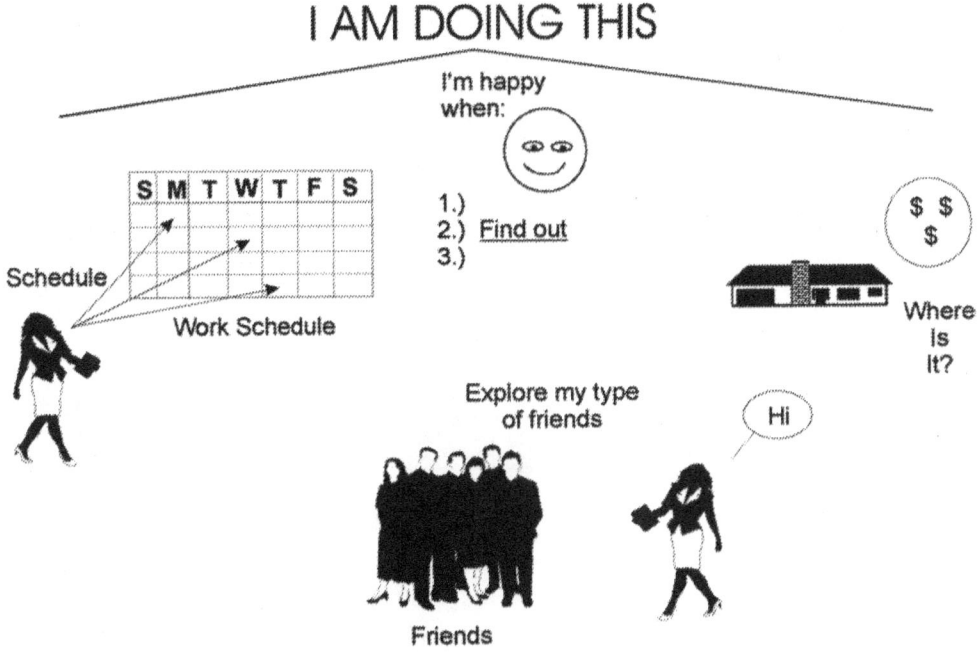

Mary's Example: Visual Summary of What To Do For My Perfect Day

Visual Summary of What I Won't Allow

2. ***Identify things that might happen that will <u>make sure your perfect day vision does NOT OCCUR</u>.*** What actions will get in the way of manifesting what you want? It can be your actions or that of others. What events? How can you get around these barriers, decrease their effect, or get rid of them? Write your answers in your journal under "*Mind Domain: Level 1 - Things I won't allow.*"

These are things that Mary will not let get in the way of creating her perfect day.

Mary's Example

I won't let the following things get in the way of doing things that help my perfect day happen:

- I schedule in time each day to do at least one thing toward my perfect day. I tell others and myself that protest because other things seem more important, that this is a requirement to make my life happen. It's just as important if not more important than other things demanding my attention.
- My husband is critical of my efforts because he tends to label dreams of the future as not realistic. I negotiated an agreement with him. He supports my scheduled time to do things for my perfect day and I will support his scheduled time to go out with the guys.

In the same way as in Step 1, create a "visual summary" of what you won't allow *and put it behind the illustration of things you are doing to bring about your perfect day. (See Mary's example visual summary on the previous page.)*

3. ***Describe the person you will have to be in order to make your perfect day happen...your <u>new identity</u>.*** What skills will you have to have, what personality characteristics, and attitudes? What actions and daily decisions will you have to do to support making your perfect day (your vision) happen? Remember to include your spirit identity of divinity experiencing humanness. Otherwise, you are telling Us that you want this identity to be forever in the future.

Mary created this new identity or self that supports her perfect day.

Mary's Example

I am divinity experiencing humanness and as such, I co-create what I want with the Creator. I commit to operate in *Being* throughout each day as best as I can in order to make the best decisions. I allow my intuitive mind to lead the way in situations that are ambiguous because it is better than my logical mind in these situations. I use my logical mind in partnership with my intuition to create the best approaches to make my perfect day happen.

I am flexible and unafraid to take risks important to my perfect day. I am creative, have fun, and have an exceptional ability to see patterns in life and how things fit together. I like people and prefer to talk with someone about my ideas and feelings because that is the way I think best and make decisions. I like to keep my options open, doing more than one thing at a time. I focus on seeking out what provides positive outcomes and *life energy* learning, while managing the negative.

I seek out and ask other people to help me, but do not expect them to take over and fix everything for me—that is my responsibility. I seek out friendships that are interdependent where each person assumes responsibility for their own actions while encouraging the growth of others and themselves. I demand a salary that is worthy of my talents. I remember that all others that I meet are also divinity experiencing humanness, and I respect them as such.

This is who I am; my identity for my perfect day vision.

---

4. ***Describe the person you can't be*** *if you want your perfect day.* Include in your description characteristics and attitudes you have that will get in the way of your perfect day. Again, write this description in the present tense.

Mary's Example

This is the self I'm not for manifesting my perfect day:

I believe I am in this world all by myself, separate from God. I have to be constantly on the watch for people and situations that could hurt me or do me harm. I don't reveal the true me because that would make me too vulnerable. So I spend a good deal of time hiding the real me, and trying to fit in.

I am afraid to take risks even if they're important to something I want very much. I am creative, but think this skill is a disadvantage in my workplace. I crave novelty and my job has little of that. So I look down on myself as an incompetent person.

I try to avoid the negative by not risking, not asking for other's help even when I need it, accommodating myself to other's needs, and generally being nice. I look at other's lives and envy what they have, but I'm too afraid to try and really change my life…it's too risky.

---

5. ***Create a picture of the self (identity) you have to be to strengthen the manifestation of your perfect day. Then create a picture of the person you can't be.*** Put your creations in your journal behind your perfect day picture and the other visual summaries.

See Mary's depictions of her new identity and the identity that won't support her perfect day on the next page. If you are working with a computer, either draw the image with your computer or scan what you drew on paper into your computer journal page.

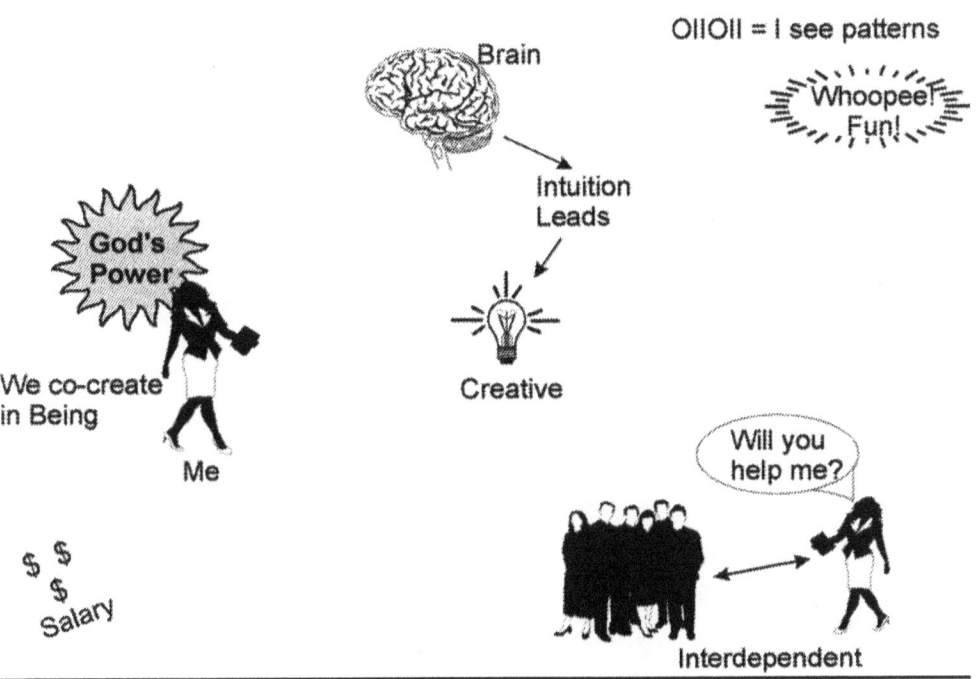

Mary's Example: My New Identity

The Identity I Can't Be

At the Mind II Level:

1. ***Using your Life Energy Journal under a section labeled the "Mind Domain: Level 2 – Beliefs," write down <u>three to five important beliefs</u> that you would have to have in order to make your perfect day vision happen.*** Some categories of important belief areas are shown in the NeuroQuantum Life Puzzle diagram. This diagram provides life areas that you should consider in identifying beliefs important to your perfect day.

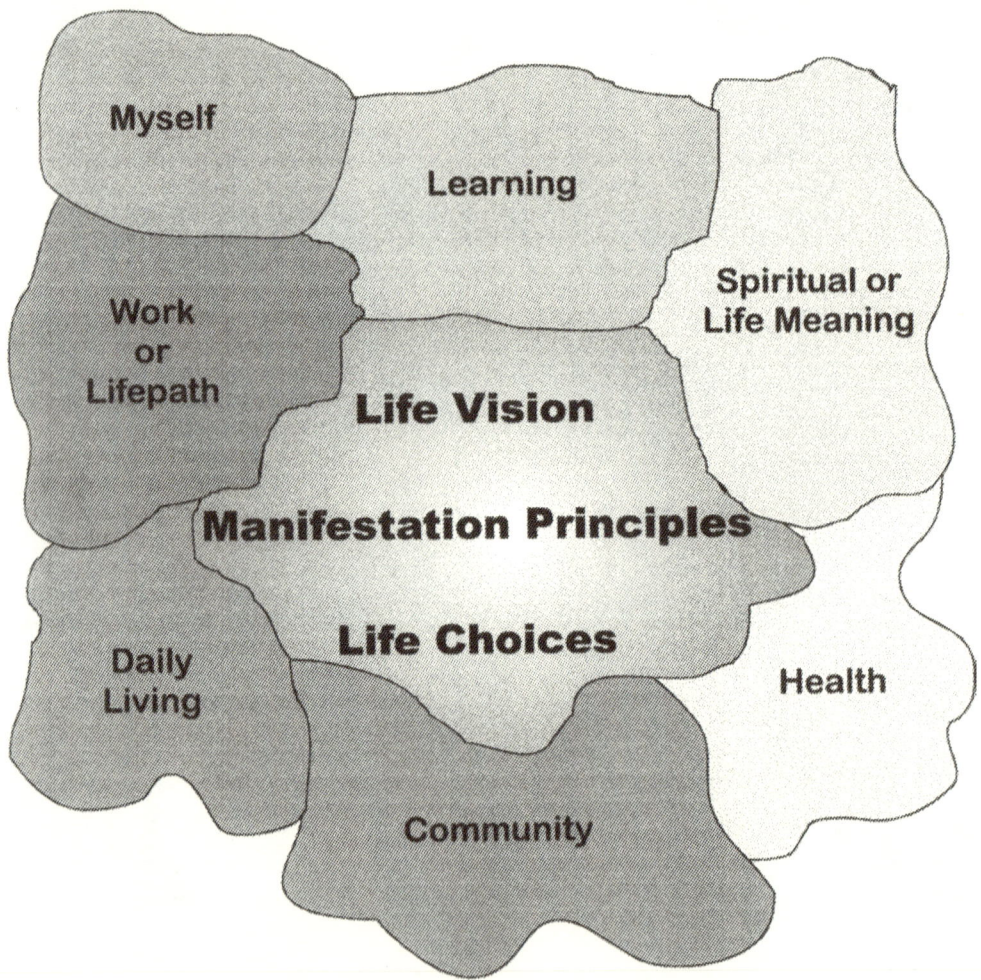

Figure 7.   NeuroQuantum Life Puzzle

Using this diagram, some example beliefs for each category are shown below:

Example beliefs under Work and/or Lifepath:

- I can make time during my workday for what is important for my perfect day.
- I can find work that is fulfilling, satisfying, and monetarily rewarding.
- I know what my life purpose is by letting my inner self show me.

Example beliefs under Learning:

- Change does not have to be painful if I listen to my intuition as well as my logical mind.
- I learn how to be the new me by taking small steps each day.
- I can manage negative events in my life and build the positive.
- I am not a victim but the creator of my life.

Example beliefs under Spiritual or Life Meaning:

- God is always with me; I am never alone.
- I am divinity experiencing humanness. As such, I create and choose what my life will be. This is easiest to do if I commit to operate within *Being* so that the Creator and my inner helpers can easily assist and support me.
- Life is only meaningful when I focus on living from the inside out, e.g., taking my power back from external sources and determining what I want from consulting within me.

Example beliefs under Health:

- My body has its own inner healer who can help me be optimally healthy if I ask it to show me how.
- *Body Consciousness* is a gateway to the Life Energy of *Being*.
- I can help solve health problems by creating a vision of the kind of health I want and then asking my inner healer to help me get there.
- I can create the time I need to have fun, relax, and do what I want to do.

Example beliefs under Myself, my Identity:

- I am a creative, vibrant, can-do person.
- I am worthwhile.
- Whatever happens in my life is my responsibility since I either create it or choose it at some level of my inner self.
- I deserve happiness and love.
- I am divinity experiencing humanness.

Example beliefs under Community:

- I have friends that are supportive of who I am; I can find even more of them.
- I can create or find groups of like-minded people who function as my community.
- I deserve to have a partner who loves and honors who I am, not who he/she wants me to be.
- Friendship is meant to support and honor who the other person is; the other person does the same for me.

Example beliefs under Daily Living:

- Abundance is the natural state of things if only I let it happen and believe I am worthy enough to have it happen to me.
- Money is neutral energy; it is neither bad nor good but helps things to happen that I want.
- Sex is the energy of the Creator in each of us.
- People are naturally good and will often live up to their best self if you expect that of them.

Mary used the NeuroQuantum Life Puzzle diagram to help her choose the following four beliefs that were especially important to supporting her vision of a perfect day. She wrote these in her journal.

<u>Mary's Example</u>

- I am divinity experiencing humanness and as such I choose and create my life in conjunction with the Creator.
- I can find work that allows a feeling of satisfaction, joy, and accomplishment.
- Change can be easy and slow, done in small steps, and enjoyable.
- I am worthy of having this life I have envisioned.

2. *In your journal under the same heading as before, write down <u>three to five beliefs you have right now that are likely to stop you</u>* from trying to manifest your perfect day vision. Reframe (reword) them so that they are no longer barriers.

Mary's Example

Barrier Beliefs:

- I have very little control over my life.
- Good jobs are few and far between and because of that, I can't risk quitting my present job.
- This process is so hard and so pie-in-the-sky that it doesn't make any sense to even try to do it. It will just get me all excited about what I want and then I'll be disappointed when I wake up to reality and know I can't have it.
- I don't have time to try and do any of this stuff.
- I'm not really worthy of having the life that I want; I have too many faults.
- Change is scary, risky, and traumatic.

Reworded Barrier Beliefs:

- My control is within me.
- Jobs that match what I want will manifest themselves. The key is to state what I want and believe that something like it will appear in the way best for me. I then need to start doing things that will make what I want more likely as a way of reinforcing my belief that it will happen.
- It's better to know what I want and try to create something like it, rather than to let other people and events define my life. It's an either/or choice. Either I create my life or someone else will.
- If something is important, I make time to do it.
- I am divinity experiencing humanness. That makes me worthwhile. I am not a flawed product. God doesn't create seconds.
- Change is the process of life; everything is always changing. It is better to know how to handle change and manage the change process so that it is pleasant, easy, and fun.

---

3. ***Decide on <u>steps, strategies, or ways</u> to make the goals listed at the Mind I Level happen.*** What do you have to do, who do you have to talk to, how are you going to make your perfect day happen NOW? Put them down in your journal under a section labeled, *"Mind Domain: Level 2 - Manifestation*

Strategies." Put what you write in the past tense as if you had already done them.

Mary needed to find out what kind of work/career would give her the flexibility to fit into her perfect day. That was one of her goals. The strategies below are ones she listed to make the goal happen. Mary wrote statements in her journal so that she would not make these steps and strategies for her perfect day WORK but FUN! If you make this work, it will never get done.

Mary's Example

I free associated things I liked to do, the type of work setting I liked, and the type of people with whom I liked to work. I just put all of these things down on paper as they occurred to me. This is what I got:

- Peaceful
- Exciting
- I feel enthusiastic about what I do
- Friends are around that get excited about my ideas
- Friends are around that are good at helping to carry out detail
- There is a flexible work schedule
- I can balance helping others with time for my own life
- I have freedom to set my own schedule

Next step: from the career section in the library, I got a book that listed all types of different careers. I went down the list and picked out ones that appealed to me ignoring practicality for the time being. After I made my list, I eliminated the ones that involved a long program of retraining, and those that didn't produce an income that was satisfactory. Then I compared this list to the characteristics that I free associated to see which ones matched these characteristics the best.

After I did this, I talked to a career counselor to narrow down what first steps needed to be taken to begin making this new work life happen.

Mary also developed other strategies that would help her accomplish her other goals. Then she wrote the following in her journal in capital letters as a reminder to herself when she started to do these steps and strategies:

- DO THESE A LITTLE BIT AT A TIME.
- DO WHAT YOU FEEL LIKE DOING ONLY.
- DON'T DO THESE IN ORDER IF YOU DON'T HAVE TO OR YOU DON'T WANT TO.
- GO WITH YOUR INTUITION AS TO WHICH STEPS AND STRATEGIES TO DO AS YOU DO THEM.

4. ***Decide on what <u>supports you are going to need</u> in order to create your
perfect day.*** Do you have friends that can provide needed information,
needed support, and/or help? Are there places where you can get the help
you need such as the library, consultants, agencies, and/or the Internet?
Write them down in your journal, again using the past tense. Put this in a
section labeled, "Mind Domain: Level 2 – Supports."

See what Mary decided to do below.

<u>Mary's Example</u>

Mary chose the career counselor, her friends, and family as necessary
supports. She wrote that she would use them to bounce ideas and ask for
emotional support when necessary. When she was asking for their help, she
would tell them exactly how to give it so there was no room for
misunderstanding. This would help her feel like she had a cheering section
who cared.

Mary also decided to use the Internet to get in-depth information about
each career she had on her final list.

---

5. ***Create a <u>visual summary</u> of what your actions and experiences would be if
you were living, doing, and letting happen the <u>positive beliefs, strategies,
and supports</u> you listed in steps 2,3, and 4.*** Use symbols, words, stick
figures, art, magazine pictures, or photos to create this illustration. Label it,
"Living positive beliefs, strategies, and supports." Put the finished product
behind the other visual summaries you did in previous steps.
 ***Similarly, create a visual summary (collage) of living out your barrier
beliefs you listed and ignoring your strategies and supports.*** What would
you feel like, what would you be doing? Label this, "Living Barrier Beliefs"
and put it behind the other visual summaries you've made. Mary's examples
are on the next page.

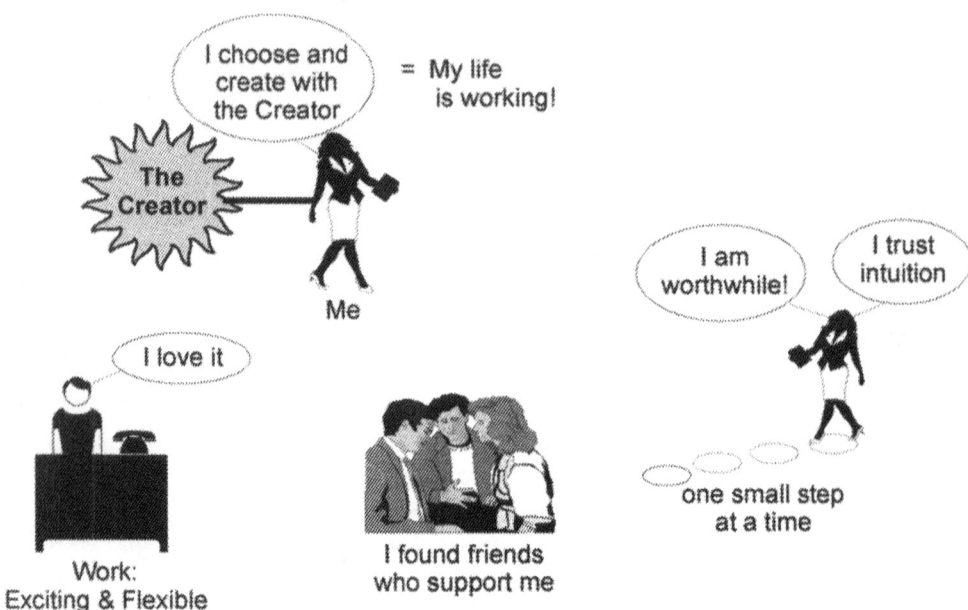

Mary's Example: Living positive beliefs, strategies, and support systems

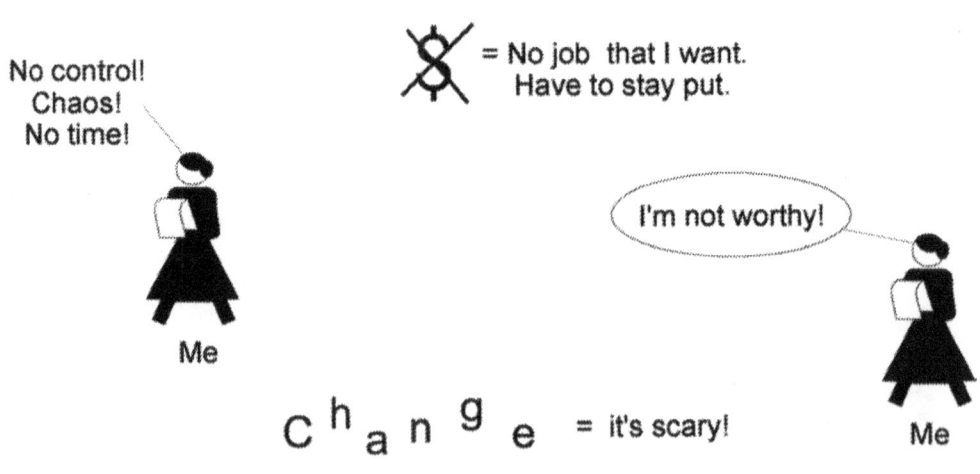

Living Barrier Beliefs

6. ***Decide on <u>cognitive skills that are critical</u> for supporting your perfect day***. Write your decisions down in your journal under the heading, "Mind Domain: Level 2 - Cognitive Skills." Some examples of important cognitive skills are thinking and decision making style, communication style, organization strategies, and relationship and community-building skills. Let Me explain more about each one.

   a) ***Thinking and Decision-Making Style***. There are various ways of thinking things through:

   - writing your ideas and conclusions out on paper
   - accessing the intuitive self and inner helpers
   - drawing or diagramming your thoughts (Figure 8 is an example of diagramming)
   - talking out your thoughts with someone else
   - mulling over ideas in your mind while relaxing
   - free associating thoughts around your focus area
   - reading about your focus area
   - setting up experiences that show you what you want to know

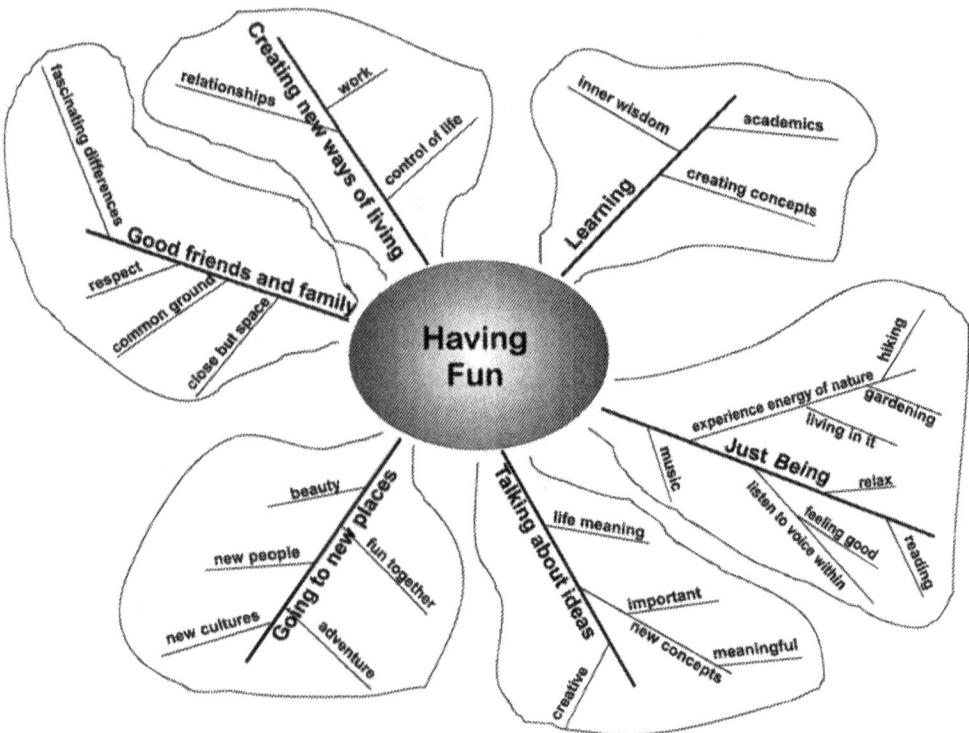

Figure 8. Mind Mapping: Diagramming Your Thoughts

All these are bona fide ways of thinking. Identify for yourself the best ways of thinking for you. As you become more conscious about creating what you want in your life, rather than passively letting things happen, thinking efficiently and making decisions is one skill that is critical to the process. So it's important for you to know how you think best. The listing above should give you a good start.

b) ***Communication Style***. (1) How should you talk about yourself, your vision of a perfect day, and your experiences to others to best support your perfect day? (2) How do you actually talk about yourself and your experiences now? Does it support your perfect day?

What you say to yourself or others reinforces your attitudes. Talking is a feedback loop to your mind, which reminds it how to react and what to think. *Your inner and outer communication must respect and be true to who you are and what your vision is.*

If you talk about yourself in defeatist terms such as "You know me, I'm just a screw up," then it does not support creating optimal living and work. Such talk will reinforce an "I can't do it" attitude in your mind. If instead, you talk about what you can do and what you are going to do, it reinforces a "can do" attitude.

If you talk about your perfect day to yourself or others as something that is "pie in the sky" or a dream, then your perfect day will never become a reality. You are telling your mind that this is something that is impossible to do. Your mind will create barriers so that your perfect day is an impossibility. In the meanwhile, your inner self and helpers will be trying to counter your attitude as best they can. The result will be a struggle with each step in making anything happen for your perfect day.

For experiences that you have, if you talk only about the negative parts, you will be encouraging only negative things to happen, including setting up barriers for your perfect day.

If you talk about how impossible the environment is around you, how incompatible with your perfect day, you will not be able to create your perfect day within your present setting.

The key is to alter your communication so that you talk about*:*

- the positives that happen to you,
- the lessons you have learned from experiences—what they taught you,
- what you can do,
- what your skills are,
- what you have accomplished, and
- the practicality of your perfect day for you.

These communications will support your perfect day because they are true to who you are and what you envision.

---

c) ***Organization Strategies.*** How are you going to organize your time to make your perfect day happen? How are you going to organize yourself, so that you get things done that need to be done each day?

If you think that your daily responsibilities have to be done first, and only when they are done, can you work on your perfect day, it will not happen. You'll never find time to do the necessary things for manifesting your vision. Instead, if you first think about where to schedule in one or two things for your perfect day, and then work around that, you will make your perfect day happen.

Also, begin to examine your daily responsibilities, what you think "has to be done," and ask if they are really important to accomplish. Re-examine your responsibilities in the light of what you want in your perfect day. Begin to eliminate those things and demands that don't fit in. Just say NO!

d) ***Relationship and Community-Building Skills.*** You cannot live in a vacuum. You decided to become human because it meant not only living as one individual but also living in relationship and community with others. In order to make your life vision happen, the necessary relationship skills and knowledge of how to build a group of people into your life that will be supportive of your dream and your new identity is a requirement.

Can you relate to others without giving up who you are? Can you relate to others well and not hide who you really are? Are you able to perceive what others want of you in a relationship or association? Can you talk to others in the style of language they can understand, e.g. using experiences they know, the type of communication style with which they feel the most comfortable? These are critical relationship skills for manifesting your vision. Look at your perfect day vision and describe the relationship skills you will have to have to support that vision when mingling with others around you.

Not only is it critical to be able to generally relate well to others while still respecting and maintaining who you are, but it is also critical to know how to bring people into your life that will support your vision and new identity. How are you going to find them, how can you "call" them to you? And once you have these strategies, how can you build small groups of people where you would have support and give support as well? This is community-building.

For both relationship skills and community-building, the previous discussion on "What You Can do To Create Optimal Living for You and Others" will help you to decide what skills you need and how to build friendships and groups that will be compatible with what you want.

Mary decided the cognitive skills described on the next page were important to support her perfect day. She put each of these skills in her journal with a description of how she would do each using the present or past tense to remind her psyche to do this NOW!

Mary's Example for Cognitive Skills Necessary to Her Life Vision

- **Thinking and Decision-Making Style**: I looked at the list of thinking and decision-making styles and decided that I think best by:

  - writing my ideas out on paper,
  - accessing my inner helpers,
  - using my intuition,
  - doing some reading on the subject if necessary,
  - talking my ideas over with others to gain perspective, and
  - trying out my ideas in a limited and easy way through seeking out or creating experiences that show what happens.

  I use these styles when thinking out things important to manifesting my perfect day.

- **Communication Style**: I talk about creating my perfect day to myself (self talk) and others in "can do" terms. When interacting with others, I make sure I am communicating in a way that is respectful to myself as well as others. In others words, I commit to being true to my new identity for my perfect day with what I say. This is hard for me only when I am so overly concerned about being supportive of others that I forget to be supportive of who I am. I try my best to do this and that's all I can ask of myself. I ask my inner helpers, especially God, to help me do this.

- **Organization Strategies:** Organization strategies are important because without them, I get distracted from doing things to manifest my vision. I love to be involved in many things at once. So I decided that I would commit to doing at least one thing each day that supports manifesting my perfect day. I make this a priority so that it doesn't get lost in all the other things I'm doing. I look at what I must do for an entire week and write my activities down. I then decide which of these activities I really <u>have</u> to do, and which I get caught up in doing. This organizational approach gives me a better idea of how to make time for what needs to be done for my perfect day.

- **Relationship and Community-Building Skills:** Two of my friends are going to support me as I work on manifesting my perfect day. I call them my Advisory Council. I want to work on building an interdependent relationship with them where I support and honor them and they support and honor me. I answered some of the questions about "creating optimal living for myself and others" in the book. That helped me better define what I wanted in a relationship. I have trouble "reading" people accurately, so I am going to a communication specialist to help me build these skills.

  For community building, I asked my two friends if they would like to meet as a group once a month or more and do some fun things together. I also asked them if they would be interested in help building a set up guideline for the group using the section on creating an optimal living to help me. They were!

---

7. *Imagine using these <u>cognitive skills</u> when needed easily and expertly. From this image, <u>create a picture</u> of how you would look when you are* doing this well. Center on drawing your facial expression and then add

symbols and words that tell what skills you are doing so easily. Put this in your journal behind your other visual summaries. Label it, "Mind Domain: Level 2 - Necessary Cognitive Skills Visual Summary." Look at the next page for an example of how to do this. *Mary drew the image on the following page for her visual summary.*

Next, imagine attempting to manifest your perfect day without these cognitive skills operating well. Draw a picture of this, putting it under the previous one you drew. (*See Mary's example on the next page.*)

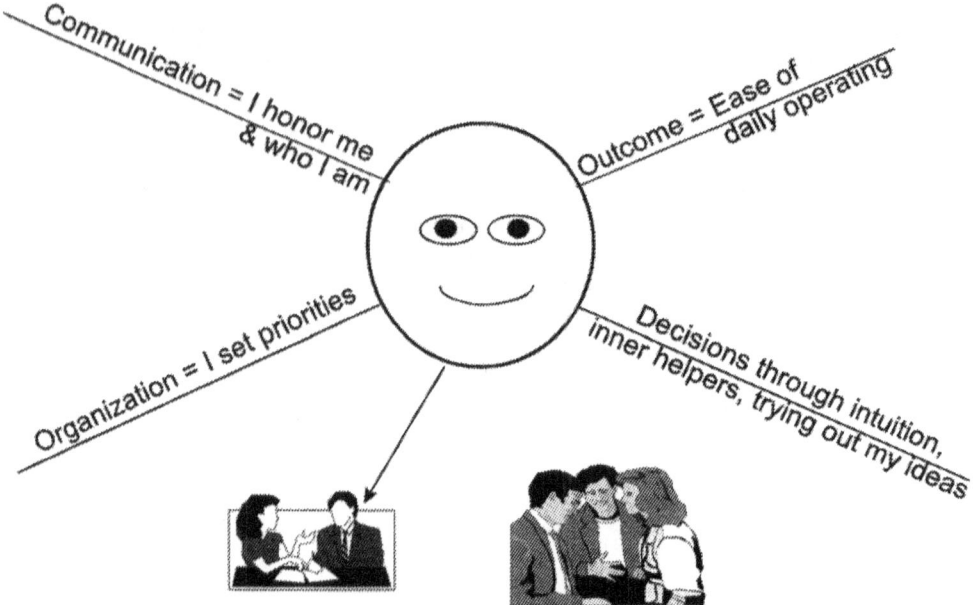

Mary's Example: **Mind Domain: Level 2 - Necessary Cognitive Skills**

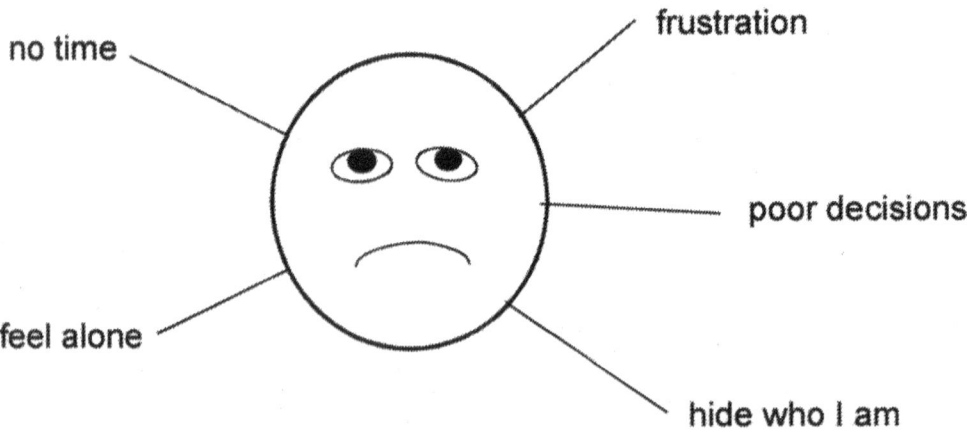

Mind Domain: Level 2 - Necessary Cognitive Skills Not Present

At the Mind III Level:

1. *Identify the <u>instinctive feeling</u> within your body and mind that indicates you are going in the <u>right direction</u> for manifesting your vision. Then identify the instinctive feeling that says you are going in the wrong direction.* Record a description of each in your Life Energy Journal under "The Mind Domain: Level 3 – Instinct."

   When you experience events and interactions with people during the day, your intuitive self is working within your deep consciousness to provide feedback about them. When you are in an experience that is bad for what you want, your intuitive self supplies inner feelings that tell you this is so, such as muscle tightness, a headache, anxiety, an off-center feeling, obsessive drive, or nausea.

   Similarly, when you experience something that is good for you, your intuitive self provides pleasant sensations such as centeredness or resonance, an immediate sense that this is right for you, and a sense of relaxation, peace, or lightness.

   Many of you ignore these sensations. Instead, you rely solely on your conscious logical mind and habitual reactions to determine what to do. This makes the learning process longer and more labored, and manifestation more difficult.

   To support your perfect day, identify the instinctive sensations that take place within your body signaling you about bad and good situations and decisions. If you have no idea what they are, observe yourself for several days and identify the feedback signals for positive and negative experiences. Once you identify both the positive and negative sensations, tell your inner helpers that you want these sensations to become stronger to help you know when you are going the right way and when you are going the wrong way for your perfect day. We will accommodate your wish and strengthen these instinctive feelings.

Dianne Greyerbiehl Ph.D.

Mary's Example

I found that when I am going in the right direction for my perfect day, I feel relaxed and centered. When I am going in the wrong direction, I often begin to get a headache as well as a tightness in my stomach, which increases the more I insist on going in that direction. I told my inner helpers that I want these feelings to be very strong so they can act as guides and signals for my conscious mind.

---

2. *Identify the <u>best ways to access your inner world</u> to enable you to increase your intuitive knowing and wisdom.* Record your answers in your Life Energy Journal under, "Mind Domain: Level 3 - Inner Wisdom."

I have talked about listening to your inner voice to provide you with the wisdom needed to make choices in your daily life. I have also talked about many ways of accessing your inner world such as meditation, automatic writing, prayer, daydreaming, drawing, etc., if you want direct communication with Us.

For supporting your perfect day vision, practice listening to your inner voice as well as watching for other signs from Us in dreams, coincidences, or people that you meet. This will help make the manifestation that you seek stronger and easier. In addition, regularly talk to Us through any method that is pleasing to you so that we can easily communicate with you to help co-create what you want.

Mary's Example

I listen to my inner voice, intuition, and my dreams because I know these are major sources of wisdom for me. I also strengthen my ability to communicate with my inner helpers through daily meditation, free association, automatic writing, and drawing out an idea when relaxed. I especially use these communication methods when I have questions about what to do.

---

3. *Create a <u>visual summary for the positive gut feeling for going in the right direction</u> along with the best way of accessing inner wisdom.* You can do this simply by listing single words or phrases that would be shorthand for

your longer description.   Put the finished product under the other visual summaries.

Next, on the same page in your journal, create a depiction representing the gut feeling you get when going in the wrong direction and what happens when you don't listen to your inner wisdom. (*See Mary's example next page.*)

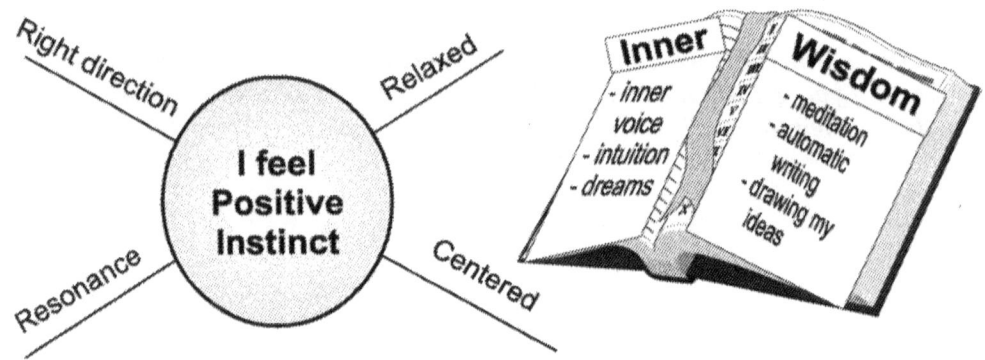

Mary's Example: Listening to My Positive Instinct and Inner Wisdom

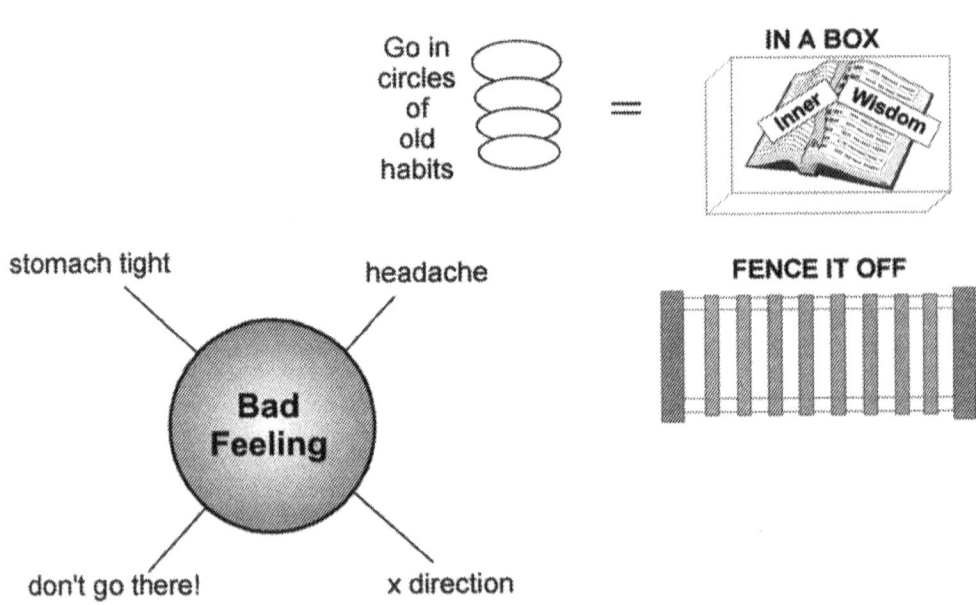

Listening to Negative Instinct and Not Following Inner Wisdom

For the Emotion Domain:

1. *Choose the <u>feelings and experiences that will support</u> your vision.* Put them down in your Life Energy Journal under "The Emotion Domain" doing so as if you were already doing them. What feelings will help your vision manifest itself? What type of experiences will help you?

2. *Identify <u>feelings and experiences that won't support</u> your vision and record them in your journal. Write them in the present tense.*

<u>**Mary's Example**</u>

Feelings of peace, joy, fun, contentment, excitement, and self-love best promote my perfect day. I encourage these emotions to be present in my daily life. The feelings that don't support my perfect day are depression, fear, and anger. When I encounter these emotions, I listen to what they are trying to tell me, rather than trying to get rid of them right away. Then I let them go.

I seek experiences that are positive but challenging situations where I have people around me that are affirming of my strengths and what I can accomplish. The type of experience that doesn't support my life vision is a negative environment where there is little support and high criticism of my actions. I avoid these situations as much as possible.

---

3. *Create a <u>visual summary for both conditions</u>—one showing emotions and experience that match your perfect day vision and one showing those that don't. (See Mary's example on the next page.)*

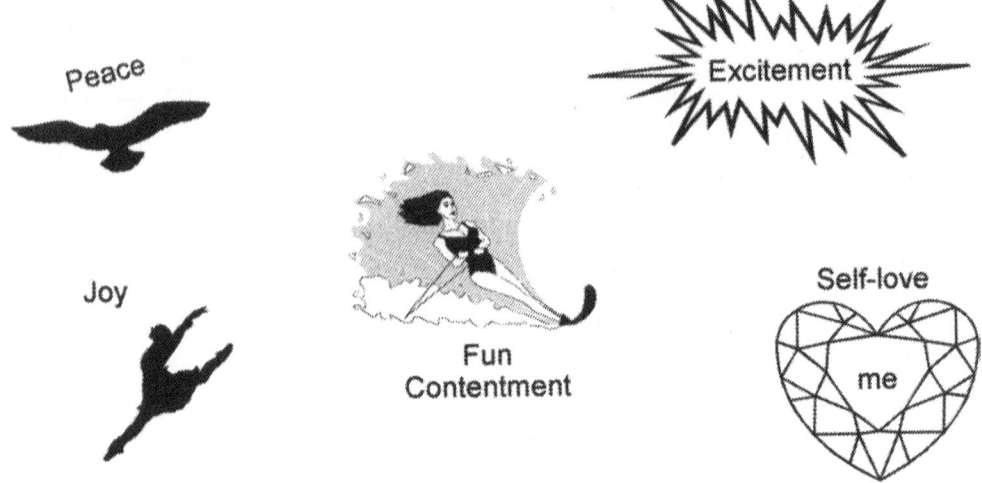

Mary's Example: Emotions That Match My Vision

Emotions That Don't Match My Vision

For the Subtle Physical Domain:

1. *Find those chakras that are not aligned with your perfect day, e.g. their energy is incompatible with your vision.* Record what they are in your journal under, "Subtle Physical Domain – Chakras." *Then change the energy of those chakras so that it is compatible with your vision. To do this, follow these steps*:

    1. Ask your *Body Consciousness* to help you find the chakras that need their energy changed to be compatible with your perfect day vision.

    2. Using Figure 4. to help you locate each of the chakras, shut down your logical mind, close your eyes, and let your *Body Consciousness* slowly guide your hand over each of the chakra centers. Allow your hand to stop at those centers that have incompatible energy for your vision. The signal to stop at a certain chakra center may be a hesitation in the forward movement of your hand, something telling you in your mind to stop, heat coming from that area, or energy pulses that hit the palm of your hand. Trust your instincts and the guidance of your *Body Consciousness*.

    3. *For those of you that cannot get the hang of operating in this intuitive way, you will be simply stopping your hand at each of the chakras and following the directions below.*

    4. Once you have chosen the chakra that needs work, imagine the color associated with it becoming very bright. (See Figure 4. for the chakras and their colors.) As it gets brighter and brighter, imagine its energy becoming stronger and more compatible with your vision. Then bring in white and gold light to strengthen this new pattern of energy. See this new pattern expanding out into the energy field associated with the chakra.

    5. Then go on to find the next chakra that needs work and repeat this whole process.

    6. Remember to record which of the chakras you worked with in your journal.

Mary's Example

Mary followed the directions for locating the chakras that needed changing to be compatible with her perfect day. She found that she felt heat at each of the last four chakra centers. She used the color associated with each center to change and strengthen its energy, imagining it becoming brighter, stronger, and more compatible with her vision. She then imagined gold and white light intertwining with the color, strengthening its new pattern. She recorded what she did under, "Subtle Physical Domain" in her journal.

---

2. ***Identify the <u>meridians</u> of the body that are incompatible with your perfect day.*** *Write them down in your journal under "Subtle Physical - Meridians." Then change the energy in these areas so that they are compatible with what you want. To do this, follow these steps:*

   1. Ask your *Body Consciousness* to help you find the meridians that need their energy changed to be compatible with your perfect day vision.

   2. Using Figure 6 to help you locate the major meridians, shut down your logical mind, close your eyes, and let your *Body Consciousness slowly* guide your hand over your body, starting with the top of your head, going down the trunk of your body, to end at your feet. Allow your hand to stop in those body areas where you feel a hesitation in the forward movement of your hand, something telling you in your mind to stop, heat coming from that area, or energy pulses that hit the palm of your hand.

   3. Once you have stopped in a certain area, imagine gold and white light coming into that area through your hand, making the energy flow easier, stronger, and more compatible with your perfect day.

   4. Then go on to find the next area of your body that needs work and repeat this whole process.

   5. *For those of you that cannot do this intuitively,* tell your *Body Consciousness* to locate those meridians that need healing in order to be compatible with your vision. Then imagine gold and while light

202

coming from a point above your head and surrounding your body. Ask your *Body Consciousness* to take over and spread the light to those areas needing work as you slowly move your hand from the top of your head to the bottom of your feet. Imagine the light going throughout your body as you move your hand down your body.

6.   Remember to record what you did in your journal.

Mary's Example

Using the directions provided, Mary found that her hand stopped around her collarbone (the kidney meridian), under her armpit (the spleen meridian), and at her chin (the central vessel). She imagined gold and white light coming to those areas and made an intention that the energy would flow easier, stronger, and more compatible with her vision. She recorded what she did in her journal.

For the Physical Domain:

1.   ***Describe a physically healthy you*** *that will best support your perfect day.* Let your mind wander and imagine this healthy you. Use the questions below to help you create this picture. Then put the description in your journal under a section labeled, "The Physical Domain."

- What would you look like if you were really healthy in a way that supports your perfect day?
- What would you physically and mentally be able to do with ease and confidence?
- How does it feel to be this healthy self? What sensations do you have that says your body and brain are functioning optimally? For example, are you feeling energetic, moving easily, feeling strong and vital, thinking effectively, and concentrating in a style that best suits your perfect day vision?

---

2. ***Describe <u>how you created</u> this physically healthy you***. The next questions are about how you went about getting this healthy. To answer these questions, just relax and let your mind free associate or daydream about what brought about this healthy you that you just described. In other words, pretend that this healthy you has really happened and you are now asking yourself, "What did I do to get here?" Ask your *Body Consciousness* and your inner helpers to help you with these answers.

- What did I do to bring about this new me?
- What exercises or physical movement am I doing during the week?
- How much rest am I getting?
- How am I getting sleep that is deep and restful?
- What am I doing for relaxation and fun each day?
- What am I feeding my body (type of food, nutritional supplements, medication)?
- How am I optimally tuning my brain's functioning so that I can concentrate, think, communicate, and remember effectively?
- Am I going to a health practitioner to help me manifest this healthy self? If so, what type of health practitioner? How does the health practitioner effectively support me and help my perfect day?

Your answers to these questions will give you the best ways of getting your body and brain functioning optimally to support your perfect day. In other words, you just developed a health program for yourself that matches your vision of a healthy you.

Record your "health program" in your journal under your description of a healthy you. Then tell your *Body Consciousness* that you want its continued help to make your body and brain function in a way that is optimal for manifesting your perfect day.

3. ***Now, imagine again this healthy you. Make a drawing, a collage, or mandala of what this you looks like***. Include in your depiction not only your healthy physical body but also your healthy subtle physical body's chakras and meridians. Put this in your journal labeling it "Physical and Subtle Physical Domain: Healthy Me," and put it behind the other visual summaries you've done.

4. ***Identify animals, plants, and minerals*** *(rocks, crystals) that make you feel energized and balanced as you think about manifesting your perfect day.* What animals would make you feel this way as you are working on your perfect day? What plants or nature settings help you the most? Are there any rocks or crystals that attract you, feel good to you, make you feel centered? Record them in your journal.

5. ***In your journal, describe*** ***choices and circumstances in your life that will*** ***not support*** ***you physically or mentally as you are attempting to manifest*** ***your perfect day.*** Here are some examples of this:

   - just going along with what others want, allowing yourself to be a victim
   - expecting others to heal you without your help
   - ignoring the health of your body
   - letting a health practitioner tell you what to do without your input
   - not getting enough rest
   - working so hard that there is little or no relaxation
   - eating poorly
   - not getting enough exercise
   - routinely associating with negative people who are critical of you
   - keeping your day so busy that you never stop running
   - scattering your energy over so many different responsibilities that you're exhausted at day's end

   Although these circumstances may seem hard to alleviate if they are part of your life now, there are always some options that will allow you to change them. Some of the options you may not like. But as long as you tell yourself there are no options, then you will manifest what you believe and your life vision will not happen.

6. ***Draw a*** ***visual image of circumstances and choices that do not support*** *a* ***healthy you for your perfect day.*** Use symbols, do a collage or mandala, draw stick figures, or draw a work of art. Whatever you feel will illustrate the things that aren't compatible with creating a healthy you. Put the result in your journal labeling it, "*Circumstances and choices that won't support a healthy me,*" and put the result behind the visual summary for a healthy you.

Along with her inner helpers and Body Consciousness, Mary co-created the following description and picture of a healthy self and health program that would be compatible with her perfect day. She also included the circumstances and choices that aren't compatible with a healthy self while trying to manifest her perfect day.

Mary's Example

I look lean and nicely muscled. My body moves with ease. My skin glows with health. I can do any of the sports and recreation activities that I like without my body feeling overly sore. I don't get colds any more. I feel energetic, strong, and vital. My brain works efficiently in my everyday life and its demands.

Three times a week, I do some type of exercising or body movement that I enjoy such as walking, dancing, roller-blading, tennis, swimming, or aerobics. Each day, I focus on listening to my inner voice as to what would be the best things for me to eat, as well as which vitamins and herbs to take. I meditate and identify different states of consciousness that help me concentrate and learn, as well as access my deeper conscious mind and its wisdom. This has helped my everyday ability to think, concentrate, and learn. I ask my *Body Consciousness* to make my body and brain function optimally each day.

I decided that Cranial Sacral therapy was important to help me balance my body. I found a therapist that believed the person's inner healer should be consulted for decisions about what to do in each session. The therapist also insisted that I make my own decisions about the direction of therapy that would best meet my needs. She keeps telling me to rely on the inner healer for these decisions.

Each day, I do something that is fun as a way of affirming how important I am. I avoid getting myself into too many projects that would bring on exhaustion, because I know exhaustion makes it more likely that I will become negative about making my perfect day a reality. I avoid negative people as much as possible.

I bought an amethyst crystal to put by my bedside because it made me feel good. I frequently do something outdoors in an area that makes me feel energized and peaceful. When I can't do this, I rely on an area in my house that I created with lots of plants, and a little indoor fountain—my indoor garden and haven for feeling peace and energy.

Mary's picture of a healthy self (physical and subtle physical) that is functioning optimally for manifesting her perfect day is on the next page. Her picture includes the things that she is doing to make her healthy. A second picture of "Circumstances and choices that don't support a healthy self" is also depicted.

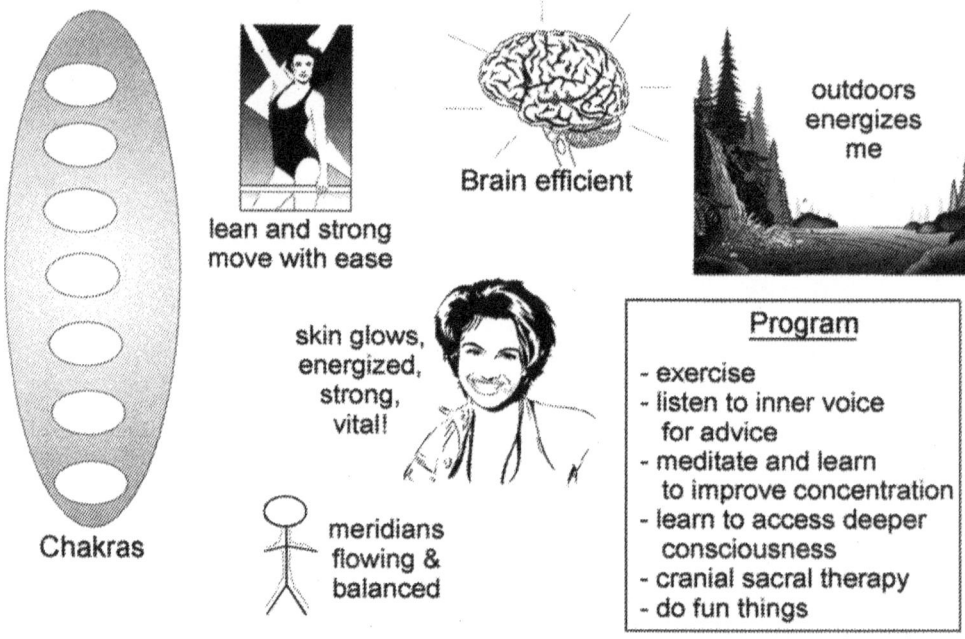

Mary's Example: My Healthy Self

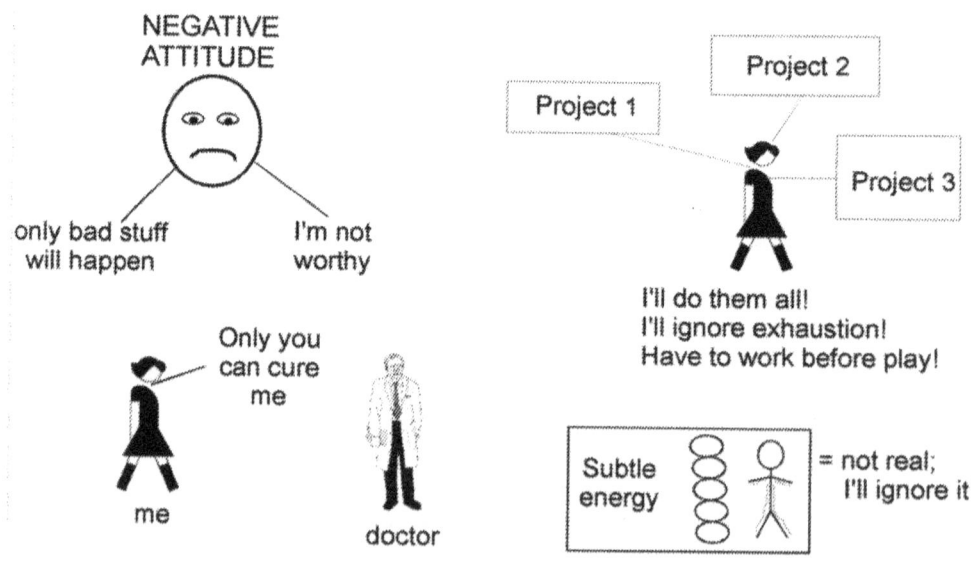

Circumstances and Choices Producing An Unhealthy Self

To Increase the Strength of Your Outline

This completes your outline of what you want. You created it in order to strengthen the energy of your vision of a perfect day and make it increasingly dense so that it will manifest in physical reality. In addition, this outline strongly and clearly tells your psyche and conscious mind what you want and what you don't want. It acts as a driving force to both your conscious and deeper conscious mind to make choices each day that will strengthen the energy within these domains. Finally, by making all domains coherent with each other, you have begun to alter your reality at an energy level. The energy defines and chooses a different lifepath and future for you.

Figure 9. on the next page shows how you have now defined both the old you and new you though completing the outline process. The Old You column lists aspects of living that you don't want that you listed for each domain. The New You column lists aspect of living you want that you created within each domain. This illustration is meant to emphasize how the domains must be compatible in order to easily manifest something in your life. As long as you keep part of the old self in control, it will interfere with creating optimal living and work. So you must increase the strength of the new you at all levels of Life Energy.

Level	Old You	New You
Spirit I **Spirit II**	Old relation to Creative Force Usually unused	New relation to Creative Force Inner helpers identified and ready to help
Spirit III	Old picture or vision of what you want	New picture or vision of what you want
Mind I **Steps**	Old steps and ways to hold vision in place	New steps and ways to manifest new vision
Mind I **Identity**	Who you think you are — skills, values, assumptions, actions - reinforce the old vision and keep it in place	A new identity is created — skills, values, assumptions, actions - that will support a new vision
Mind II **Beliefs**	Your beliefs match and support the old vision	Beliefs are created that match and support the new vision
Mind II **Strategies**	Your coping strategies match your old vision,	Coping strategies are developed that will help manifest your new vision.
Mind II **Cognitive** **Skills**	The way you think, remember, perceive and communicate match and support the old vision	Thinking, remembering, perceiving and communicating styles and strategies are developed to match and support the new vision
Mind III **Intuitive** **Instinct**	Your instincts and intuitive wisdom have been trained to match your old vision	New instincts and intuitive wisdom are identified and trained to support your new vision
Emotion	Experiences of daily life are chosen and reinforced to match old vision,	Experiences of daily life are identified and chosen to match new vision.
Subtle **Energy**	Energy patterns in the mind and body are configured to support the old vision	New energy patterns are created and old ones released so that the new vision is supported. Access to *Being* is initiated.
Physical **Body**	Your health matches your old vision and supports it	Your health is adjusted to support your new vision. Body Consciousness is used to bring optimal health.

Figure 9. The Old and New You

To further increase the density, strength, and guiding force of the energy of your outline, do the following steps*:*

1. *Concentrate on your Five-Domain Outline.* Look at or listen to your perfect day. Next, skim the other parts of your outline that correspond to the "new you" by first going through your visual summaries and then skimming the narrative sections of your Life Energy Journal. This strengthens your intention to manifest your outline at both the deeper conscious and conscious levels of your mind. *Do not focus on the "old you" summaries.* You don't want to strengthen that energy!

2. *When you complete this, go back to your perfect day. Imagine it already in place and a reality. Imagine*:

   - the *context* of the day (what the surroundings are around you),
   - your *internal state* (how you are feeling in this perfect day),
   - your *external behavior* (what you and others are doing, what experiences are happening, to whom you're talking),
   - your *cognitive processes* (what you are thinking, deciding to do, what your attention focuses on the most), and
   - how *I and your inner helpers* are aiding you in manifesting this day.
   - Hold this image for about five to ten minutes and then let it go.

   -OR-

   Instead of visually and experientially trying to meditate on your perfect day, write about it. Write about your experience of a perfect day as if it has already happened and you are writing down your observations. Include the same elements in your description as I described for your visual/experiential meditation—context of the day, your internal state, your external behavior, your cognitive processes, and how I and your inner helpers are helping you co-create your perfect day.

   -OR-

   Talk about your perfect day instead of visually imagining it or writing about it. Record yourself talking about your perfect day as if it has already happened and you are reporting your observations. Include the same elements in your description as I described earlier—context, internal state, external behavior, cognitive processes, and I and your inner helpers. You can re-record this each time or you can simply play back what you have

211

recorded and listen to it with some soft music playing in the background that will relax you. The deep relaxation while listening will deepen the effect of your audiotape.

The Day-to-Day Manifestation of What You Want: Daily Living Choices

The Five-Domain Outline you just created is critical to your daily living. It provides you with an ongoing energy framework within which you make choices, learn, live life, and grow more toward manifesting optimal living as divinity experiencing humanness. In other words, the outline, once created, is not something you have completed and then just cast aside. Rather, it is a living piece of artwork for your life. *You change it, refer to it, and build it according to what you learn and choose each day. It is an ongoing work of art and a process by which you can live your life optimally.*

Now we will talk about how to go about implementing your Domain Outline on a day-to-day basis. Do the following daily, or less frequently depending on your need. Label this section of your Life Energy Journal, "Daily Living Choices."

Step 1. Begin to carry out the goals, steps, and strategies you recorded in your outline under the Mind Domain. Do the same for your health program in the Physical Domain. Do this a little bit at a time. You do not want to make this work; you want it to be fun and easy. Pick something to do each day in the Mind Domain as well as one thing from your health program. Do whatever seems easiest and most fun.

As you implement things to help your perfect day occur, observe what happens each day or for whatever short period you choose. In your Life Energy Journal under "Observations," write down or verbally record a summary of what you observed and date it. Describing your observations in this way activates your *Observer Self.* You can also simply go over what happened in your mind, but when you are starting out with this process, it is better to record it in some permanent fashion. Writing or recording better activates the *Observer Self.*

Remember, the *Observer Self* is able to detach from the experience as it is happening so that you can see what is taking place. This pulls you out of your normal reaction patterns and makes you conscious enough so that you can choose what you want to do rather than just react.

Ask your deeper consciousness to help you as well as your inner helpers and Me. It is important you don't feel alone.

Mary's Example for Step 1

OBSERVATIONS, MARCH 7: I resolved that today I would explore getting closer to Kimmy to see if we could possibly become interdependent friends. I met her for lunch and we talked about a lot of things. Bottom line, I think it's possible we could work into that kind of friendship. Later on, my friend Ann called me and dumped a whole load of negative stuff. I couldn't get a word in edgewise. This happens too often with her but I haven't figured out how to stop her—scared of hurting her feelings. I was drained after the conversation. Then I had to get something done for John, my boss. Deadline project. So I spent the rest of the day running around desperately trying to finish it by tomorrow. I should have told him I needed more time, but he was so insistent that he needed it right away that I was afraid to say anything. I know I'm not going to get much sleep tonight.

MARCH 9: Today good day. Things worked—met Kimmy for lunch again. Nice woman. We decided to form a support "group" for each other and meet on a regular basis. We seemed to be trying to change our lives in similar ways. Boss was pleased with my work and said so. Felt good to get his praise. Maybe I rely on outside praise too much. Have to think about that.

Step 2. Find what's working and what isn't. Review what you have written, recorded, or thought about asking what worked and what didn't. You might ask which of your choices during the day (or whatever period of time you picked) were compatible with your perfect day outline and which weren't. By doing this, you are noting your successes as well as things that didn't work.

Mary's Example for What's Working and What Isn't

Looking at her observations, Mary saw that her steps toward setting up a friendship with Kimmy were compatible with her vision. Mary also saw that depending on her boss for praise and being afraid to tell him when she needed help was giving up her power.

Step 3. Strengthen what's working. For those things that are successes, why were you able to manifest them? When you think you know the answer, put it into your journal under a section marked, "Why It Worked." Until you answer the question, "why," you won't be able to consciously repeat your successes. You need to learn to do this so that manifesting your perfect day it not a struggle, but rather an easy, creative process.

To further strengthen the energy of your successes and your perfect day, ask your internal helpers and Myself to constantly strengthen the Life Energy within each of the five reality domains that is aligned with your perfect day and your successes. Then, do the following things:

1. ***Meditate on your perfect day, inserting the successes you had in your meditation.*** Imagine it already in place and a reality that contains the following elements:

   - the *context* of the day (what the surroundings are around you),
   - your *internal state* (how you are feeling in this perfect day, e.g. emotions),
   - your *external behavior* (what you and others are doing, what experiences are happening, who you're talking to),
   - your *cognitive processes* (what you are thinking, deciding to do, what your attention focuses on the most), and
   - how *I and your inner helpers* are aiding you in manifesting this day.

Make this as vivid and real as possible and do this for about five to ten minutes, then let it go.

-OR-

Write about your perfect day, inserting your successes as if they have already happened. Instead of meditating, write about your experience of a perfect day and your successes as if they have happened and you are writing down your observations. Include the same elements in your description as I described for meditation—your successes, context of the day, your internal state, your external behavior, your cognitive processes, and how I and your inner helpers are helping you co-create your perfect day.

-OR-

Talk about your perfect day instead of visually imagining it or writing about it. Record yourself talking about your perfect day as if it has already happened and you are reporting your observations. Include the same elements in your description as I described earlier—your success, context, internal state, external behavior, cognitive processes, and I and your inner helpers. You can re-record this each time or you can simply play back what you have recorded and listen to it with some soft music playing in the background that will relax you. Deep relaxation while listening will deepen the effect of your audiotape.

2. ***Next, ask your deeper consciousness which levels of Life Energy especially need further strengthening at this moment in time.*** For those that are identified, ask what is the best way to strengthen them. *To do this, use one of the three following approaches to communicate with your deeper self:*

   a) *After stating your question while in a relaxed state of mind, write down the answer with your non-dominant hand or use your computer to receive the answer from your deeper self.* More specifically, first ask your deeper consciousness and Me which domains need strengthening to best support your perfect day vision. Of those domains needing more energy, ask Us how to strengthen them and wait for the answer to come through your fingertips.

   b) *Use your intuition.* Relax as deeply as possible. Use relaxing music as well as an intention to clear the way for communication with Me and your inner helpers. Ask Us to have the domains that need strengthening pop into your mind. Then, for each domain, ask to have an idea for strengthening its energy also appear in your mind.

   c) *Use muscle testing. To do this*:

   1. Make a circle with your left index finger and thumb as if you are making an "Okay" sign. Hold them together firmly.

   2. Put your right index finger and thumb together in the same way, and then link the two circles together as illustrated in Figure 10. Attempt to pull your two circles apart just to the point of actually

coming apart. You want to maintain the link without it pulling apart to give you a sense of your normal muscle strength.

3. Tell your *Body Consciousness* and deeper self that a "yes" response will be an inability to pull the two circles apart. A "no" response will be easily breaking apart the two circles when you attempt to pull them apart.

4. Train your fingers, *Body Consciousness* and deeper consciousness to respond in this way through practicing on responses to which you know the true answer. For example, for Dianne, "yes" responses would be correct to the following statements: I am a woman, I have a Ph.D., I am married, and I have two children. The following statements would be "no" answers for Dianne: I am a man, I am not married, I like details, and I have no children. For each of the statements, Dianne would train her finger and muscles to respond in the appropriate way— "yes" (circles staying together) for true statements and "no" (circles coming apart) for false.

5. After this, you are ready to go through and make statements or ask questions about which domains are in need of strengthening, using your fingers in the same manner as you did in the training session. Trust your *Body Consciousness* and your deeper conscious to help you receive the correct answer through aiding the muscles in your fingers to reply correctly.

6. Once you learn which domains need help, you can go down a list of things you could do to boost the energy of those domains.
   For example, suppose the Subtle Physical Domain needs strengthening according to your muscle response. You can then go down a list on paper, or one created in your head, of things you could to help this domain strengthen the Life Energy manifesting your perfect day. Let's say the list is as follows:

   - Chakra balancing
   - Acupuncture
   - Working with your *Body Consciousness* to move your body in ways beneficial to the subtle energy of your perfect day vision
   - Something else

Go down the list asking your deeper consciousness to give you a "yes" response for something on this list. Point to the first one and then muscle test (try to pull your fingers apart). If you get a "yes" response, stop going down the list. If not, go on to the next one, continuing down the list until you get a "yes" response. Then stop.

If you get a "yes" response for "something else," you will have to generate other possibilities in your head. Ask your deeper consciousness/inner helpers and Me to help you do this. Then, for each of the possibilities that pop into your mind, muscle test to see what the answer is. Or you could ask for a response to come through your non-dominant hand using paper and a pencil.

Step 1: Form an "Okay" sign with your thumb and index finger.

Step 2: Attempt to pull them apart.

Figure 10. A Method of Muscle Testing

Mary's Example

Mary decided that she was able to reach out to Kimmy because she believed her inner helpers and the All were guiding her. When she met Kimmy, she had a feeling of ease and centeredness that she felt were her helpers telling her to reach out for a relationship with Kimmy. She wrote this down in her journal under "WHY IT WORKED."

She decided to further strengthen her perfect day so she imagined a day when her friendships and married life were based on interdependence. She added to that image other important elements of her perfect day. (She kept her mandala in front of her as she did this visualization to help remind her of her vision and what it was.)

She then muscle tested which domains needed strengthening. The answer was the Mind Domain - Beliefs. Mary had a list of possible strengthening affirmations and beliefs that she used to find specific beliefs that she needed to concentrate on to increase the power of the Mind Domain. She then asked how to strengthen these beliefs. To find the answer, she decided not to make a list of possibilities and muscle test which one. Instead, she used her intuition and had an idea pop into her head of drawing a picture of her carrying out these beliefs in her daily life. She did that.

Step 4. Decrease what's not working. For those things that are not working, determine why not. Put your answer in your journal under, "Why It Didn't Work." Here is where all the information on negative manifestation in Chapter 4 applies. Nothing happens by accident. You bring about what happens to you either through actively creating it, or through accepting it at some level of your consciousness. So when you ask why, remember that you are dealing with a part of yourself that is generating this negative experience for your learning—your negative teacher self.

Respond to this self in the following way:

- ***Ask this self what the message is.*** What is this negative experience trying to tell you? It certainly is pointing out what you don't want, but your negative teacher is also trying to show you some assumptions or beliefs you have that have created this circumstance. Ask what these beliefs are? Put them in your journal under, "Why It Didn't Work" and then reword them so that they are compatible with your perfect day. Put the reworded version in your journal.

- ***Ask if this is a part of yourself you haven't accepted.*** Sometimes your negative teacher may be trying to show you that there is a part of yourself, a shadow self, that you haven't accepted. If you don't accept a negative part of you, such as sometimes wanting to control everything around you, then you will attract people to you that will reflect this very aspect of you. Examine yourself, asking if you have ever manifested the type of behavior you observed in what didn't work. If you have, accept this part of yourself as doing the best it could at the time. Once you do this, the people showing this behavior will begin to disappear from your life.

Record the discovery of any shadow self in the same section in your journal.

- ***Is there a gift that has come out of this experience?*** For example, have you learned to be more assertive due to the confrontations you have had to manage? Record this gift in your journal.

After asking these questions, let the negative energy go by asking your inner helpers and Myself to unblock and eliminate this energy within each of the five domains. Then do <u>one</u> of the following:

> ***Think of the negative experience and/or belief(s) that you want to let go.*** Tell your negative teacher self that you wish to eliminate this negative energy since you have listened to the message it brought. Then remove all the labels that you put on your experience, remove all feelings and sensations, and see the labels and feelings just floating away. This dissipates the negative energy in the Mind and Emotion Domains. (I adapted this strategy from Dianne's knowledge and training in Quantum Psychology.)
> Now, again think of the negative experience or belief, and use your index finger to *slowly* trace a square, triangle, or diagonal in the air in front of your face. Have your eyes follow your finger as it moves, continuing to think of the experience and/or belief at the same time. Keep on doing this figure until you no longer have any feelings left for this experience or belief. If one type of movement pattern doesn't seem to be working, try another. For example, if you tried a square, go to a triangle. Or try moving your finger in a circle while your eyes follow. A circle is often a very powerful release pattern. The movement of your finger followed by your eyes dissipates the negative energy at a subtle

physical and physical level. (I adapted this approach from Dianne's knowledge and training in a counseling method called, Eye Movement Integration.)

-OR-

Use the description of the core purpose process to find out what the core purpose of the negative belief or behavior is. Once you find the core purpose, it naturally dissipates the negative Life Energy.

-OR-

Ask if a specific Life Energy Domain or Domains needs healing or transforming to more positive energy at this moment in time. If so, how? To do this, I recommend using the same types of approach that I described before. *That is, do <u>one</u> of the following*:

o *After asking your question, write the response with your non-dominant hand or use your computer*.

o **Use your intuition.**

o *Use muscle testing*. Remember once you learn which domains need help, you can go down a list of things you could do to heal the energy of those domains. *(In Chapter 4, there are a number of suggestions for transforming negative Life Energy into positive for each domain.)*

Here is how Mary went through this step.

<u>Mary's Example</u>

Mary asked herself why she gave up her power to her boss. The answer was that she had a belief that this man would hurt her if she didn't placate him. Another belief told her that he had all the power and she didn't have any. She wrote this down in her journal under WHY IT DIDN'T WORK. She then reworded the beliefs in the following manner:

I create my own reality. The best way of coping with that reality is to be true to myself. I also have all the skills necessary to cope with what I create including

---

speaking to my boss in a language that he understands and respects.

For the shadow self, she decided that she did get bossy when she felt safe, usually in her family structure. She talked to this shadow self and told it that she knew it was trying to cope the best it knew how, but that it would be better able to cope if it respected the other person more when she needed something.

The gift from this situation was one where she was being given the opportunity to develop a way of better balancing her life through being more assertive.

After discovering these things, she used the directions in number 1 to dissipate the negative energy of the beliefs and the shadow self that she found.

Step 5. Make sure of what you want. Look at your vision of a perfect day and the rest of your outline. Is there anything that you want to change, add, or delete based on your experiences? Look at your perfect day vision and the accompanying "new you" visual summaries asking these questions. Then, scan the rest of your outline at the Mind, Emotion, and Physical domains asking the same questions. Make sure all of your domains are aligned with any changes in your perfect day vision.

If you have changed your perfect day, think of the Subtle Physical Domain— your chakras and their corresponding energy fields as well as your meridians. Ask your *Body Consciousness* to change and strengthen any energy in these areas that need it in order to be compatible with your changed vision.

This is how your outline becomes a working piece of art that represents your life vision. It changes as you change. It stays in place as you stay in place. It represents where you are now and what your vision is today—not tomorrow or somewhere in the future. It is what you see as being a perfect day from your present status of learning and growth. So the outline changes and grows. It is dynamic, as you are dynamic. It becomes a living piece of artwork reminding you of your optimal life and aligning energy to manifest your vision.

Mary's Example

Into my perfect day, I need to add that my husband and I will develop a more interdependent relationship. Right now, I feel like I'm giving far more than I'm getting.

Mary then added two beliefs to the Mind II area writing them as if they were already fact.

- John and I have all the skills we need for an interdependent married relationship.
- John and I are creating an interdependent relationship more and more each day.

Then Mary told her Body Consciousness to strengthen any area of her subtle physical body that needed help in being compatible with her amended vision.

Step 6. Operate in Being. Commit to operate in Being and all that it implies. You are divinity experiencing humanness who creates and co-creates the life experiences that manifest.

After altering her perfect day, finding out what worked and what didn't, strengthening her success, and letting go the negative, Mary made a commitment to the Creator in the form of a prayer.

Mary's Example

I believe that I am divinity experiencing humanness, that I create my own reality in co-creation with You, the All. I commit to co-creating my life with You and my inner helpers within the core energy of *Being*. Help me to operate from this energy each moment of my day.

Step 7. Determine what you do NOW. *While relaxing into Being, ask your deeper self, your inner helpers, and Me what you should do right now to further your perfect day. Answer these questions:*

- What can I do now to go forward with manifesting my perfect day— what actions?
- How can I best handle any negative energy that is manifested?
- What support can I build around me right now to help me manifest my perfect day?
- What am I going to do to create joy and happiness for me now? (Refresh your memory about what creates happiness by scanning Chapter 5.)

Mary heard the answers to the four questions above within her mind as she relaxed within Being.

Mary's Example

Actions for today: practice relaxing in *Being* as you are at work. If negative energy comes, *Being* is the easiest place to manage it and refocus it to the positive.

Her new friend Kimmy could be a great support for resting in Being, if she let her know what she was trying to do. (Mary often saw Kimmy at work.) Her husband, John, could provide affirmation for her at the beginning of the day and after work. To make sure she was going to manifest joy for herself that day, Mary chose to think of her perfect day in spare moments of the day.

Continue to go through this seven-step process within the time period that is comfortable for you—each day, every other day, each week. As you get more adept with this process, you can begin to do many of the steps in your head, rather than writing them down. You can then use writing as a process for particularly complex events or difficult problems.

This process helps to focus and strengthen your overall energy and actions so that manifestation of your perfect day becomes a reality more quickly. It also helps to decrease the strength of daily events that pull you away while re-focusing you on your version of the perfect day.

The Specifics for Manifesting What You Want: Moment-to-Moment

When you are living your daily life, how do you stay connected to your inner self, inner helpers, and Me? There are three major parts of your consciousness that make up who you are as you react moment-to-moment: The *Present Self*, the *Observer Self*, and the *Best Self*.

The *Present Self* is your psyche as well as your conscious mind and body as you are right now. It is the self that enables you to experience life in human reality and it operates predominantly in the Physical, Subtle Physical, and Emotion Domains. *Body Consciousness* is included within this self, feeding back the state of your body and emotions from moment-to-moment. It is also an access point to the deeper conscious part of you.

The *Observer Self* is that part of your consciousness that stays apart from your experiences and observes what is taking place. This is the same *Observer Self* we have been talking about throughout this book. It allows you to make choices by making your reactions and behavior conscious rather than automatic. It operates primarily within the Mind Domain. It is a second access point to the deeper conscious part of you.

The *Best Self* encompasses the deeper part of your consciousness, which includes your soul, your Higher Self, your guides, your guardian angel, other interested non-physical beings, and Myself. The purpose of the *Best Self* is to provide you with a vision of the most optimal choices for your intentions and life purposes.

These three selves constantly interact forming a seamless whole that is you. Your present dominant philosophy would tell you that these selves are separate and disconnected from one another. Your present philosophy would have you believe that only one can operate at a time. The truth is that each of these selves are individual but not separate from each other. They are, therefore, constantly present and operating at the same time—interacting constantly.

If you believe that these selves are really separate and disconnected from each other, you will manifest reality that corresponds to your belief. It will seem to you that only one operates at a time and that your *Present Self* seems to predominate most of the time. It will seem that you get caught in the day's events, reacting to what comes your way using well-learned reactions. You will think that you are making unique decisions and plans, but most of them will be based on the well-learned patterns of thinking and behavior that define you. The result will be a feeling of separateness and vulnerability in what you do.

If you believe that these selves are not separate but part of one system that makes up who you are, then you will manifest the reality that corresponds to this belief. You will be able to consciously feel the presence of each self, more or less, depending on the demands of the moment. All three will be simultaneously working together in your conscious mind like a well-tuned orchestra, producing experiences, observing them, and then deciding whether those experiences match your present vision. This model enables you to rise above learned reactions when you want to choose a new response. It also keeps your wisdom resources and co-creative power consciously present through the presence of your *Best Self*.

So it is important to believe that the *Present Self*, the *Observer Self*, and the *Best Self* are connected and within your conscious reach as you operate from moment-to-moment.

Believe in this multiple you and believe in your extended resources and co-creative helpers. Remind yourself of this belief at the beginning of each day and simply commit to resting within this you. This commitment and belief will allow the optimal operation of all three selves and provide a safety net all day long. Just listen for your internal messages as you go through the day. You are never alone. Just let Us know what your intentions are for the day and we will help you manifest them.

Summary of NeuroQuantum Thinking and its Stages

To summarize the NeuroQuantum Thinking process, use the three stages that I just presented to you to create the life and work that you want. That is, make a Five-Domain Outline so that you have a cohesive picture and energy system for creating optimal living and work for yourself. Then go through the seven-step process daily or for whatever short period of time you choose. These seven steps fine-tune your outline as is needed to fit the learning you create each day to fulfill you life purpose and intentions. Finally, remind yourself as you go about living your daily life that there are three selves within you that are present at all times to help you with moment-to-moment observation and decision-making. This process is pictured in the drawing on the next page. With NeuroQuantum Thinking, you are in charge of creating your life as divinity experiencing humanness!

Stage I

Spirit Domain
  – Create a life journal
  – Describe God and your relationship
  – Decide on inner helpers and energy forms to communicate with
  – Create a positive vision of what you want

Mind Domain
  – Create goals and a personal identity that matches your perfect day
  – Identify beliefs, strategies, and skills to manifest your perfect day

Emotion Domain
  – Choose feelings and experiences to support your vision

Subtle Physical Domain
  – Find and align energy chakras and meridians to support your vision

Physical Domain
  – Describe a physically healthy you
  – Choose things that make you feel energized

Communication

Feedback

Communication

Feedback

Stage II

Seven Step Process
  1. Implement and observe your outlined steps and strategies
  2. Decide what is working and what is not
  3. Strengthen what is working
  4. Decrease what is not working
  5. Make certain of what you want in your outline
  6. Commit to operate in Being each day
  7. Decide what you must do each day to enhance your perfect day, manage any negative energy, and create happiness for you

Stage III

Moment to Moment Daily Management
Allow simultaneous interaction of the Best Self, Observer Self, and Present Self

Communication

Feedback

NQT Model Summary

Summary

- There are five domains of Life Energy with nine levels that define human reality: Spirit I, II, III, Mind I, II, III, Emotion, Subtle Physical, and Physical. Each of the domains:

    1. Contain their own type of Life Energy
    2. Includes the core energy of *Being* as well as negative and positive Life Energy
    3. Have their own reality that include unique rules of operation
    4. Have different sizes and power with the largest and most powerful being Spirit followed in decreasing power and size by Mind, Emotion, Subtle Physical, and Physical Domains
    5. Must fit together or be coherent when you are trying to manifest a specific outcome

- The first step in creating the life you want is to use these five domains to build an outline of what you want. Starting with an intention in the Spirit Domain, the outline builds in goals, psychological identity, beliefs, cognitive strategies, feelings, experiences, subtle energies, and a physical health program that matches the intention or vision of what is wanted. This produces manifestation.

- **At the Spirit I Level,** to produce the beginning of an outline:

    1. Get a notebook that will serve as your Life Energy journal or create one on your computer.
    2. Describe who you want Me to be and write the description in your journal.
    3. Decide on what you want your relationship with Me to be.
    4. In your journal, create a drawing of who you want Me to be and the relationship you want with Me.
    5. Decide on Who I'm not and what you don't want from Our relationship. Describe this in your journal and then make a picture of this undesirable relationship.

- **At the Spirit II Level,** to add to the outline:

    1. Decide on what inner helpers you believe in and want to communicate with to help you as you implement your new vision or intention. Put this in your journal.

2. Decide on which non-physical energy forms you don't believe, as well as those you don't want to communicate with.

- **At the Spirit III Level,** add to the outline in the following manner:

    1. Ask your soul and the various parts of your psyche to help create a positive vision of what you want your life to be through creating a perfect day.
    2. Draw a picture of your perfect day, dividing it into sections labeled Personal, Work, Relationships, and Necessary Resources.
    3. Describe what kind of life you don't want.
    4. Make a picture of the life you don't want.

- **At the Mind I Level**:

    1. Using your Life Energy journal, create goals or things you can do to make your perfect day happen NOW.
    2. Identify things that might happen that would make sure your perfect day vision does NOT OCCUR.
    3. Describe the person you will have to be in order to make your perfect day happen—your new identity.
    4. Describe the person you can't be if you want your perfect day.
    5. Create a picture of the self you have to be to strengthen the manifestation of your perfect day. Then create a picture of the person you can't be.

- **At the Mind II Level**:

    1. Using your Life Energy journal, write down three to five beliefs that you would have to have in order to make your perfect day vision happen.
    2. In your journal, write down three to five beliefs you have right now that are likely to stop you from trying to manifest your perfect day. Reword them so that they are no longer barriers.
    3. Decide on steps, strategies, or ways to make the goals listed at the Mind I Level happen.
    4. Decide on what supports you are going to need in order to create your perfect day.
    5. Create a visual summary of what your actions and experience would be if you were living, doing, and letting happen the positive beliefs, strategies, and supports you listed in steps 2–4.

6. Decide on cognitive skills that are critical for supporting your perfect day.
7. Imagine yourself demonstrating these cognitive skills when needed easily and expertly. From this image, create a picture of how you would look when you are doing this well.

- **At the Mind III Level:**

   1. Identify the instinctive feeling within your body and mind that indicates you are going in the right direction for manifesting your vision. Then, identify the instinctive feeling that says you are going in the wrong direction. Record a description of each in your Life Energy Journal.
   2. Identify the best ways to access your inner world to enable you to increase your intuitive wisdom.
   3. Create a visual summary for your positive gut feeling along with the best way of accessing inner wisdom.

- **For the Emotion Domain**:

   1. Choose the feelings and experiences that will support your vision.
   2. Identify feelings and experiences that won't support your vision.
   3. Create a visual summary for both conditions.

- **For the Subtle Physical Domain**:

   1. Find the chakras that are not aligned with your perfect day, i.e., their energy is incompatible with your vision. Then, realign their energy so that it fits your vision.
   2. Identify the meridians of the body that are incompatible with your perfect day. Change the energy in these areas so they are compatible with what you want.

- **For the Physical Domain**:

   1. Describe a physically healthy you that will best support your perfect day.
   2. Describe how you created this physically healthy you.
   3. Now imagine again this healthy you and make a drawing, collage, or mandala of what this you looks like.

4. Choose animals, plants, and minerals (rocks, crystals) that make you feel energized and balanced as you think about manifesting your perfect day.
5. In your journal, describe choices and circumstances in your life that will not support you physically or mentally as you are working on manifesting your perfect day.
6. Draw a visual image of circumstances and choices that do not support a healthy you.

- **After your outline is complete, to manage daily living choices, do the following**:

1. Begin to implement your steps and strategies in your outline. Observe what actually happens in your life. Write them down or record your observations.
2. From these observations, decide what's working and what isn't.
3. Strengthen what's working.
4. Decrease what's not working.
5. Given these experiences, make sure of what you want by reviewing your outline.
6. Commit to operate in *Being* each day.
7. Decide what you must do during the day that:

   a) helps your perfect day move forward,
   b) best manages any negative energy,
   c) supports you in your positive efforts, and
   d) creates joy and happiness for you.

- **To manage your day from moment-to-moment,** allow the simultaneous interaction of the *Present, Observer*, and *Best Selves*.

Dianne's Experience

The three levels of the NQT Model—the Five-Domain Outline, the seven-step Daily Choices process, and the Moment-to- Moment mindset—provides a way of operating each day in order to manifest what is wanted. Parts of the three processes are similar to other advice written in self-help books, but the unique aspect of the NQT system is the presence of all three within the same framework for manifesting the life you want.

When I originally made my "outline," I soon got bored staring at it trying to envision it being a reality. And when I get bored, I usually stop doing whatever is bringing on the boredom, even with the best of intentions. I also felt that during the day, my perfect day got lost in the pressures of everyday life.

The seven-step process for daily choices solved this problem. It gave me a way of orienting myself for the day or over short periods of time. It gave me a progress report, a plan of action that was easy to accomplish, kept me focused in the NOW rather than in the past or future, and gave me a way of making my outline a continuing work of art through changing and adjusting it as I grew more insightful about what I really wanted. In other words, it kept me connected to my inner reality and power. It gave me a way to live creatively and learn how to turn my life around without such a struggle response all the time.

The moment-to-moment process made my learning even easier by giving me a feeling that I was never alone, that I was truly connected to my soul, inner helpers, and All That Is. It gave me a great sense of peace and security even when I was experiencing one of those "delightful" negative learning experiences!

I'm still learning how to build "optimal living" for myself. But my life has become one hundred fold better than it was before I used this process. I feel that learning is fun and an adventure—most of the time. When I don't feel that way, when I feel lost or frightened or angry, it isn't long before my inner voice reminds me that the negative is just a part of the creative process. That I have choices and that my helpers and I to help steer my course forward toward my intentions are creating these feelings or experiences. I feel that I am being carried in the hand of God.

Life Energy Experience

Follow the steps provided in this chapter to begin building optimal living and work. Although completion of the Five-Domain Outline takes some time, you will only have to spend this much effort once. After you have it completed, you will simply be adjusting the outline to match any addition, change, or deletion that you choose for your perfect day vision. So spend the initial time doing it well.

Do not try to implement your vision before completing the Five-Domain Outline. Focusing your energy on your perfect day is good, but implementing any of the steps and strategies before getting the entire outline is completed, will set you up for struggle and frustration. The reason is that you will not have completed aligning all of the five domains, so there will be some parts that are not coherent with your vision. This will make manifestation harder because the energy will not be at its strongest.

Once you have completed your outline, your perfect day vision is already in the process of being manifested. To accelerate and reinforce its manifestation, use the seven-step process described under "Day to Day Manifestation of What

You Want". Use "the Specifics for Manifesting What You Want: Moment –to-Moment to guide your daily living behavior and choices.

I and your inner helpers are always with you. Remember that as you go about this great adventure of creating the life and work you want.

Dianne Greyerbiehl Ph.D.

References

Andreas, C. with Andreas, T. (1994). *Core Transformation*. Moab, Utah: Real People Press.

Buzan, T. with Buzan, B. (1994). *The Mind Map Book*. New York: Penguin Books.

Csikszentmihalyi, M. (1990). *Flow: The Psychology of Optimal Experience*. New York: Harper and Row Publishers.

Dawes, N. (1991). *Shiatsu for Beginners.* Roseville, CA: Prima Publishing.

Klein, R. (1998). Eye Movement Integration. A workshop presented by AIM Seminars/AHTA, Inc.

Myers, D. (1992). *The Pursuit Of Happiness*. New York: William Marrow and Company, Inc.

Tiller, W. (1997). *Science and Human Transformation*. Walnut Creek, Calif.: Pavior Publishing.

Wolinsky, S. (1991). *Trances People Live: Healing Approaches to Quantum Psychology*. Falls Village, CT: The Bramble Company.

Dianne Greyerbiehl Ph.D.

About the Author

Dianne Henney Greyerbiehl holds a master's in business administration, and a doctorate in speech-language pathology and cognitive psychology, specializing in communication, memory, and consciousness. She is a member of the American Speech-Language-Hearing Association and the American Counseling Association. She has been on the faculty of higher education institutions as a teacher, administrator, neurocognitive trainer, communication therapist, lifestyle planner, and organizational consultant. Currently, through her Life Coaching Institute, a neurocognitive training and life coaching center, she teaches people how to use their thinking, communication, and deeper consciousness to create what they want while managing negative and positive energies to their advantage.

Dr. Greyerbiehl's years of research into life meaning and how to create positive living environments led to delving into deeper consciousness to find better answers, both for herself and her clients. The present book is the result of this search for truth. Through the development of the NeuroQuantum Thinking framework, she has discovered that it is possible to build greater personal power, life meaning, and optimal living so that it becomes a permanent way of life. Formerly a resident of Annapolis, Maryland, she and her husband now make their home in the foothills of the Blue Ridge Mountains in South Carolina. She may be reached at http://home.att.net/~lifecoaching.

www.ingramcontent.com/pod-product-compliance
Lightning Source LLC
Chambersburg PA
CBHW030303290526
45785CB00001B/200